ASPEN PUBLISHERS

Casenote™ *Legal Briefs*

DEBTORS AND CREDITORS

Keyed to Courses Using

Warren and Westbrook's
The Law of Debtors and Creditors

Sixth Edition

Wolters Kluwer
Law & Business

AUSTIN BOSTON CHICAGO NEW YORK THE NETHERLANDS

This publication is designed to provide accurate and authoritative information in regard to the subject matter covered. It is sold with the understanding that the publisher is not engaged in rendering legal, accounting, or other professional services. If legal advice or other expert assistance is required, the services of a competent professional person should be sought.

— From a Declaration of Principles adopted jointly by a Committee of the American Bar Association and a Committee of Publishers and Associates

a Wolters Kluwer business
http://lawschool.aspenpublishers.com

Aspen Publishers
Attn: Permissions Dept.
76 Ninth Avenue, 7th Floor
New York, NY 10011-5201

To contact Customer Care, e-mail customer.care@aspenpublishers.com, call 1-800-234-1660, fax 1-800-901-9075, or mail correspondence to:

Aspen Publishers
Attn: Order Department
P.O. Box 990
Frederick, MD 21705

Printed in the United States of America.

4 5 6 7 8 9 0

ISBN 978-0-7355-7875-3

About Wolters Kluwer Law & Business

Wolters Kluwer Law & Business is a leading provider of research information and workflow solutions in key specialty areas. The strengths of the individual brands of Aspen Publishers, CCH, Kluwer Law International and Loislaw are aligned within Wolters Kluwer Law & Business to provide comprehensive, in-depth solutions and expert-authored content for the legal, professional and education markets.

CCH was founded in 1913 and has served more than four generations of business professionals and their clients. The CCH products in the Wolters Kluwer Law & Business group are highly regarded electronic and print resources for legal, securities, antitrust and trade regulation, government contracting, banking, pension, payroll, employment and labor, and healthcare reimbursement and compliance professionals.

Aspen Publishers is a leading information provider for attorneys, business professionals and law students. Written by preeminent authorities, Aspen products offer analytical and practical information in a range of specialty practice areas from securities law and intellectual property to mergers and acquisitions and pension/benefits. Aspen's trusted legal education resources provide professors and students with high-quality, up-to-date and effective resources for successful instruction and study in all areas of the law.

Kluwer Law International supplies the global business community with comprehensive English-language international legal information. Legal practitioners, corporate counsel and business executives around the world rely on the Kluwer Law International journals, loose-leafs, books and electronic products for authoritative information in many areas of international legal practice.

Loislaw is a premier provider of digitized legal content to small law firm practitioners of various specializations. Loislaw provides attorneys with the ability to quickly and efficiently find the necessary legal information they need, when and where they need it, by facilitating access to primary law as well as state-specific law, records, forms and treatises.

Wolters Kluwer Law & Business, a unit of Wolters Kluwer, is headquartered in New York and Riverwoods, Illinois. Wolters Kluwer is a leading multinational publisher and information services company.

Format for the Casenote Legal Brief

Nature of Case: This section identifies the form of action (e.g., breach of contract, negligence, battery), the type of proceeding (e.g., demurrer, appeal from trial court's jury instructions) or the relief sought (e.g., damages, injunction, criminal sanctions).

Fact Summary: This is included to refresh your memory and can be used as a quick reminder of the facts.

Rule of Law: Summarizes the general principle of law that the case illustrates. It may be used for instant recall of the court's holding and for classroom discussion or home review.

Facts: This section contains all relevant facts of the case, including the contentions of the parties and the lower court holdings. It is written in a logical order to give the student a clear understanding of the case. The plaintiff and defendant are identified by their proper names throughout and are always labeled with a (P) or (D).

Palsgraf v. Long Island R.R. Co.

Injured bystander (P) v. Railroad company (D)

N.Y. Ct. App., 248 N.Y. 339, 162 N.E. 99 (1928).

NATURE OF CASE: Appeal from judgment affirming verdict for plaintiff seeking damages for personal injury.

FACT SUMMARY: **Helen Palsgraf (P) was injured on R.R.'s (D) train platform when R.R.'s (D) guard helped a passenger aboard a moving train, causing his package to fall on the tracks. The package contained fireworks which exploded, creating a shock that tipped a scale onto Palsgraf (P).**

RULE OF LAW

The risk reasonably to be perceived defines the duty to be obeyed.

FACTS: Helen Palsgraf (P) purchased a ticket to Rockaway Beach from R.R. (D) and was waiting on the train platform. As she waited, two men ran to catch a train that was pulling out from the platform. The first man jumped aboard, but the second man, who appeared as if he might fall, was helped aboard by the guard on the train who had kept the door open so they could jump aboard. A guard on the platform also helped by pushing him onto the train. The man was carrying a package wrapped in newspaper. In the process, the man dropped his package, which fell on the tracks. The package contained fireworks and exploded. The shock of the explosion was apparently of great enough strength to tip over some scales at the other end of the platform, which fell on Palsgraf (P) and injured her. A jury awarded her damages, and R.R. (D) appealed.

ISSUE: Does the risk reasonably to be perceived define the duty to be obeyed?

HOLDING AND DECISION: (Cardozo, C.J.) Yes. The risk reasonably to be perceived defines the duty to be obeyed. If there is no foreseeable hazard to the injured party as the result of a seemingly innocent act, the act does not become a tort because it happened to be a wrong as to another. If the wrong was not willful, the plaintiff must show that the act as to her had such great and apparent possibilities of danger as to entitle her to protection. Negligence in the abstract is not enough upon which to base liability. Negligence is a relative concept, evolving out of the common law doctrine of trespass on the case. To establish liability, the defendant must owe a legal duty of reasonable care to the injured party. A cause of action in tort will lie where harm, though unintended, could have been averted or avoided by observance of such a duty. The scope of the duty is limited by the range of danger that a reasonable person could foresee. In this case, there was nothing to suggest from the appearance of the parcel or otherwise that the parcel contained fireworks. The guard could not reasonably have had any warning of a threat to Palsgraf (P), and R.R. (D) therefore cannot be held liable. Judgment is reversed in favor of R.R. (D).

DISSENT: (Andrews, J.) The concept that there is no negligence unless R.R. (D) owes a legal duty to take care as to Palsgraf (P) herself is too narrow. Everyone owes to the world at large the duty of refraining from those acts that may unreasonably threaten the safety of others. If the guard's action was negligent as to those nearby, it was also negligent as to those outside what might be termed the "danger zone." For Palsgraf (P) to recover, R.R.'s (D) negligence must have been the proximate cause of her injury, a question of fact for the jury.

ANALYSIS

The majority defined the limit of the defendant's liability in terms of the danger that a reasonable person in defendant's situation would have perceived. The dissent argued that the limitation should not be placed on liability, but rather on damages. Judge Andrews suggested that only injuries that would not have happened but for R.R.'s (D) negligence should be compensable. Both the majority and dissent recognized the policy-driven need to limit liability for negligent acts, seeking, in the words of Judge Andrews, to define a framework "that will be practical and in keeping with the general understanding of mankind." The Restatement (Second) of Torts has accepted Judge Cardozo's view.

Quicknotes

FORESEEABILITY A reasonable expectation that change is the probable result of certain acts or omissions.

NEGLIGENCE Conduct falling below the standard of care that a reasonable person would demonstrate under similar conditions.

PROXIMATE CAUSE The natural sequence of events without which an injury would not have been sustained.

Party ID: Quick identification of the relationship between the parties.

Concurrence/Dissent: All concurrences and dissents are briefed whenever they are included by the casebook editor.

Analysis: This last paragraph gives you a broad understanding of where the case "fits in" with other cases in the section of the book and with the entire course. It is a hornbook-style discussion indicating whether the case is a majority or minority opinion and comparing the principal case with other cases in the casebook. It may also provide analysis from restatements, uniform codes, and law review articles. The analysis will prove to be invaluable to classroom discussion.

Issue: The issue is a concise question that brings out the essence of the opinion as it relates to the section of the casebook in which the case appears. Both substantive and procedural issues are included if relevant to the decision.

Holding and Decision: This section offers a clear and in-depth discussion of the rule of the case and the court's rationale. It is written in easy-to-understand language and answers the issue presented by applying the law to the facts of the case. When relevant, it includes a thorough discussion of the exceptions to the case as listed by the court, any major cites to the other cases on point, and the names of the judges who wrote the decisions.

Quicknotes: Conveniently defines legal terms found in the case and summarizes the nature of any statutes, codes, or rules referred to in the text.

Note to Students

Aspen Publishers is proud to offer *Casenote Legal Briefs*—continuing thirty years of publishing America's best-selling legal briefs.

Casenote Legal Briefs are designed to help you save time when briefing assigned cases. Organized under convenient headings, they show you how to abstract the basic facts and holdings from the text of the actual opinions handed down by the courts. Used as part of a rigorous study regimen, they can help you spend more time analyzing and critiquing points of law than on copying bits and pieces of judicial opinions into your notebook or outline.

Casenote Legal Briefs should never be used as a substitute for assigned casebook readings. They work best when read as a follow-up to reviewing the underlying opinions themselves. Students who try to avoid reading and digesting the judicial opinions in their casebooks or online sources will end up shortchanging themselves in the long run. The ability to absorb, critique, and restate the dynamic and complex elements of case law decisions is crucial to your success in law school and beyond. It cannot be developed vicariously.

Casenote Legal Briefs represents but one of the many offerings in Aspen's Study Aid Timeline, which includes:

- *Casenote Legal Briefs*
- *Emanuel Law Outlines*
- *Examples & Explanations* Series
- *Introduction to Law* Series
- Emanuel *Law in a Flash* Flashcards
- Emanuel *CrunchTime* Series

Each of these series is designed to provide you with easy-to-understand explanations of complex points of law. Each volume offers guidance on the principles of legal analysis and, consulted regularly, will hone your ability to spot relevant issues. We have titles that will help you prepare for class, prepare for your exams, and enhance your general comprehension of the law along the way.

To find out more about Aspen Study Aid publications, visit us online at *http://lawschool.aspenpublishers.com* or email us at *legaledu@wolterskluwer.com.* We'll be happy to assist you.

Free access to Briefs online!

Download cases from this Casenote Legal Brief. Simply fill out this form for full access to this useful feature provided by Loislaw. Learn more about Loislaw services on the inside front cover of this book or visit *www.loislawschool.com.*

Name		**Phone** ( )
Address		**Apt. No.**
City	**State**	**ZIP Code**
Law School		**Year** (check one) ☐ 1st ☐ 2nd ☐ 3rd

Cut out the UPC found on the lower left-hand corner of the back cover of this book. Staple the UPC inside this box. Only the original UPC from the book cover will be accepted. No photocopies or store stickers are allowed.

Attach UPC inside this box.

Email (Print legibly or you may not get access!)
Title of this book (course subject)
Used with which casebook (provide author's name)

Mail the completed form to:

Aspen Publishers, Inc.
Legal Education Division
Casenote Online Access
130 Turner Street, Building 3, 4th Floor
Waltham, MA 02453-8901

I understand that online access is granted solely to the purchaser of this book for the academic year in which it was purchased. Any other usage is not authorized and will result in immediate termination of access. Sharing of codes is strictly prohibited.

Signature ______________________

Upon receipt of this completed form, you will be emailed codes with which to access the briefs for this Casenote Legal Brief. Online briefs are not available for all titles. For a full list of Casenote Legal Brief titles, please visit *http://lawschool.aspenpublishers.com.*

Make a photocopy of this form and your UPC for your records.

For detailed information on the use of the information you provide on this form, please see the PRIVACY POLICY at www.aspenpublishers.com.

How to Brief a Case

A. Decide on a Format and Stick to It

Structure is essential to a good brief. It enables you to arrange systematically the related parts that are scattered throughout most cases, thus making manageable and understandable what might otherwise seem to be an endless and unfathomable sea of information. There are, of course, an unlimited number of formats that can be utilized. However, it is best to find one that suits your needs and stick to it. Consistency breeds both efficiency and the security that when called upon you will know where to look in your brief for the information you are asked to give.

Any format, as long as it presents the essential elements of a case in an organized fashion, can be used. Experience, however, has led *Casenotes* to develop and utilize the following format because of its logical flow and universal applicability.

NATURE OF CASE: This is a brief statement of the legal character and procedural status of the case (e.g., "Appeal of a burglary conviction").

There are many different alternatives open to a litigant dissatisfied with a court ruling. The key to determining which one has been used is to discover *who is asking this court for what.*

This first entry in the brief should be kept as *short as possible.* Use the court's terminology if you understand it. But since jurisdictions vary as to the titles of pleadings, the best entry is the one that addresses who wants what in this proceeding, not the one that sounds most like the court's language.

RULE OF LAW: A statement of the general principle of law that the case illustrates (e.g., "An acceptance that varies any term of the offer is considered a rejection and counteroffer").

Determining the rule of law of a case is a procedure similar to determining the issue of the case. Avoid being fooled by red herrings; there may be a few rules of law mentioned in the case excerpt, but usually only one is *the* rule with which the casebook editor is concerned. The techniques used to locate the issue, described below, may also be utilized to find the rule of law. Generally, your best guide is simply the chapter heading. It is a clue to the point the casebook editor seeks to make and should be kept in mind when reading every case in the respective section.

FACTS: A synopsis of only the essential facts of the case, i.e., those bearing upon or leading up to the issue.

The facts entry should be a short statement of the events and transactions that led one party to initiate legal proceedings against another in the first place. While some cases conveniently state the salient facts at the beginning of the decision, in other instances they will have to be culled from hiding places throughout the text, even from concurring and dissenting opinions. Some of the "facts" will often be in dispute and should be so noted. Conflicting evidence may be briefly pointed up. "Hard" facts must be included. Both must be *relevant* in order to be listed in the facts entry. It is impossible to tell what is relevant until the entire case is read, as the ultimate determination of the rights and liabilities of the parties may turn on something buried deep in the opinion.

Generally, the facts entry should not be longer than three to five *short* sentences.

It is often helpful to identify the role played by a party in a given context. For example, in a construction contract case the identification of a party as the "contractor" or "builder" alleviates the need to tell that that party was the one who was supposed to have built the house.

It is always helpful, and a good general practice, to identify the "plaintiff" and the "defendant." This may seem elementary and uncomplicated, but, especially in view of the creative editing practiced by some casebook editors, it is sometimes a difficult or even impossible task. Bear in mind that the *party presently* seeking something from this court may not be the plaintiff, and that sometimes only the cross-claim of a defendant is treated in the excerpt. Confusing or misaligning the parties can ruin your analysis and understanding of the case.

ISSUE: A statement of the general legal question answered by or illustrated in the case. For clarity, the issue is best put in the form of a question capable of a "yes" or "no" answer. In reality, the issue is simply the Rule of Law put in the form of a question (e.g., "May an offer be accepted by performance?").

The major problem presented in discerning what is *the* issue in the case is that an opinion usually purports to raise and answer several questions. However, except for rare cases, only one such question is really the issue in the case. Collateral issues not necessary to the resolution of the matter in controversy are handled by the court by language known as *"obiter dictum"* or merely *"dictum."* While dicta may be included later in the brief, they have no place under the issue heading.

To find the issue, ask *who wants what* and then go on to ask *why did that party succeed or fail in getting it.* Once this is determined, the "why" should be turned into a question.

The complexity of the issues in the cases will vary, but in all cases a single-sentence question should sum up the issue. *In a few cases,* there will be two, or even more rarely, three issues of equal importance to the resolution of the case. Each should be expressed in a single-sentence question.

Since many issues are resolved by a court in coming to a final disposition of a case, the casebook editor will reproduce the portion of the opinion containing the issue or issues most relevant to the area of law under scrutiny. A noted law professor gave this advice: "Close the book; look at the title on the cover." Chances are, if it is Property, you need not concern yourself with whether, for example, the federal government's treatment of the plaintiff's land really raises a federal question sufficient to support jurisdiction on this ground in federal court.

The same rule applies to chapter headings designating sub-areas within the subjects. They tip you off as to what the text is designed to teach. The cases are arranged in a casebook to show a progression or development of the law, so that the preceding cases may also help.

It is also most important to remember to *read the notes and questions* at the end of a case to determine what the editors wanted you to have gleaned from it.

HOLDING AND DECISION: This section should succinctly explain the rationale of the court in arriving at its decision. In capsulizing the "reasoning" of the court, it should always include an application of the general rule or rules of law to the specific facts of the case. Hidden justifications come to light in this entry; the reasons for the state of the law, the public policies, the biases and prejudices, those considerations that influence the justices' thinking and, ultimately, the outcome of the case. At the end, there should be a short indication of the disposition or procedural resolution of the case (e.g., "Decision of the trial court for Mr. Smith (P) reversed").

The foregoing format is designed to help you "digest" the reams of case material with which you will be faced in your law school career. Once mastered by practice, it will place at your fingertips the information the authors of your casebooks have sought to impart to you in case-by-case illustration and analysis.

B. Be as Economical as Possible in Briefing Cases

Once armed with a format that encourages succinctness, it is as important to be economical with regard to the time spent on the actual reading of the case as it is to be economical in the writing of the brief itself. This does not mean "skimming" a case. Rather, it means reading the case with an "eye" trained to recognize into which "section" of your brief a particular passage or line fits and having a system for quickly and precisely marking the case so that the passages fitting any one particular part of the brief can be easily identified and brought together in a concise and accurate manner when the brief is actually written.

It is of no use to simply repeat everything in the opinion of the court; record only enough information to trigger your recollection of what the court said. Nevertheless, an accurate statement of the "law of the case," i.e., the legal principle applied to the facts, is absolutely essential to class preparation and to learning the law under the case method.

To that end, it is important to develop a "shorthand" that you can use to make margin notations. These notations will tell you at a glance in which section of the brief you will be placing that particular passage or portion of the opinion.

Some students prefer to underline all the salient portions of the opinion (with a pencil or colored underliner marker), making marginal notations as they go along. Others prefer the color-coded method of underlining, utilizing different colors of markers to underline the salient portions of the case, each separate color being used to represent a different section of the brief. For example, blue underlining could be used for passages relating to the rule of law, yellow for those relating to the issue, and green for those relating to the holding and decision, etc. While it has its advocates, the color-coded method can be confusing and time-consuming (all that time spent on changing colored markers). Furthermore, it can interfere with the continuity and concentration many students deem essential to the reading of a case for maximum comprehension. In the end, however, it is a matter of personal preference and style. Just remember, whatever method you use, underlining must be used sparingly or its value is lost.

If you take the marginal notation route, an efficient and easy method is to go along underlining the key portions of the case and placing in the margin alongside them the following "markers" to indicate where a particular passage or line "belongs" in the brief you will write:

- N (NATURE OF CASE)
- RL (RULE OF LAW)
- I (ISSUE)
- HL (HOLDING AND DECISION, relates to the RULE OF LAW behind the decision)
- HR (HOLDING AND DECISION, gives the RATIONALE or reasoning behind the decision)
- HA (HOLDING AND DECISION, APPLIES the general principle(s) of law to the facts of the case to arrive at the decision)

Remember that a particular passage may well contain information necessary to more than one part of your brief, in which case you simply note that in the margin. If you are using the color-coded underlining method instead of margin notation, simply make asterisks or checks in the margin next to the passage in question in the colors that indicate the additional sections of the brief where it might be utilized.

The economy of utilizing "shorthand" in marking cases for briefing can be maintained in the actual brief writing process itself by utilizing "law student shorthand" within the brief. There are many commonly used words and phrases for which abbreviations can be substituted in your briefs (and in your class notes also). You can develop abbreviations that are personal to you and which will save you a lot of time. A reference list of briefing abbreviations can be found on page xii of this book.

C. Use Both the Briefing Process and the Brief as a Learning Tool

Now that you have a format and the tools for briefing cases efficiently, the most important thing is to make the time spent in briefing profitable to you and to make the most advantageous use of the briefs you create. Of course, the briefs are invaluable for classroom reference when you are called upon to explain or analyze a particular case. However, they are also useful in reviewing for exams. A quick glance at the fact summary should bring the case to mind, and a rereading of the rule of law should enable you to go over the underlying legal concept in your mind, how it was applied in that particular case, and how it might apply in other factual settings.

As to the value to be derived from engaging in the briefing process itself, there is an immediate benefit that arises from being forced to sift through the essential facts and reasoning from the court's opinion and to succinctly express them in your own words in your brief. The process ensures that you understand the case and the point that it illustrates, and that means you will be ready to absorb further analysis and information brought forth in class. It also ensures you will have something to say when called upon in class. The briefing process helps develop a mental agility for getting to the *gist* of a case and for identifying, expounding on, and applying the legal concepts and issues found there. The briefing process is the mental process on which you must rely in taking law school examinations; it is also the mental process upon which a lawyer relies in serving his clients and in making his living.

Abbreviations for Briefs

acceptance .... acp
affirmed .... aff
answer .... ans
assumption of risk .... a/r
attorney .... atty
beyond a reasonable doubt .... b/r/d
bona fide purchaser .... BFP
breach of contract .... br/k
cause of action .... c/a
common law .... c/l
Constitution .... Con
constitutional .... con
contract .... K
contributory negligence .... c/n
cross x
cross-complaint .... x/c
cross-examination .... x/ex
cruel and unusual punishment .... c/u/p
defendant .... D
dismissed .... dis
double jeopardy .... d/j
due process .... d/p
equal protection .... e/p
equity .... eq
evidence .... ev
exclude .... exc
exclusionary rule .... exc/r
felony .... f/n
freedom of speech .... f/s
good faith .... g/f
habeas corpus .... h/c
hearsay .... hr
husband .... H
in loco parentis .... ILP
injunction .... inj
inter vivos .... I/v
joint tenancy .... j/t
judgment .... judgt
jurisdiction .... jur
last clear chance LCC
long-arm statute .... LAS
majority view .... maj
meeting of minds .... MOM
minority view .... min
Miranda warnings .... Mir/w
Miranda rule .... Mir/r
negligence .... neg
notice .... ntc
nuisance .... nus
obligation .... ob
obscene .... obs
offer .... O
offeree .... OE
offeror .... OR
ordinance .... ord
pain and suffering .... p/s
parol evidence .... p/e
plaintiff .... P
prima facie .... p/f
probable cause .... p/c
proximate cause .... px/c
real property .... r/p
reasonable doubt .... r/d
reasonable man .... r/m
rebuttable presumption .... rb/p
remanded .... rem
res ipsa loquitur .... RIL
respondeat superior .... r/s
Restatement .... RS
reversed .... rev
Rule Against Perpetuities .... RAP
search and seizure .... s/s
search warrant .... s/w
self-defense .... s/d
specific performance .... s/p
statute of limitations .... S/L
statute of frauds .... S/F
statute .... S
summary judgment .... s/j
tenancy in common .... t/c
tenancy at will .... t/w
tenant .... t
third party .... TP
third party beneficiary .... TPB
transferred intent .... TI
unconscionable .... uncon
unconstitutional .... unconst
undue influence .... u/e
Uniform Commercial Code .... UCC
unilateral .... uni
vendee .... VE
vendor .... VR
versus v
void for vagueness .... VFV
weight of the evidence .... w/e
weight of authority .... w/a
wife .... W
with .... w/
within .... w/i
without prejudice .... w/o/p
without .... w/o
wrongful death .... wr/d

Table of Cases

A
ACLI Government Securities, Inc. v. Rhoades...... 10
Andrews University v. Merchant 17
Associates Commercial Corp. v. Rash.............. 45

B
Bakersfield Westar, Inc., In re 98
Bank of America National Trust & Savings Assn. v. 203 North LaSalle Street Partnership....... 115
Bay Plastics, Inc., In re............................... 11
Bear Stearns High-Grade Structured Credit Strategies Master Fund, Ltd., In re............ 155
Bernhard Steiner Pianos USA, Inc., In re......... 136
Board of Directors Telecom Argentina, S.A., In re . 157
Bowling, In re.. 77
Burgess, In re.. 16

C
Carolee's Combine, In re 99
Carter, In re.. 51
Channel Master Holdings, Inc., In re............. 117
Chase Manhattan Mortgage Corp. v. Shapiro 80
Cluck, United States v. 39
Commodity Futures Trading Commission v. Weintraub 142
Commonwealth Edison v. Denson................... 7
Credit Bureau of Broken Bow v. Moninger 5

D
Dana Corp., In re (351 B.R. 96 (2006)).......... 119
Dana Corp., In re (358 B.R. 567 (2006)) 121
Denochick, In re..................................... 82
Dow Corning Corp. (I), In re...................... 145
Dow Corning Corp. (II), In re 146

E
Earth Lite, In re..................................... 72
Enron Corp., In re 148

F
Faberge Restaurant of Florida, Inc., In re 61
Fairchild Aircraft Corp., In re 128
Farm Credit of Central Florida, ACA v. Polk........ 67
Farrar-Johnson, In re 55
FCC v. NextWave Personal Communications, Inc. . 129
Figter Ltd., In re 112

G
Garland Corp., In re 74
Gerdes v. Kennamer................................. 4
Gibraltor Amusements, In re........................ 60
Granfinanciera, S.A. v. Nordberg 144

H
HAL, Inc., In re 73
Heintz v. Jenkins.................................... 2
Hill, In re.. 35
Howe, In re 133
Hubbard Power & Light, Inc., In re 75
Huelbig, In re 57

I
Image Worldwide, Ltd., In re 96

J
Jamesway Corp., In re.............................. 92
Johnson, In re 24

K
Kagenveama, In re.................................. 53
Kane v. Johns-Manville Corp. 126
Kimbro, In re.. 22
Krystal Cadillac-Oldsmobile-GMC Truck, Inc., In re.. 91

L
Lanza, In re 31
Lee, In re 138
Loral Space & Communications, Ltd., In re 123

M
Made in Detroit, Inc., Debtor, In re 103
Malek, In re....................................... 114
Malkus, Inc., Debtor, In re....................... 102
Martin, In re 141
Maxwell Communication Corp. PLC, In re........ 161
McGrath v. Riddell................................ 159
McLean Industries, Inc. (I), In re................ 152
McLean Industries, Inc. (II), In re 153
McNamara, Debtor, In re Robert W. 32
Metromedia Fiber Network, Inc., In re 135
Milbank, In re.. 38
Miller, Debtor, In re Patricia M. 37
Mitchell, In re....................................... 27
MJ Metal Products, Inc., In re.................... 116
Murphy, In re 56

N
Network Solutions, Inc. v. Umbro International, Inc. 8
Nissan Motor Acceptance Corp. v. Baker.......... 18
Nivens, In re.. 89
Northwest Airlines Corp., In re................... 113

O
Orkin, In re.. 15

P
Paglia, Debtor, In re 41
Palidora, In re...................................... 28
Pendlebury, In re 40
Pizzi, In re.. 25
PPI Enterprises (U.S.), Inc., In re 110
Pysz, In re.. 78

Q
QMECT, Inc. In re 87

R
Radden, In re 44
Reed, In re.................................... 29, 30
Riodizio, Inc., In re................................. 93
Rogers Development Corp., In re 69

S
San Miguel, In re 58
Seitles, United States v. 68
SGL Carbon Corporation, In re..................... 70
Shapiro v. Saybrook Manufacturing Co., Inc. 76
Sharon Steel Corp., In re 71
Sharp v. Dery 14
Sharpe, In re....................................... 33

Shaw, In re 21
Shreves, In re 85
SI Restructuring, In re 100
Signature Combs, Inc. v. United States 124
Silverman, In re 62
SK-Palladin Partners, L.P. v. Platinum Entertainment, Inc. 105
SONICblue Inc., In re 139
Stewart, In re 83

T Taddeo, In re 49
Till v. SCS Credit Corporation 47
TWA Inc. Post Confirmation Estate 94
Twyne's Case 9

U United States Lines, Inc., In re 147
U.S. Truck Co., Inc., In re 107
U.S.H. Corp., In re 131

V Video Depot, Ltd., In re 97

W Walsh, In re 26
Webb v. Erickson 6
Wild Bills, Inc., In re 90
Wyant, In the Matter of 52

X X. v. Schenkius (Receiver for Y) 154

CHAPTER 1

Collection Without Courts

Quick Reference Rules of Law

PAGE

1. Federal Statutory Controls on Nonjudicial Collection. A lawyer who regularly tries to obtain payment of consumer debts through legal proceedings is a debt collector to whom federal law applies. (Heintz v. Jenkins) *2*

Heintz v. Jenkins

Bank legal counsel (D) v. Debtor (P)

514 U.S. 291 (1995).

NATURE OF CASE: Appeal from judgment in Fair Debt Collection Practices Act suit.

FACT SUMMARY: After she defaulted on a car loan, Jenkins (P) sued Heintz (D), a lawyer for the bank's law firm, claiming he violated the Fair Debt Collection Practices Act by falsely representing the balance due on the debt.

RULE OF LAW

A lawyer who regularly tries to obtain payment of consumer debts through legal proceedings is a debt collector to whom federal law applies.

FACTS: After Jenkins (P) borrowed money from a bank to buy a car, she defaulted on the loan. The bank's law firm (D) then sued Jenkins (P) to recover the balance due. In an effort to settle the suit, Heintz (D), a lawyer with that law firm (D), wrote a letter to Jenkins's (P) lawyer, listing an amount due on the loan, which included an amount for insurance that the bank took out on the car. Jenkins (P) brought suit against Heintz (D) and the firm (D), alleging that the letter violated the Fair Debt Collection Practices Act in that it made a false representation of the amount of her debt. Heintz (D) argued that the letter could not be a violation of the Act because the Act did not apply to litigation-related activities conducted by attorneys. The appellate court held that it did apply, and Heintz (D) appealed.

ISSUE: Is a lawyer who regularly tries to obtain payment of consumer debts through legal proceedings a debt collector to whom federal law applies?

HOLDING AND DECISION: (Breyer, J.) Yes. A lawyer who regularly tries to obtain payment of consumer debts through legal proceedings is a debt collector to whom federal law applies. Although Congress initially exempted lawyers from the Act, that exemption was repealed in its entirety. The plain language of the Act itself says nothing about retaining the exemption in respect to litigation. While some members of Congress have expressed the fear that repeal of the exemption would limit lawyers' ability to contact third parties in order to facilitate settlements, proposed language to keep litigation activities outside the Act's scope was never enacted. Thus, the Seventh Circuit's ruling that the Act applies to attorneys who regularly engage in consumer-debt-collection activity, even when that activity consists of litigation, is affirmed.

ANALYSIS

The exemption in the original 1977 version of the statute said that the term "debt collector" did not include "any attorney-at-law collecting a debt as an attorney on behalf of and in the name of a client." When Congress repealed this exemption in its entirety in 1986, it created no narrower, litigation-related exemption to fill the void. Thus, it seems clear that Congress intended that lawyers be subject to the Act where the Act's definition of "debt collector" applies to their activities.

Quicknotes

DEFAULT Failure to carry out a legal obligation.

EXEMPTION Colloquial term usually used to refer to a deduction not keyed to actual expenditures.

CHAPTER 2

State Law Debt Collection

Quick Reference Rules of Law

PAGE

1. **Collection in Other Jurisdictions.** A court may statutorily use "other means," including execution and surrender of documents, to aid a creditor in collecting a judgment debt. (Gerdes v. Kennamer) *4*

2. **Priorities.** Physical seizure of personal property is not required to complete a valid and effective levy on the property. (Credit Bureau of Broken Bow v. Moninger) *5*

3. **Garnishment.** Under extraordinary circumstances, a defaulting garnishee may be relieved from a default judgment against him. (Webb v. Erickson) *6*

4. **Restrictions on Wage Garnishment.** Payroll deductions required under a support order should be included when computing the percentage reduction of a debtor's disposable earnings. (Commonwealth Edison v. Denson) *7*

5. **Creative Garnishment.** Internet domain names are not valuable intangible property and are not subject to garnishment. (Network Solutions, Inc. v. Umbro International, Inc.) *8*

6. **Origins of Fraudulent Conveyance Law.** A transfer solely to defeat the rights of other creditors where possession remains in the debtor is fraudulent and void. (Twyne's Case) *9*

7. **Development of the Uniform Fraudulent Transfer Act.** A fraudulent conveyance is one made with actual intent to hinder, delay, or defraud present or future creditors or is one made without receipt of fair consideration and which has the effect of rendering the conveyor insolvent. (ACLI Government Securities, Inc. v. Rhoades) *10*

8. **Leveraged Buyouts.** The selling shareholders of a constructive fraudulent transfer rendering the debtor insolvent are accountable to creditors. (In re Bay Plastics, Inc.) *11*

Gerdes v. Kennamer

Judgment debtor (D) v. Judgment creditor (P)

Tex. App., 155 S.W.3d 541 (2004).

NATURE OF CASE: Appeal from turnover order.

FACT SUMMARY: The Gerdeses (D) refused to comply with the court-ordered turnover of stock certificates evidencing ownership in a Mexican entity. The stock was to satisfy a judgment held by Kennamer (P).

RULE OF LAW

A court may statutorily use "other means," including execution and surrender of documents, to aid a creditor in collecting a judgment debt.

FACTS: Roger and Carolyn Gerdes (D), husband and wife, owned 50 percent of stock in a Mexican entity. This entity held title to a large tract of land in Mexico. Kennamer (P) was a judgment creditor of the Gerdeses (D) and sought to collect a $915,392.65 judgment from the Gerdeses (D). Kennamer (P) could only collect if he could reach the Mexican land. In accordance with Tex. Civ. Prac. & Rem. Code Ann. § 31.002 (Vernon 1997), the trial court ordered the Gerdeses (D) to turn over their stock. The Gerdeses (D) refused and the court ordered them to do so a second time at a contempt hearing on the first refusal. The contempt hearing recessed for one month with the order that Roger Gerdes (D) was to deliver the documents with his and his wife's signatures. Gerdes (D) still refused to comply. When the hearing reconvened, the court signed a third turnover order and found Roger Gerdes (D) in contempt for non-compliance with the first two orders. The Gerdeses (D) appealed, claiming the order is beyond the scope of the court's power because stock was never issued, and the court order required the Gerdeses (D) to execute nonexistent documents in addition to turning documents over.

ISSUE: May a court statutorily use "other means," including execution and surrender of documents, to aid a creditor in collecting a judgment debt?

HOLDING AND DECISION: (Castillo, J.) Yes. A court may statutorily use "other means," including execution and surrender of documents, to aid a creditor in collecting a judgment debt. The documents required to be executed were part of the appellate record and were available at the hearing. Gerdes (D) argued that the court could not compel the turnover of nonexistent documents, but the court's powers are not so limited. § 31.002 provides that a court may use "other means" to allow a judgment creditor to collect. "Other means" may include document execution. Gerdes (D) has not demonstrated that he has no authority to sign the documents or that he cannot obtain his wife's signature. Gerdes (D) also claims that Kennamer (P) did not satisfy the second prong of § 31.002; namely, that the property cannot be attached through ordinary legal process. The holding of stock certificates by third parties prevents attachment through ordinary legal process, so this argument also fails. The Gerdeses' appeal is overruled.

ANALYSIS

The trial court in the Gerdes case was not reaching in requiring the Gerdeses to execute documents. The statute at issue, § 31.002, was designed to give judgment creditors the opportunity to collect judgments because debtors can be creative in hiding attachable properties. Kennamer would not have been able to satisfy his judgment without the Gerdeses' land in Mexico and the Gerdeses simply tried to avoid allowing him to reach it. The Supreme Court of Texas denied review in this case in May 2005.

Quicknotes

ATTACHMENT The seizing of the property of one party in anticipation of, or in order to satisfy, a favorable judgment obtained by another party.

BANKRUPTCY ESTATE Created by the filing of a petition in bankruptcy and includes all legal and equitable interests of the debtor in property as of that time.

JUDGMENT CREDITOR A creditor who has obtained an enforceable judgment against a debtor and who may collect on that debt once the debtor has been given notice of the action.

POST-PETITION After bankruptcy petition has been filed.

TURNOVER ORDER Court order to judgment debtor to turn over property to debtor's control.

Credit Bureau of Broken Bow v. Moninger

Lien creditor (P) v. Debtor (D)

Neb. Sup. Ct., 204 Neb. 679, 284 N.W.2d 855 (1979).

NATURE OF CASE: Appeal from order awarding proceeds of sheriff's sale.

FACT SUMMARY: Credit Bureau of Broken Bow (P) appealed from an order affirming a judgment awarding the proceeds from a sheriff's sale of Moninger's (D) truck to the Bank (D), contending that the sheriff's levy of execution made the Bureau (P) a lien creditor superior in interest to the Bank (D).

RULE OF LAW

Physical seizure of personal property is not required to complete a valid and effective levy on the property.

FACTS: The Bureau (P) obtained a default judgment against Moninger (D). Subsequently, Moninger (D) renewed a prior note with the Bank (D) secured in part by a security agreement on Moninger's (D) pickup truck. No security interest was entered into at that time. In June 1978, on the request of the Bureau (P), a writ of execution was issued. On July 7, 1978, the deputy sheriff receiving the writ examined the motor vehicle title records and found no lien on the pickup. He proceeded to Moninger's (D) place of work, informed Moninger (D) that he was executing on the pickup, grabbed hold of the vehicle and stated, "I execute on the pickup for the county of Custer." The deputy sheriff was informed that money had been borrowed from the Bank (D) against the vehicle and that the Bank (D) had title to it. On July 10, 1978, after being informed of the events of the 7th, the Bank (D) and Moninger (D) executed a security agreement on the vehicle that was filed and noted on the title to the vehicle. The vehicle was physically seized on July 13, 1978, and the vehicle was sold on August 14, 1978. The sheriff filed a motion for a determination of the division of proceeds from the sale and was joined in the motion by the Bank (D). The court ruled that the sheriff had knowledge of the possible lien against the vehicle as of July 7, 1978, and that the Bank (D) had a valid lien as of that date. The court awarded the proceeds to the Bank (D). The district court for Custer County affirmed. The Bureau (P), contending that its interest was superior to the Bank's (D) interest and alleging discrepancies in the written order, appealed.

ISSUE: Is physical seizure of personal property required to complete a valid and effective levy on the property?

HOLDING AND DECISION: (Brodkey, J.) No. Physical seizure of personal property is not required to complete a valid and effective levy on the property. Manual interference with the chattel is not necessary. So long as the officer in possession of the writ exerts his dominion over the property by virtue of the writ, a valid levy occurs. Thus, a valid levy occurred before the Bank (D) perfected its security interest in the vehicle. The valid levy gives the Bureau (P) the status of a lien creditor, whose interest is superior to that held by the Bank (D), an unperfected security interest. [The court also concluded that the knowledge of the possible lien by the deputy sheriff could not be imputed to the Bureau (P).] Thus, the Bureau (P) has prior rights to the proceeds of the sheriff's sale. Reversed.

ANALYSIS

The jurisdictions are split over the rule of law in the present case; some require actual seizure of the property for a valid and effective levy. Where possession of the property by the creditor is not required, if the levied-upon goods are left in the hands of the debtor for an unreasonably long time with the creditor's consent, the creditor's lien will be lost. The creditor's allowing the debtor to continue to use the goods as he did before the levy is often construed as evidence of fraud, causing the court in any later action to set aside the first judgment lien in favor of subsequent creditors.

Quicknotes

LEVY The collection or assessment of a tax; the legal process pursuant to which property is seized and sold in order to satisfy a debt.

LIEN CREDITOR A creditor whose interest is secured pursuant to a lien on certain property.

SECURITY INTEREST An interest in property that may be sold upon a default in payment of the debt.

UNPERFECTED Not executed, completed or finished; unmarketable.

Webb v. Erickson

Judgment holder (P) v. Debtor (D)

Ariz. Sup. Ct. 134 Ariz. 182, 655 P.2d 6 (1982).

NATURE OF CASE: Appeal from decision reversing decision to vacate and set aside default.

FACT SUMMARY: Bates (D) appealed from a decision reversing the trial court's decision to vacate and set aside a default and to quash a writ of garnishment served on his employer, contending that extraordinary circumstances justified relief from his position as a defaulting garnishee.

RULE OF LAW

Under extraordinary circumstances, a defaulting garnishee may be relieved from a default judgment against him.

FACTS: Webb (P) obtained a default judgment against Carl and Nancy Erickson (D). Carl Erickson (D) earned commissions as a real estate agent. Erickson (D) had in fact sold a home to Bates (D). To collect on his judgment, Webb (P) served a writ of garnishment on Bates (D) naming him as a garnishee-defendant in an action based upon the judgment against Erickson (D). The writ and summons served contained no information as to how the garnishee should answer or appear. The evidence showed that at the time of service of process, Bates (D) was beset by a number of severe marital and physical problems. Apparently, Bates (D) encountered several lengthy hospital stays, was divorced, and lost custody of his children. He never answered the writ. Webb (P) obtained a default judgment against Bates (D), but notice was not mailed to Bates (D), nor was execution attempted. Approximately three years later, Webb (P) sought to negotiate the default with Bates (D). No settlement was reached, and Webb (P) served a writ of garnishment on Bates's (D) employer, garnishing Bates's (D) wages, and seeking to collect on the Erickson (D) debt. Upon motion by Bates (D), the default judgment was vacated and the writ of garnishment was quashed. This decision was reversed on appeal, and from the reversal, Bates (D) appealed.

ISSUE: Under extraordinary circumstances, may a defaulting garnishee be relieved from a default judgment against him?

HOLDING AND DECISION: (Feldman, J.) Yes. Under extraordinary circumstances, a defaulting garnishee may be relieved of a default judgment against him. More liberality should be shown in setting aside a default judgment against a garnishee as opposed to a defendant. He is a disinterested third party so far as being benefited, but is a most interested third party so far as the danger of being injured is concerned. In the present case, Bates's (D) physical, medical, and marital difficulties were substantial. The confusing nature of the entire proceeding, as well as the fact that the papers served made no mention of how or where to answer, may have contributed to Bates's (D) failure to appreciate the significance of the papers served upon him. The circumstances of this case create a unique situation, and it cannot be said that the trial court abused its discretion in setting aside the default. [The court also found that Bates (D) might have a meritorious defense to the action.] Vacated.

ANALYSIS

The garnishee may defend against the garnishor in a number of ways. The garnishee may choose to challenge the validity of the debt owed the garnishor by the debtor, or the garnishee may have the option of offsetting the debt by an obligation of the judgment debtor owed the garnishee.

Quicknotes

DEFAULT JUDGMENT A judgment entered against a defendant due to his failure to appear in a court or defend himself against the allegations of the opposing party.

GARNISHEE A party against whom a garnishment has been ordered; party holding the property of a judgment creditor who is directed to hold the property until a court determination of the proper disposition thereof.

Commonwealth Edison v. Denson

Creditor (P) v. Garnishee (D)

Ill. App. Ct., 144 Ill. App. 3d 383, 494 N.E.2d 1186 (1986).

NATURE OF CASE: Appeal by an employer from two separate wage deduction orders against two of the employer's employees.

FACT SUMMARY: When Caterpillar (D) included its employee's (D) previously filed support garnishment in calculating the amount due to Edison (P), that employee's judgment creditor, Edison (P) contended that support order deductions should be excluded when computing the percentage reduction of a debtor's disposable earnings.

RULE OF LAW

Payroll deductions required under a support order should be included when computing the percentage reduction of a debtor's disposable earnings.

FACTS: Two separate garnishment actions were brought against employees (D) of Caterpillar Tractor Company (Caterpillar) (D). The first action was brought by Commonwealth Edison (Edison) (P) against Denson (D). Caterpillar (D) forwarded a check to Edison (P), but declined to deduct the full 15 percent of Denson's (D) gross earnings as Caterpillar (D) was already withholding money from his wages pursuant to a previously filed support order. Caterpillar (D) contended that no garnishment was allowed that would exceed the lesser of 15 percent of gross earnings or the amount by which the weekly disposable earnings exceeded thirty times the federal minimum hourly wage. Edison (P) argued that the payroll deductions under the prior support order should not be included when computing the percentage reduction of a debtor's disposable earnings. The trial court ruled in favor of both plaintiffs. Caterpillar (D) appealed.

ISSUE: Should payroll deductions required under a support order be included when computing the percentage reduction of a debtor's disposable earnings?

HOLDING AND DECISION: (Stouder, J.) Yes. Payroll deductions required under a support order should be included when computing the percentage reduction of a debtor's disposable earnings. There is no basis, either in the language of the federal and state statutes or in their legislative history, to support the argument that support garnishments should be considered entirely independent of judgment creditor garnishment. Edison (P) argued that the statutes thus construed may help debtors to evade payment of their debts if they collusively procure orders of support that exceed the statutory maximums. This point was considered and indeed vigorously debated in Congress prior to the passage of the Consumer Credit Protection Act. This court is hardly free to tamper with the way in which Congress has chosen to balance the interests of the debtor, his family, and his creditors. Reversed and remanded with directions.

ANALYSIS

Since the Consumer Credit Protection Act does not establish any order of priority among garnishments, the court of appeal applied state law. Under Illinois law, support order garnishments have priority over judgment creditor garnishments regardless of the timing of those garnishments. The garnishment restriction provision of the Consumer Credit Protection Act, 15 U.S.C. § 1671, et seq., preempts state laws insofar as state laws would permit recovery in excess of 25 percent of an individual's disposable earnings.

Quicknotes

GARNISHMENT Satisfaction of a debt by deducting payments directly from the debtor's wages before the wages are paid to him by his employer; due process requires that the debtor be first given notice and an opportunity to be heard.

Network Solutions, Inc. v. Umbro International, Inc.

Garnishee (D) v. Judgment creditor (P)

Va. Sup. Ct. 529 S.E.2d 80 (2000).

NATURE OF CASE: Review of garnishment summons.

FACT SUMMARY: Umbro International, Inc. (P) sought to garnish Internet domain names that a judgment debtor had registered with Network Solutions, Inc. (NSI) (D).

RULE OF LAW

Internet domain names are not valuable intangible property and are not subject to garnishment.

FACTS: Network Solutions (NSI) (D) managed certain Internet domain name registrations. When Umbro International, Inc. (Umbro) (P) obtained a judgment against a creditor who had registered thirty-eight domain names with NSI (D), Umbro (P) alleged the domain names were valuable property and were subject to garnishment. The court ordered the sheriff's office to sell the domain names and NSI (D) to transfer the domain name registrations to the successful bidders. NSI (D) appealed, claiming that a domain name registration was the product of a contract for services between the registrar and the registrant, and that a contract for services was not a liability and could not be garnished.

ISSUE: Are Internet domain names valuable intangible property subject to garnishment?

HOLDING AND DECISION: (Kinser, J.) No. Internet domain names are not valuable intangible property and are not subject to garnishment. A domain name registration is the product of a contract for services. Where the property to be garnished is in the form of a contract right, the judgment creditor does not step into the shoes of the judgment debtor and become a party to the contract, but merely has a right to the value of the contract right. Reversed, and garnishment summons dismissed.

DISSENT: (Compton, J.) The trial court correctly ruled that the judgment debtor had a possessory interest in the domain names it had registered with NSI (D). The exclusive right to use the domain names was a valuable asset and would be subject to garnishment. This right existed separate and apart from NSI's (D) various services.

ANALYSIS

This was a case of first impression. NSI (D) successfully argued that whatever rights the judgment creditor had in the domain names did not exist separate and apart from NSI's (D) services that made the domain names operational Internet addresses. A garnishment summons may be issued with respect to a liability on any person other than the judgment debtor. Here no liability was found to exist.

Quicknotes

CONTRACT An agreement pursuant to which a party agrees to act, or to forbear from acting, in exchange for performance on the part of the other party.

GARNISHMENT Satisfaction of a debt by deducting payments directly from the debtor's wages before the wages are paid to him by his employer; due process requires that the debtor be first given notice and an opportunity to be heard.

JUDGMENT CREDITOR A creditor who has obtained an enforceable judgment against a debtor and who may collect on that debt once the debtor has been given notice of the action.

POSSESSORY INTEREST The right to possess particular real property to the exclusion of others.

Twyne's Case

Creditor (P) v. Debtor and creditor (D)

3 Coke 806, 76 Eng. Rep. 809 (Star Chamber, 1601).

NATURE OF CASE: Action to recover debt by execution and sale.

FACT SUMMARY: Pierce (D) secretly executed a deed in trust to Twyne (D) of all his personal property to satisfy his debt.

RULE OF LAW

A transfer solely to defeat the rights of other creditors where possession remains in the debtor is fraudulent and void.

FACTS: Pierce (D) owed Twyne (D) £400 and C. (P) £200. C. (P) instituted suit on the debt and applied for a writ of execution. Pierce (D) secretly transferred all of his property to Twyne (D), although he retained possession of the property in trust. C. (P) obtained a judgment and levied on Pierce's (D) property, which was worth approximately £300. Twyne (D) prevented execution alleging that he owned the property. C. (P) brought suit alleging that the transfer was made solely to defraud him. Twyne (D) alleged that the transfer was genuine/bona fide and was made for good consideration, i.e., satisfaction of the £400 debt. The court found that a secret transfer of all Pierce's (D) property that was made pending the writ, the debtor retaining possession, bore all the indices of a fraud on creditors. The transfer was voided, and C. (P) was allowed to attach.

ISSUE: Is a secret transfer in trust, made solely to defeat the rights of other creditors, fraudulent?

HOLDING AND DECISION: (Sir Thomas Egerton, Lord Keeper of the Great Seal) Yes. To be deemed a nonfraudulent transfer, it must be for good consideration and bona fide. While good consideration is present herein, the court below believed that no bona fide transfer took place. This court concurs. Pierce (D) retained both possession and use of the property. Pierce (D) was to hold it until the debt to Twyne (D) was paid. The transfer was merely a device to prevent C. (P) from executing his judgment. A secret transfer where the debtor retains possession in trust is presumptively fraudulent when it involves all or substantially all of the debtor's assets and other creditors exist. It is especially true when another creditor has instituted suit. Affirmed.

ANALYSIS

A transfer made without good consideration under similar circumstances as above is also deemed fraudulent. The presence of a trust is not required. The creditor may go after the transferee who has obtained possession of the debtor's property. If Twyne (D) had actually obtained the possession and use of Pierce's property, C. (P) could not prevail unless he could establish that Twyne (D) was really holding the property in trust for Pierce (D). A debtor can favor any of his creditors by giving preference to their debt without being guilty of fraud.

Quicknotes

BONA FIDE In good faith.

FRAUD A false representation of facts with the intent that another will rely on the misrepresentation to his detriment.

LEVY The collection or assessment of a tax; the legal process pursuant to which property is seized and sold in order to satisfy a debt.

ACLI Government Securities, Inc. v. Rhoades

Creditor (P) v. Debtor (D)

653 F. Supp. 1388 (S.D.N.Y. 1987).

NATURE OF CASE: Action to set aside fraudulent conveyances.

FACT SUMMARY: Nine days after a jury verdict against him was rendered, and one day before judgment for $1.5 million was entered, Rhoades (D) conveyed his 60 percent interest in sixty-eight acres of New York property to his sister (D).

RULE OF LAW

A fraudulent conveyance is one made with actual intent to hinder, delay, or defraud present or future creditors or is one made without receipt of fair consideration and which has the effect of rendering the conveyor insolvent.

FACTS: ACLI Government Securities (ACLI) (P) won a $1.5 million jury verdict against Daniel Rhoades (D). Daniel (D) practiced law and commingled his finances with his sister Norma (D). Together, in 1959, they purchased sixty-eight acres in Putnam County, New York, as tenants-in-common, with Daniel (D) having a three-fifths interest and Norma (D) a two-fifths interest; the 1983 appraised value of the property was $325,000. The day before ACLI's (P) judgment was to be entered against Daniel (D), he conveyed his interest in the Putnam County property to Norma (D) for one dollar. Norma (D) testified that the conveyance by Daniel (D) was to repay her for a half-million dollars in treasury bonds she had entrusted to him but were never returned, but there was no other evidence that this was truly a debt between them. Daniel (D) owned only three other assets, which he asserted could be used to satisfy ACLI's (P) judgment against him: two relatively worthless properties and 425 acres of undeveloped land in South Carolina which by appraisal was worth about $212,500.

ISSUE: Will a conveyance be set aside as fraudulent if the debtor actually intended to hinder, delay, or defraud his creditors, or if it rendered the debtor insolvent and was made for inadequate consideration?

HOLDING AND DECISION: (Lasker, J.) Yes. A fraudulent conveyance is one made with actual intent to hinder, delay, or defraud present or future creditors or is one made without receipt of fair consideration and which has the effect of rendering the conveyor insolvent. ACLI (P) first contended that Daniel's (D) conveyance to Norma (D) was made without fair consideration and rendered Daniel (D) insolvent. ACLI (P), as creditor, had the burden of establishing that unfairness of consideration unless, as here, evidence was presented as to the nature and value of consideration having been within the transferee's control. The evidence presented by Daniel (D) did not establish that the Putnam property was transferred to satisfy an antecedent debt. The transaction between Daniel (D) and Norma (D) was closer to a bailment, the Rhoades's (D) personal and professional finances had been inextricably commingled, and the debt was not proportionate to Daniel's (D) interest in the property. Nor was Daniel's (D) interest in the South Carolina property sufficient to satisfy ACLI's (P) judgment; so the Putnam transfer rendered Daniel (D) insolvent. ACLI (P) also contended that Daniel (D) actually intended to defraud it by the Putnam conveyance. ACLI (P) bore the burden of proving this by clear and convincing circumstantial evidence including: (1) close relationship between the parties to the transaction; (2) secrecy and haste of sale; (3) inadequacy of consideration; (4) transferor's knowledge of creditor's claim and his inability to pay it. Here, Daniel (D) and Norma (D) were siblings who had practiced law together for forty years; the conveyance was in secret, contrary to court order one day prior to entry of judgment; only $1 was given for three-fifths interest in the Putnam property; and Daniel (D) knew he could not pay the judgment. Conveyance ordered set aside as fraudulent.

ANALYSIS

This case relies on New York's enactment of the Uniform Fraudulent Transfer Act, which was promulgated in 1984 to replace the 1918 Uniform Fraudulent Conveyance Act. Section 5(a) of UFTA carries over the UFCA provisions of "presumptive" or "constructive" fraud and allows an innocent conveyance by the debtor to be set aside if the exchange was for unfairly low consideration at a time when the debtor was insolvent. Sections 4(a)(1) and (2) provide "quasi-constructive" grounds for fraud where a debtor had guilty intent or was negligent in making the conveyance.

Quicknotes

CONVEYANCE The transfer of property, or title to property, from one party to another party.

In re Bay Plastics, Inc.

Debtor (P) v. Selling shareholders (D)

187 B.R. 315 (Bankr. C.D. Cal. 1995).

NATURE OF CASE: Plaintiff's motion for summary judgment in adversary proceeding in bankruptcy.

FACT SUMMARY: The trustee (P) of an insolvent corporation claimed that the selling shareholders (D) in a leveraged buyout (LBO) had engaged in a fraudulent transfer.

RULE OF LAW

The selling shareholders of a constructive fraudulent transfer rendering the debtor insolvent are accountable to creditors.

FACTS: The shareholders of Bay Plastics (D) sold their stock in an LBO. As a result, Bay Plastics (P) filed for bankruptcy. The bankruptcy trustee (P), standing in the shoes of a creditor, claimed that the shareholders (D) had violated the California version of the Uniform Fraudulent Transfer Act. The Bay Plastics shareholders (D) claimed that the debtor was not a qualifying pre-transaction creditor.

ISSUE: Are the selling shareholders of a constructive fraudulent transfer rendering the debtor insolvent accountable to creditors?

HOLDING AND DECISION: (Bufford, J.) Yes. The selling shareholders of a constructive fraudulent transfer rendering the debtor insolvent are accountable to creditors. Here, the Bay Plastics shareholders (D) acted in bad faith. The various pieces of this transaction were collapsed into one integral transaction, in which the funds went to the selling shareholders (D), not to Bay Plastics or its new parent BPI (P). The loan obligation, in contrast, was undertaken by Bay Plastics (P), which also provided the security for the loan. Bay Plastics (P) received no reasonably equivalent value for the security interest it gave. It was appropriate to apply fraudulent transfer law to an LBO. The debtor had a massive requirements contract with Bay Plastics (P) and was a present creditor for purposes of fraudulent transfer law. Motion granted.

ANALYSIS

Leveraged buyouts are frequently used in corporate takeovers. Old equity holders may finance the takeover, leading to what is known as seller financing. Many of these transactions were found to be fraudulent transfers in the 1980s and 1990s.

Quicknotes

BANKRUPTCY TRUSTEE Individual charged with the administration of the bankruptcy estate.

LEVERAGED BUYOUT A transaction whereby corporate outsiders purchase the outstanding shares of a publicly held corporation mostly with borrowed funds.

SECURITY INTEREST An interest in property that may be sold upon a default in payment of the debt.

Note: There are no principal cases in Chapter 3 of the casebook.

CHAPTER 4

Elements Common to Consumer Bankruptcies

Quick Reference Rules of Law

1. **Property of the Estate.** A bonus plan under which a debtor has no contractual right to payment does not provide the bankruptcy trustee an enforceable right to the bonus check if and when it is received. (Sharp v. Dery) *14*

2. **Property of the Estate.** Employee retirement benefits under ERISA-qualified pension plans are excluded from a debtor's bankruptcy estate. (In re Orkin) *15*

3. **Property of the Estate.** Licenses issued by state agencies are property for bankruptcy purposes. (In re Burgess) *16*

4. **The Automatic Stay.** Educational loans are not excepted from the automatic stay provision of the federal bankruptcy laws. (Andrews University v. Merchant) *17*

5. **The Automatic Stay.** After receiving notice of an automatic bankruptcy stay, a secured creditor is required to turn over the collateral without first receiving adequate protection. (Nissan Motor Acceptance Corp. v. Baker) *18*

Sharp v. Dery

Trustee (P) v. Debtor (D)

253 B.R. 204 (Bankr. E.D. Mich. 2000).

NATURE OF CASE: Appeal of turnover order.

FACT SUMMARY: Debtor (D) received a bonus check from his employer two months after filing a Chapter 7 petition. The Trustee (P) of the bankruptcy estate argued that the bonus funds were part of the estate, while Debtor (D) contended that he had no interest in the funds at the time of the petition.

RULE OF LAW

A bonus plan under which a debtor has no contractual right to payment does not provide the bankruptcy trustee an enforceable right to the bonus check if and when it is received.

FACTS: Debtor (D) filed a Chapter 7 petition on December 21, 1998, thus creating a bankruptcy estate on that day. On February 22, 1999, Debtor's (D) employer gave Debtor (D) a bonus check based on a percentage of Debtor's (D) salary. The bonus plan under which Debtor (D) received his bonus gave the employer complete discretion over whether to issue bonuses at all, when, and to whom, but no discretion as to the amount of the bonus because it was based on a salary percentage. To receive a bonus, Debtor (D) had to be employed in good standing January 1 through December 31 of the bonus year. When Debtor (D) received his bonus in February, the Trustee (P) of the bankruptcy estate claimed it was part of Debtor's (D) pre-petition property because Debtor (D) was expecting the bonus as of the petition date. The trial court ordered Debtor (D) to turn over the bonus funds to Trustee (P) to hold in escrow pending Debtor's (D) appeal.

ISSUE: Does a bonus plan under which a debtor has no contractual right to payment provide the bankruptcy trustee an enforceable right to the bonus check if and when it is received?

HOLDING AND DECISION: (Gadola, J.) No. A bonus plan under which a debtor has no contractual right to payment does not provide the bankruptcy trustee enforceable right to the bonus check if and when it is received. State law determines whether property is part of a bankruptcy estate. A debtor must have a legal or equitable interest in property at the petition-filing date for it to be part of the estate. On December 21, the filing date here, Debtor (D) was not entitled to a bonus. At the very least, he needed to remain an "employee in good standing" at the time the employer declared a bonus. The employer could also have declined to issue bonuses at all. *Vogel v. Palmer*, 57 B.R. 332 (Bankr. W.D. Va. 1986), while not binding on this court, is squarely on point. The *Vogel* court did not find the bonus to be part of the estate property because the employee had to be employed and satisfactorily performing his job at bonus time, and payment of the bonus was entirely within the employer's discretion. Debtor (D) here had to be employed in "good standing" (i.e., satisfactorily performing) and employer had discretion to issue the bonus or not. Michigan law holds that employees forfeit bonus rights if they fail to fulfill a contractually mandated condition of bonus receipt. As of December 21, Debtor (D) still had to fulfill conditions of the bonus plan. It is a well-established principle that if Debtor's (D) continued services were required, the bonus funds fall outside of the estate. Trustee's (P) argument for pre- and post-petition apportionment fails because Debtor (D) never had any legal or equitable interest in the property until post-petition (i.e., upon receipt). As Debtor (D) had no interest in the property, Trustee (P) had no interest. Reversed.

ANALYSIS

It is the trustee's duty to retain as much of the debtor's property for the bankruptcy estate as is financially feasible. Creditors are entitled to recover what the court offers and the trustee can only do that through vigilant organization of debtor's assets and liabilities. The trustee cannot, however, snatch away every bit of money that comes into a debtor's possession unless that asset was originally part of debtor's estate at the time of the petition filing. This allows the debtor to truly make a fresh start and acquire new monies and assets post-petition without fear of trustee attachment.

Quicknotes

BANKRUPTCY ESTATE Created by the filing of a petition in bankruptcy and includes all legal and equitable interests of the debtor in property as of that time.

BANKRUPTCY TRUSTEE Individual charged with the administration of the bankruptcy estate.

CHAPTER 7 BANKRUPTCY A legal proceeding whereby a debtor, who is unable to pay his debts as they become due, is relieved of his obligation to pay his creditors by liquidation and distribution of his remaining assets.

ESCROW A written contract held by a third party until the conditions therein are satisfied, at which time it is delivered to the obligee.

TURNOVER ORDER Court order to judgment debtor to turn property over to debtor's control.

In re Orkin

Bankruptcy trustee (P) v. Debtor (D)

170 B.R. 751 (Bankr. D. Mass. 1994).

NATURE OF CASE: Action to determine if a specific asset belonging to the debtor is property of the estate.

FACT SUMMARY: Orkin (D) filed a Chapter 7 bankruptcy petition in which he contended that the retirement plan provided by his sole proprietor real estate business was not part of the bankruptcy estate.

RULE OF LAW
Employee retirement benefits under ERISA-qualified pension plans are excluded from a debtor's bankruptcy estate.

FACTS: As the sole proprietor of a real estate business, Orkin (D) established a retirement plan into which he transferred his individual retirement account. Under the terms of the plan, Orkin (D) was the employer, sole employee, and sole participant. After filing a Chapter 7 bankruptcy petition, Orkin (D) claimed that the retirement plan was excluded under § 541(c)(2) of the Bankruptcy Code from the bankruptcy estate. The Bankruptcy trustee (P) disagreed since the retirement plan did not contain a transfer restriction enforceable under either state or federal nonbankruptcy law.

ISSUE: Are employee retirement benefits under ERISA-qualified pension plans excluded from a debtor's bankruptcy estate?

HOLDING AND DECISION: (Hillman, J.) Yes. Employee retirement benefits under ERISA-qualified pension plans are excluded from a debtor's bankruptcy estate. To comply with ERISA and qualify for tax benefits, a pension plan must, among other things, include a restriction prohibiting assignment and alienation of pension benefits. Under the law of this circuit, a person functioning as the employer cannot be a covered employee under ERISA. Thus, Orkin's (D) interest under the pension plan is not ERISA-qualified. In light of this, the transfer restriction contained in his plan is not a restriction enforceable under federal law that will serve to exclude the plan's assets from the bankruptcy estate. Further, the restriction on transfer contained in the plan is easily terminable by Orkin (D) on sixty days' notice, with all funds reverting to him. Under those circumstances, the plan does not contain a restriction on the transfer of a beneficial interest of the debtor in a trust that is enforceable under Massachusetts spendthrift trust law. Hence, those assets cannot be excluded under state law exemptions either. Therefore, the Trustee's (P) objection to the claimed exemption is sustained.

ANALYSIS

Other courts have also held that "ERISA-qualified" means that a plan satisfies both ERISA and the Internal Revenue Code. This approach has been criticized because creditors could reach a plan benefit if an employer failed to amend a plan to comply with a change in the tax law. A third requirement often imposed is that a plan must also have an enforceable nonalienation provision. In the case above, the court found such a requirement to be unnecessary. Because the court found the plan was not ERISA-qualified, it did not need to decide the compliance with the IRC issue.

Quicknotes

BANKRUPTCY ESTATE Created by the filing of a petition in bankruptcy and includes all legal and equitable interests of the debtor in property as of that time.

BANKRUPTCY TRUSTEE Individual charged with the administration of the bankruptcy estate.

CHAPTER 7 BANKRUPTCY A legal proceeding whereby a debtor, who is unable to pay his debts as they become due, is relieved of his obligation to pay his creditors by liquidation and distribution of his remaining assets.

ERISA Employee Retirement Income Security Act of 1974.

SOLE PROPRIETORSHIP A business owned by an individual and not considered a separate entity for tax purposes; tax liability is incurred on behalf of the business by the owner.

TRUST The holding of property by one party for the benefit of another.

In re Burgess

Debtor (P) v. Bankruptcy court (D)

234 B.R. 793 (Bankr. D. Nev. 1999).

NATURE OF CASE: Appeal from denial of debtor's request that the revocation of his license to operate a legal brothel be undone.

FACT SUMMARY: When a bankruptcy court held that a license to operate a brothel was not property for purposes of federal bankruptcy law, the license-holder appealed.

RULE OF LAW
Licenses issued by state agencies are property for bankruptcy purposes.

FACTS: A Debtor (P) who owned and operated a legal brothel in Storey County, Nevada filed for Chapter 11 bankruptcy. The Storey County Commission and Sheriff did not like the Debtor's (P) continuing association with the Hell's Angels and revoked the Debtor's (P) brothel license soon afterwards. When the Debtor (P) sought to undo the revocation of the license, the Bankruptcy court (D) held that the license was not property, but rather a personal privilege.

ISSUE: Are licenses issued by state agencies property for bankruptcy purposes?

HOLDING AND DECISION: (Reed, J.) Yes. Licenses issued by state agencies are property for bankruptcy purposes. The license at issue in this case has enormous value to the estate; without it, there would be no business left to reorganize. The congressional goal of encouraging reorganizations is met by a broad definition of property. Reversed and remanded.

ANALYSIS

The court found that the license at issue here was similar to a liquor license or a license to operate a casino, which had been held to be property. The very same license had been held to be property for due process purposes in the same debtor's civil rights case. Many state-created privileges are considered property for bankruptcy purposes.

Quicknotes

CHAPTER 11 BANKRUPTCY A legal proceeding whereby a debtor, who is unable to pay his debts as they become due, is relieved of his obligation to pay his creditors through reorganization and payment from future income.

CHAPTER 11 REORGANIZATION A plan formulated pursuant to Chapter 11 of the Bankruptcy Code whereby a debtor, who is unable to pay his debts as they become due, is relieved of his obligation to pay his creditors through reorganization and payment from future income.

Andrews University v. Merchant

University-creditor (D) v. Student-debtor (P)

958 F.2d 738 (6th Cir. 1992).

NATURE OF CASE: Appeal from a judgment holding indebtedness dischargeable in bankruptcy action.

FACT SUMMARY: After Merchant (P) defaulted on her student loan and filed for bankruptcy, she asked for a copy of her transcript, which Andrews University (D) refused to give her, leading Merchant (P) to bring this action, alleging that such refusal violated the automatic stay provision of the bankruptcy laws.

RULE OF LAW

Educational loans are not excepted from the automatic stay provision of the federal bankruptcy laws.

FACTS: While attending Andrews University (the University) (D), Merchant (P) received a student loan. The loan program gave the bank full recourse against the University (D) in the event of a default on the loan. When Merchant (P) defaulted, the University (D) paid the bank, becoming the sole creditor for Merchant's (P) educational expenses. After Merchant (P) filed a Chapter 7 bankruptcy, she requested a copy of her academic transcript from the University (D), which refused to provide it. Merchant (P) brought this proceeding, claiming that the University's (D) refusal violated the automatic stay provision of the bankruptcy laws. The University (D) argued that the educational loan was excepted from discharge; therefore, it had a right to withhold the transcript. The district court found the indebtedness dischargeable. Thus, the University (D) was in violation of the automatic stay, but the court refused to hold the University (D) in contempt. The University (D) appealed.

ISSUE: Are educational loans excepted from the automatic stay provision of the federal bankruptcy laws?

HOLDING AND DECISION: (Johnstone, J.) No. Educational loans are not excepted from the automatic stay provision of the federal bankruptcy laws. Refusal to issue a transcript until a debtor pays a pre-petition debt is an act to collect, assess, or recover a pre-petition debt and thus a violation of 11 U.S.C. § 362(a)(6). Although Merchant's (P) educational debts are not dischargeable, they are not listed within the exceptions to the automatic stay. Thus, the automatic stay applies to creditors of education loans and remains in effect until a discharge is granted or denied. Therefore, the University (D) violated § 362(a). Accordingly, the judgment holding the indebtedness dischargeable is reversed. However, the judgment refusing to hold the University (D) in contempt is affirmed.

ANALYSIS

By excepting educational loans from discharge, Congress has determined that the continued solvency of educational funding and financial aid programs override the need to provide debtors with a fresh start in their financial affairs. Congress, however, has not excepted educational loans from the automatic stay provision. In *In re Smith,* 876 F.2d 524 (6th Cir. 1989), the Sixth Circuit held that the automatic stay provision was to be broadly interpreted and that it was self-executing. Thus, it automatically takes effect when a petition is filed in bankruptcy.

Quicknotes

AUTOMATIC STAY Upon the filing of a voluntary bankruptcy petition, creditors are prohibited from attempting to recover payment from the debtor or his property.

Nissan Motor Acceptance Corp. v. Baker

Creditor (D) v. Debtors (P)

239 B.R. 484 (Bankr. N.D. Tex. 1999).

NATURE OF CASE: Appeal of damages award for violation of bankruptcy stay.

FACT SUMMARY: When the Bakers (P) filed for bankruptcy under Chapter 7, the auto finance company repossessed and sold their pickup truck.

RULE OF LAW

After receiving notice of an automatic bankruptcy stay, a secured creditor is required to turn over the collateral without first receiving adequate protection.

FACTS: The Bakers (P) were behind in their payments to Nissan Motor Acceptance Corp. (Nissan) (D) when they filed a Chapter 7 bankruptcy petition. At that time, they stated they intended to reaffirm their debt to Nissan (D). Nissan (D) repossessed the pickup truck. When Nissan (D) was later informed of the bankruptcy, Nissan (D) sought relief from the automatic stay, and then sold the car. The bankruptcy court did not know the car had been sold and eventually granted Nissan's (D) motion. The Bakers (P) claimed that Nissan (D) had violated the stay by selling their truck, and filed an adversary proceeding for damages for violation of the automatic stay. The bankruptcy court found the sale of the car was a willful violation of the stay and awarded actual and punitive damages, as well as attorney fees. Nissan (D) appealed.

ISSUE: After receiving notice of an automatic bankruptcy stay, is a secured creditor required to turn over the collateral without first receiving adequate protection?

HOLDING AND DECISION: (Kendall, J.) Yes. After receiving notice of an automatic bankruptcy stay, a secured creditor is required to turn over the collateral without first receiving adequate protection. Here Nissan's (D) action in selling the car was a violation of its obligation under § 542(a) of the Bankruptcy Code. The bankruptcy court's award of actual damages, punitive damages, and attorney fees was not clearly erroneous. Affirmed.

ANALYSIS

The automatic stay provision of the Bankruptcy Code serves to preserve the status quo. The bankruptcy court had given Nissan (D) the option of satisfying the damages part of the judgment by delivering a new truck to the Bakers (P). The court held that creditors could not engage in self-help to retain property as adequate protection.

Quicknotes

ACTUAL DAMAGES Measure of damages necessary to compensate victim for actual injuries suffered.

AUTOMATIC STAY Upon the filing of a voluntary bankruptcy petition, creditors are prohibited from attempting to recover payment from the debtor or his property.

CHAPTER 7 BANKRUPTCY A legal proceeding whereby a debtor, who is unable to pay his debts as they become due, is relieved of his obligation to pay his creditors by liquidation and distribution of his remaining assets.

COLLATERAL Property that secures the payment of a debt.

PUNITIVE DAMAGES Damages exceeding the actual injury suffered for the purposes of punishment, deterrence and comfort to plaintiff.

CHAPTER 5

Liquidation Bankruptcy

Quick Reference Rules of Law

		PAGE
1.	**Eligibility.** The court may dismiss a debtor's Chapter 7 petition for "substantial abuse" under the Bankruptcy Code if the debtor has the ability to at least partially repay creditors, but seeks to avoid doing so in order to maintain an excessive lifestyle. (In re Shaw)	*21*
2.	**Income and Expenses.** A debtor may claim the "vehicle ownership expense" on the means test form under the means test of 11 U.S.C. § 707(b)(2)(A)(ii)(I) for a vehicle that is not encumbered by debt or subject to a lease. (In re Kimbro)	*22*
3.	**Property Exempt from Seizure.** For purposes of the "motor vehicle" bankruptcy exemption, the motor vehicle claimed to be exempt need not necessarily be an automobile. (In re Johnson)	*24*
4.	**Property Exempt from Seizure.** Lottery winnings are nonexempt assets that must be liquidated to pay creditors in a bankruptcy proceeding. (In re Pizzi)	*25*
5.	**Valuation of Exempt Property.** Assets claimed as exempt should be appraised according to their liquidation value. (In re Walsh)	*26*
6.	**Valuation of Exempt Property.** Fair market value is the valuation standard to be applied to exempt property in bankruptcy cases. (In re Mitchell)	*27*
7.	**Proceeds and Tracing Exempt from Seizure.** (1) Arizona's exemption laws do not apply to paid wages. (2) Arizona's exemption laws apply to court-ordered child support payments that can be traced back to their exempt source. (In re Palidora)	*28*
8.	**Exemption Planning.** Nonexempt property may be converted into exempt real property prior to bankruptcy. (In re Reed)	*29*
9.	**Exemption Planning.** A debtor may be denied discharge under the Bankruptcy Code if he has transferred property with intent to hinder, delay, or defraud a creditor or has failed to explain satisfactorily any loss of assets. (In re Reed)	*30*
10.	**Disputed Claims.** The party objecting to a proof of claim, which is prima facie evidence of its validity and amount, bears the burden of going forward with proof of the claim's validity. (In re Lanza)	*31*
11.	**Exceptions to Discharge.** A court must grant a debtor's discharge unless the debtor himself or someone acting on his behalf conceals, destroys, transfers, or removes debtor property within one year of the petition filing date with the intent to defraud creditors or the court. (In re Robert W. McNamara, Debtor)	*32*
12.	**Exceptions to Discharge.** The trappings of wealth, demeanor, and an extravagant lifestyle, together with an oral representation by the debtor that he has sufficient funds to repay a debt, do not rise to the level of false pretenses, false representation, or actual fraud such that the debt is nondischargeable pursuant to 11 U.S.C. § 523(a)(2)(A). (In re Sharpe)	*33*
13.	**Exceptions to Discharge.** Under 11 U.S.C. § 523(a)(2)(B), a creditor's reliance on a fraudulent written representation of a debtor's financial condition is not reasonable where the creditor's normal business practices deviate from reasonable industry standards and where the creditor ignores "red flags" concerning the misrepresentation. (In re Hill)	*35*

14. **Exceptions to Discharge.** A court may grant a partial student loan discharge under 11 U.S.C. § 105(a) if the Brunner criteria are met for a finding of undue hardship. (In re Patricia M. Miller, Debtor) *37*

15. **Exceptions to Discharge.** A bankrupt's pretenses need not be expressed in words, and a deliberately created falsehood is the same as a spoken falsehood. (In re Milbank) *38*

16. **No Discharge, and Worse—Bankruptcy Crimes.** Circumstances, which may be inconclusive if considered separately, may, by their number and joint operation, be sufficient to constitute conclusive proof. (United States v. Cluck) *39*

17. **Reaffirmation of Secured Debt.** The bankruptcy court will make an independent inquiry as to whether a voluntary post-petition reaffirmation agreement between debtor and creditor is in the best interests of the debtor only when the debtor is unrepresented by counsel. (In re Pendlebury) *40*

18. **Reaffirmation of Unsecured Debt.** (1) Creditors may not "act to collect" discharged debts from debtors. (2) Creditors may accept voluntary repayment from debtors. (In re Paglia, Debtor) *41*

In re Shaw

Court consideration of bankruptcy petition

311 B.R. 180 (Bankr. M.D.N.C. 2003).

NATURE OF CASE: Action in bankruptcy under Chapter 7.

FACT SUMMARY: The Shaws filed for Chapter 7 bankruptcy in an apparent effort to protect their house and three vehicles from creditors. Over the years, the Shaws had amassed hundreds of thousands of dollars in secured and unsecured debt.

RULE OF LAW

The court may dismiss a debtor's Chapter 7 petition for "substantial abuse" under the Bankruptcy Code if the debtor has the ability to at least partially repay creditors, but seeks to avoid doing so in order to maintain an excessive lifestyle.

FACTS: The Shaws, husband and wife, had a combined monthly income of approximately $7,800. Although Mrs. Shaw experienced a brief period of unemployment, both Shaws are fully employed. The couple spent years, however, with their consumer spending far exceeding their income, thus amassing hundreds of thousands of dollars in secured and unsecured debt. The Shaw family had three cars, a large home, four telephone lines including two mobile phones, an adult son living rent-free at home, and a daughter in college. In an effort to protect the three cars and their principal residence, the Shaws filed for Chapter 7 bankruptcy. The Shaws submitted a family budget of over $6,000 per month, leaving no disposable income. They stipulated that $130,000 of their debt was consumer debt. The court scheduled the matter to determine whether Chapter 7 bankruptcy petition should be dismissed under § 707(b) of the Code for "substantial abuse."

ISSUE: May the court dismiss a debtor's Chapter 7 petition for "substantial abuse" under the Bankruptcy Code if the debtor has the ability to at least partially repay creditors, but seeks to avoid doing so in order to maintain an excessive lifestyle?

HOLDING AND DECISION: (Carruthers, J.) Yes. The court may dismiss a debtor's Chapter 7 petition for "substantial abuse" under the Bankruptcy Code if the debtor has the ability to at least partially repay creditors, but seeks to avoid doing so in order to maintain an excessive lifestyle. Congress did not define "substantial abuse," but the Fourth Circuit adopted a test in *In re Green,* 934 F.2d 568 (1991). A court must consider the "totality of the circumstances," potential ability to repay the debt, and the five *Green* factors. Here, the Shaws do have the ability to repay at least a portion of the unsecured debt because their income remains high and their expenses can be significantly reduced. Their proposed budget is excessive given that the Shaws have no practical need for such a large principal residence, three cars, four phone lines, or college expenses. The amount of $2,000 per month could go toward a Chapter 13 plan. The Shaws have admittedly lived beyond their means for years, and are not filing for bankruptcy after an unexpected or tragic event. Their petition cannot be considered filed in good faith when the Shaws seek to maintain their excessive lifestyle at the expense of their creditors. The court does not find that the Shaws intended to mislead parties with inadvertent discrepancies on their inventory, but their proposed budget is unacceptable. Considering the totality of the circumstances, it is a substantial abuse of the Bankruptcy Code to allow these debtors to file under Chapter 7. They may decide whether a Chapter 13 petition should be filed. Dismissed.

ANALYSIS

The income of the Shaws was approximately six times that of the typical petitioner. Courts tend to look askance at debtors with lavish lifestyles simply seeking to avoid the repayment consequences of a life of excess. Chapter 7 is ideally protection for those in need of asset preservation because of a calamity rather than a lifestyle choice.

Quicknotes

CHAPTER 7 BANKRUPTCY A legal proceeding whereby a debtor, who is unable to pay his debts as they become due, is relieved of his obligation to pay his creditors by liquidation and distribution of his remaining assets.

CHAPTER 13 BANKRUPTCY Debtor may modify plan at any time before the completion of the payments under such plan.

GOOD FAITH COMPLIANCE A sincere or unequivocal intention to fulfill an obligation or to comply with specifically requested conduct.

SECURED CLAIM A claim, the repayment of which is secured by collateral sufficient to repay the debt owed.

UNSECURED CLAIM A claim, the repayment of which is not secured by collateral sufficient to repay the debt owed.

In re Kimbro

Trustee (P) v. Debtor (D)

2008 Bankr. Lexis 1692 (6th Cir. BAP 2008).

NATURE OF CASE: Appeal from judgment for debtor permitting deduction of vehicle ownership expense under the means test.

FACT SUMMARY: The trustee (P) contended that the Kimbros (D) were not permitted to claim under the means test an ownership expense for a vehicle that they owned and that was not encumbered by debt or subject to a lease.

RULE OF LAW

A debtor may claim the "vehicle ownership expense" on the means test form under the means test of 11 U.S.C. § 707(b)(2)(A)(ii)(I) for a vehicle that is not encumbered by debt or subject to a lease.

FACTS: In calculating their monthly disposable income under the means test of 11 U.S.C. § 707(b)(2)(A)(ii)(I), the Kimbros (D)—the debtors in bankruptcy—claimed $332 for a vehicle they owned that was not encumbered by debt or subject to a lease. The trustee (P) challenged this deduction and the bankruptcy court's confirmation of the plan. The means test states that "The debtor's monthly expenses shall be the debtor's applicable monthly expense amounts specified under the National Standards and Local Standards, and the debtor's actual monthly expenses for the categories specified as Other Necessary Expenses issued by the Internal Revenue Service (IRS) for the area in which the debtor resides[.]" "National and Local Standards" refers to the standards used by IRS for revenue officers to determine a taxpayer's ability to pay a delinquent tax. The IRS Local Transportation Standards, which vary by census region, provide "Ownership Costs" amounts for the debtor's "first car" and "second car." Relying on the Internal Revenue Manual, Financial Analysis Handbook (IRM), which does not allow taxpayers to claim an ownership expense for a vehicle for which they do not make payments, the trustee (P) contended that this same rule was incorporated into the means test. The bankruptcy court rejected the trustee's (P) position and held that the Kimbros (D) were allowed to deduct the ownership expense amounts in the applicable Local Transportation Standards. The Circuit Court Bankruptcy Appellate Panel (Panel) granted review.

ISSUE: May a debtor claim the "vehicle ownership expense" on the means test form under the means test of 11 U.S.C. § 707(b)(2)(A)(ii)(I) for a vehicle that is not encumbered by debt or subject to a lease?

HOLDING AND DECISION: (Rhodes, J.) Yes. A debtor may claim the "vehicle ownership expense" on the means test form under the means test of 11 U.S.C. § 707(b)(2)(A)(ii)(I) for a vehicle that is not encumbered by debt or subject to a lease. First, there is no express language in the statute conditioning deductibility of a vehicle ownership expense on the debtor having debt or a lease on the vehicle. Second, the IRM is not statutorily incorporated into the means test. Third, Congress intended to incorporate only the specific IRS expense standards and not the IRM. Fourth, the IRS Local Transportation Standard does not require a debtor to have a debt or lease payment to deduct a vehicle ownership expense in the bankruptcy means test. Fifth, revenue officers have substantial discretion under the IRM, and such discretion is inconsistent with the purpose of the means test, which is intended to provide a uniform standard and to eliminate judicial discretion. If the IRM were used to determine the amounts of expenses, the means test would become a highly discretionary test, due to revenue officers' substantial discretion under the IRM. The process for a revenue officer of applying IRM guidelines for tax collection purposes is a highly discretionary process that is very much like the highly discretionary process that bankruptcy judges utilized before the 2005 amendments to the bankruptcy code when determining a debtor's net disposable income. However, Congress gave no indication with the 2005 amendments that it desired such a discretionary process to continue. To the contrary, the legislative history shows that Congress desired to effect a bright-line test in determining disposable income. Sixth, the trustee's (P) premise is incorrect, since revenue officers have substantial discretion to consider and allow any expenses above the standards. Finally, every debtor who owns a vehicle incurs expenses arising from the ownership of the vehicle regardless of whether the debtor incurs a debt or lease payment associated with the vehicle. Affirmed.

DISSENT: (Fulton, J.) The Panel misconstrues the word "applicable" in the first sentence of 11 U.S.C. § 707 (b)(2)(A)(ii)(I). The Panel assumes that a debtor can just look up the "applicable" dollar amount set forth in the IRS's tables. However, if "applicable" is to have any meaning at all, the debtor must look to the IRS's guidelines regarding the use of the tables set forth in the National Standards and Local Standards to determine the amount of expenses that may be "applied" to reduce the debtor's monthly income. If Congress had intended that the amount be the amount listed in the tables, it would not have had to include the word "applicable" in the statute; it could have just stated that "The debtor's monthly expenses shall be the debtor's monthly expense amounts specified under the National Standards and Local Standards. . . ." By adding the word "applicable," Congress intended that the debtor refer to IRS guidelines. The reality is that one cannot just look up a dollar amount

Continued on next page.

in the tables without additional IRS guidance. The only other approach, such as that taken by the Panel, is to impose pre-existing assumptions and prejudices about how the tables are to be navigated.

ANALYSIS

The position espoused by the Panel in this case is a minority position. The majority of bankruptcy courts and the overwhelming majority of appellate courts across the United States that have considered this issue, including the Eighth and Ninth Circuit Bankruptcy Appellate Panels, have concluded that a vehicle ownership expense is applicable only if a debtor is in fact incurring such an expense.

Quicknotes

BANKRUPTCY TRUSTEE Individual charged with the administration of the bankruptcy estate.

In re Johnson

Trustee (P) v. Debtor (D)

14 B.R. 14 (Bankr. W.D. Ky. 1981).

NATURE OF CASE: Trustee's challenge to debtor's claimed exemption.

FACT SUMMARY: The trustee (P) objected to Johnson's (D) claimed exemption of his 1969 Dodge bus, contending that the "motor vehicle" exemption was intended to be synonymous with "automobile."

RULE OF LAW
For purposes of the "motor vehicle" bankruptcy exemption, the motor vehicle claimed to be exempt need not necessarily be an automobile.

FACTS: Johnson (D) petitioned for bankruptcy, and the trustee (P) was appointed to administer the estate. Johnson (D) claimed as exempt his 1969 Dodge bus, which had a seating capacity of sixty passengers. The trustee (P) objected to the claimed exemption, contending that the "motor vehicle" exemption was meant to apply only to automobiles.

ISSUE: For purposes of the "motor vehicle" bankruptcy exemption, must the motor vehicle claimed exempt be an automobile?

HOLDING AND DECISION: (Deitz, J.) No. For purposes of the "motor vehicle" bankruptcy exemption, the motor vehicle claimed exempt need not necessarily be an automobile. The motor vehicle exemption no longer limits the uses to which a motor vehicle might be put. The record is silent as to the size of Johnson's (D) family or his transportation needs. In this era of motorized evolution, we must conclude that a bus and an automobile are species of the genus "motor vehicle." Johnson's (D) claimed exemption should stand.

ANALYSIS

The court in its opinion seemed to be irritated that this issue was even litigated, comparing its decision sarcastically to cases of great moment, such as *Marbury v. Madison*, 1 Cranch 137, 2 L.Ed. 60 (1803). An unchallenged assumption in the present case was that the bus in question had a value not exceeding $2,500.

Quicknotes

BANKRUPTCY TRUSTEE Individual charged with the administration of the bankruptcy estate.

EXEMPTION Colloquial term usually used to refer to a deduction not keyed to actual expenditures.

In re Pizzi

Lottery winner-debtor (P) v. Bankruptcy trustee (D)

153 B.R. 357 (Bankr. S.D. Fla. 1993).

NATURE OF CASE: Action to determine the assets subject to liquidation to pay creditors in a bankruptcy proceeding.

FACT SUMMARY: When Pizzi (P) filed this Chapter 7 bankruptcy proceeding, she contended that her lottery winnings were annuity payments and thus exempt, under Florida law, from liquidation to pay her creditors.

RULE OF LAW

Lottery winnings are nonexempt assets that must be liquidated to pay creditors in a bankruptcy proceeding.

FACTS: After Pizzi (P) won the Connecticut state lottery, she incurred substantial debt, ultimately resulting in the filing of a Chapter 7 petition. Pizzi (P) claimed that the remainder of her annual lottery payments were an annuity contract and therefore exempt, under Florida law, from the assets that must be liquidated to pay her creditors. Her exemption claim was challenged by the bankruptcy trustee (D) and by two bank creditors (D).

ISSUE: Are lottery winnings nonexempt assets that must be liquidated to pay creditors in a bankruptcy proceeding?

HOLDING AND DECISION: (Mark, J.) Yes. Lottery winnings are nonexempt assets that must be liquidated to pay creditors in a bankruptcy proceeding. It would be inequitable for a debtor to obtain loans in reliance upon her lottery winnings and then discharge these obligations without turning over the winnings to her estate. Moreover, the annuity contract purchased by Connecticut lists the state as the "owner" and "beneficiary" of the contract. In addition, the income stream flowing directly to Pizzi (P) is not an annuity at all, but prize winnings stemming from the winning of the lottery. The Connecticut lottery regulations never refer to the winnings as proceeds of an annuity contract, and the winner is never referred to as the beneficiary or payee of an annuity contract. Thus, the objections, filed by the trustee (D) and the bank creditors (D) to Pizzi's (P) claim of exemption, will be sustained.

ANALYSIS

The definition of an annuity under Florida law was addressed by the Florida Supreme Court in *In re McCollam,* 612 So. 2d 572 (1993). *McCollam* involved the damage settlement stemming from a wrongful death action resulting from a fatal automobile accident. Under the terms of the agreement, Travelers Insurance Company purchased an annuity contract. The debtor was listed as the beneficiary and payee under the contract. Travelers' debt obligation to the debtor was liquidated and discharged by the amount of each successive annuity payment. Utilizing a broad definition of annuity, the court concluded that the contract at issue was within the statutory exemption.

Quicknotes

ANNUITY The payment or right to receive payment of a fixed sum periodically, for a specified time period.

CHAPTER 7 BANKRUPTCY A legal proceeding whereby a debtor, who is unable to pay his debts as they become due, is relieved of his obligation to pay his creditors by liquidation and distribution of his remaining assets.

LIQUIDATION The reduction to cash of all assets for distribution to creditors.

In re Walsh

Trustee (P) v. Debtor (D)

5 B.R. 239 (Bankr. D.D.C. 1980).

NATURE OF CASE: Action by trustee in bankruptcy for hearing on application for appraisal.

FACT SUMMARY: In Tyler's (P) action as trustee in bankruptcy against the debtor, Walsh (D), for hearing on an application for appraisal, Tyler (P) sought an appraisal of assets, claimed by Walsh (D) to be exempt under 11 U.S.C. § 522, at fair market value rather than liquidation value.

RULE OF LAW

Assets claimed as exempt should be appraised according to their liquidation value.

FACTS: Walsh (D), a debtor in bankruptcy under Chapter 7 of the Bankruptcy Code, claimed property as exempt under 11 U.S.C. § 522. Tyler (P), the trustee in bankruptcy, then filed an action against Walsh (D), seeking an appraisal of the assets claimed exempt by Walsh (D) at fair market value, rather than liquidation value, on which basis a previous appraisal was made.

ISSUE: Should assets claimed as exempt be appraised according to their liquidation value?

HOLDING AND DECISION: (Whelan, J.) Yes. Assets claimed as exempt should be appraised according to their liquidation value. Fair market value, the price at which a willing seller and a willing buyer will trade, assumes agreement between an owner willing but not obliged to sell for cash and a buyer desirous but not compelled to purchase. Here, Tyler (P) argues that the § 522 (a)(1) definition of value, that is, fair market value, should be construed literally and independently of the Chapter 7 context rather than taking into consideration the liquidation context and the goals of the Code as a whole. Walsh (D), however, argues that the definition of "market" on the day a bankruptcy petition is filed, is, invariably, an eventual bankruptcy sale. Thus, the assets claimed as exempt should be appraised according to their liquidation value. The purpose of valuation under exemption provisions is ultimately to determine whether such property is subject to liquidation by the trustee because it is in excess of specified monetary amount. Therefore, the term "market value" as it is used to define value in § 522 must be interpreted in the liquidation context in a Chapter 7 case. Application for appraisal denied.

ANALYSIS

The 1978 Bankruptcy Code provided for federal exemptions, and the 1898 Bankruptcy Act incorporated state exemptions into the debtor's protections in bankruptcy. Now a debtor may choose either the state or the federal exemptions, depending on the debtor's circumstances. As part of the compromise allowing this choice, states were authorized to "opt out" of the federal scheme. In opt-out states, a debtor filing for bankruptcy can therefore only exempt property protected under that state's laws.

Quicknotes

CHAPTER 7 BANKRUPTCY A legal proceeding whereby a debtor, who is unable to pay his debts as they become due, is relieved of his obligation to pay his creditors by liquidation and distribution of his remaining assets.

FAIR MARKET VALUE The price of particular property or goods that a buyer would offer and a seller would accept in the open market following full disclosure.

LIQUIDATION The reduction to cash of all assets for distribution to creditors.

In re Mitchell

Creditor (P) v. Debtor (D)

103 B.R. 819 (Bankr. W.D. Texas 1989).

NATURE OF CASE: Objection to claim of exempt property in Chapter 7 bankruptcy proceeding.

FACT SUMMARY: Creditor First City (P) contended that the court should use fair market value for Mrs. Mitchell's (D) diamond wedding ring, while the Mitchells (D) argued in favor of a lower liquidation valuation.

RULE OF LAW

Fair market value is the valuation standard to be applied to exempt property in bankruptcy cases.

FACTS: The Mitchells (D) filed for Chapter 7 bankruptcy. Among the items they claimed exempt as "clothing reasonably necessary for the family" was a 6.18 carat diamond ring. Mr. Mitchell (D) had purchased the ring as a twenty-fifth anniversary present since he had been unable to purchase a real diamond ring at the time of their wedding. Mrs. Mitchell (D) wore the ring continuously, and the ring showed significant wear and tear. Mr. Mitchell (D) bought the ring for $30,000. First City (P) claimed that the ring had a fair market value of $36,000. The Mitchells (D) presented evidence that all that they could get for the ring if forced to liquidate it would be $7,800. The Mitchells (D) also claimed other exemptions totaling $48,357. First City (P) contested the acceptance of the ring as an exemption and argued that the ring should be valued at its fair market price. The Mitchells (D) claimed that the ring should be valued at the price that the liquidation market would bear.

ISSUE: Is fair market value the valuation standard to be applied to exempt property in bankruptcy cases?

HOLDING AND DECISION: (Clark, J.) Yes. Fair market value is the valuation standard to be applied to exempt property in bankruptcy cases. The Texas property code allows debtors to retain personal property necessary to the survival of the family or individual. The legislature has set a limit on the property they can keep. The debtor is not entitled to keep everything simply because it is approved by the court as personal property. The Mitchells (D) must choose among the list of items admitted by the court, up to the statutory limit, which means they will have to choose between necessary items and the ring. Both the federal and state statutes specify the use of fair market value; that value is $36,000.

ANALYSIS

The Texas statute applied in this case (which was later modified to include jewelry as an exempt category) was not intended to maintain a debtor's quality of life, but merely to prevent the debtor from becoming destitute. The purpose of exemptions was to prevent debtors from turning to the state for public assistance. However, allowing the Mitchells to use the lower valuation standard in this case would have prevented their creditors from being repaid out of the value of that asset.

Quicknotes

CHAPTER 7 BANKRUPTCY A legal proceeding whereby a debtor, who is unable to pay his debts as they become due, is relieved of his obligation to pay his creditors by liquidation and distribution of his remaining assets.

FAIR MARKET VALUE The price of particular property or goods that a buyer would offer and a seller would accept in the open market following full disclosure.

In re Palidora

Bankruptcy trustee (P) v. Debtors (D)

310 B.R. 164 (Bankr. D. Ariz. 2004).

NATURE OF CASE: Challenge to claim of exemption.

FACT SUMMARY: The Palidoras (D) had slightly over $2,000 in their bank accounts upon filing for Chapter 7 bankruptcy protection. The funds came in part from Frank Palidora's (D) wages and in part from child support paid to Sondra Palidora (D). The Chapter 7 Trustee (P) moved for the turnover of those funds.

RULE OF LAW

(1) Arizona's exemption laws do not apply to paid wages.

(2) Arizona's exemption laws apply to court-ordered child support payments that can be traced back to their exempt source.

FACTS: The Palidoras (D), husband and wife, petitioned for Chapter 7 bankruptcy protection. At the time they filed, they had $2,194.80 in their bank accounts. The Chapter 7 Trustee (P) moved for turnover of the funds, but the Palidoras (D) argued that the funds were exempt because they were from Frank Palidora's (D) wages and $1,000 in child support paid to Sondra Palidora (D) for the benefit of a minor child.

ISSUE:

(1) Do Arizona's exemption laws apply to paid wages?

(2) Do Arizona's exemption laws apply to court-ordered child support payments?

HOLDING AND DECISION: (Haines, J.)

(1) No. Arizona's exemption laws do not apply to paid wages, but do apply to court-ordered child support payments that can be traced back to their exempt source. Arizona's exemption laws apply to 75 percent of a debtor's "disposable income," as defined in A.R.S. § 33.1131 (A), including "that remaining portion of a debtor's wages, salary or compensation." The distinction for exemption purposes is whether "wages, salary or compensation" includes what is due to the employee or what has already been paid to the employee. The Arizona Court of Appeals, however, has held that the exemption applies to "earnings" and not "monies" already paid. Frank Palidora (D) received the monies as paid compensation and was not expecting them as earnings. Arizona's construction of the exemption laws is binding on this court, so the wages paid to Frank Palidora (D) are not exempt for purposes of Chapter 7.

(2) Yes. As to child support, Arizona law implies that child support payments are to be held in trust for the support, present or future, of the minor child. The support payments do not become the property of the estate, and are thus exempt. Additionally, Arizona expressly exempts by statute child support payments received by a debtor, if the payments are made pursuant to a court order. Payments already in a debtor's account must be able to be traced back to the source and demonstrably paid pursuant to a court order. Here, no such tracing back or determination can be made. If traceable and a court order exists, the child support is exempt. The support is otherwise not exempt. No finding can be made here absent additional facts being placed before the court. Sustained as to the objection to the claim of wage exemption, decision pending on claim of exemption for child support payments.

ANALYSIS

Tracing the source of proceeds is a requirement for an exemption claim. It can become a difficult puzzle if the original property has been converted several times (e.g., using child support payments from one account to purchase a crib, later selling that crib for cash, and depositing the cash into a different account).

Quicknotes

CHAPTER 7 BANKRUPTCY A legal proceeding whereby a debtor, who is unable to pay his debts as they become due, is relieved of his obligation to pay his creditors by liquidation and distribution of his remaining assets.

CLAIM OF EXEMPTION Privilege granted to judgment debtor allowing debtor to hold property of a certain class or to a certain amount free from levy or sale on execution or attachment.

In re Reed

Trustee (P) v. Debtor (D)

12 B.R. 41 (Bankr. N.D. Tex. 1981).

NATURE OF CASE: Action to challenge exemptions in bankruptcy.

FACT SUMMARY: Reed (D) sold nonexempt property to close acquaintances and applied the proceeds to liens on exempt property, prompting the trustee to sue to set aside the exemptions to preclude fraudulent transfers.

RULE OF LAW
Nonexempt property may be converted into exempt real property prior to bankruptcy.

FACTS: Just prior to filing bankruptcy, Reed (D) sold items of personal property to friends at far below their value. He applied the proceeds to a lien on his home, thus converting the value of nonexempt property into exempt property. The trustee (P) sued to preclude the conversion as fraudulent.

ISSUE: May the value of nonexempt property be converted into exempt property prior to bankruptcy?

HOLDING AND DECISION: (Brister, J.) Yes. The value of nonexempt property may be converted into exempt real property prior to bankruptcy. Had the conversion been to exempt personal property, it could have been set aside. However, the legislature did not include the exemption as applied to real property in its prohibition of conversion to frustrate creditors. Therefore, the transactions were valid.

ANALYSIS

This case illustrates that some transactions, even if facially fraudulent, may survive debt collection techniques. The case turns upon the perceived sanctity of the homestead and the court's reluctance to establish precedent, which would open the door to jeopardizing the exemption.

Quicknotes

LIEN A claim against the property of another in order to secure the payment of a debt.

In re Reed

Creditor bank (P) v. Debtor (D)

700 F.2d 986 (5th Cir. 1983).

NATURE OF CASE: Appeal from denial of discharge under § 727 of the Bankruptcy Code.

FACT SUMMARY: In Texas Bank's (P) action against Reed (D) for denial of discharge under § 727 of the Bankruptcy Code, Texas Bank (P) alleged that Reed (D) effected transfer designed to convert nonexempt property into exempt property less than two weeks before bankruptcy with the intent to hinder, delay, and defraud creditors.

RULE OF LAW

A debtor may be denied discharge under the Bankruptcy Code if he has transferred property with intent to hinder, delay, or defraud a creditor or has failed to explain satisfactorily any loss of assets.

FACTS: Reed (D) opened a men's wear shop, financing this venture in part by obtaining a loan from Texas Bank (P), which was guaranteed by the Small Business Administration. After a year, Reed (D) knew that his business was insolvent and met with Texas Bank (P), the Small Business Administration, and his major trade creditors. Reed (D) signed an agreement to turn over management of the store to a consulting firm, and the creditors agreed to postpone collection efforts if Reed (D) promised to resume payment on his debts. Reed's (D) business continued to fail, Reed (D) signed a foreclosure agreement surrendering the store to Texas Bank (P), and Reed (D) then filed voluntary petitions for bankruptcy. Just before filing for bankruptcy, Reed (D) sold $19,586.83 in personal assets and applied the proceeds to reduce the mortgages on his family residence, which was exempt from creditor's claims under Texas law. In Texas Bank's (P) action against Reed (D), Texas Bank (P) alleged that Reed (D) had effected the transfer of assets in order to convert nonexempt property to exempt property less than two weeks before filing for bankruptcy with the intent to hinder, delay, and defraud creditors. The bankruptcy judge agreed with Texas Bank's (P) allegations and denied Reed (D) discharge under 11 U.S.C. § 727(a)(5). Reed (D) appealed.

ISSUE: May a debtor be denied discharge under the Bankruptcy Code if he has transferred property with intent to hinder, delay, or defraud a creditor or failed to explain satisfactorily any loss of assets?

HOLDING AND DECISION: (Rubin, J.) Yes. A debtor may be denied discharge under the Bankruptcy Code if he has transferred property with intent to hinder, delay, or defraud a creditor or he has failed to explain satisfactorily any loss of assets. Here, the evidence amply supports the bankruptcy court's findings that Reed (D) had actual intent to defraud. Reed's (D) whole pattern of conduct evinces that intent. His rapid conversion of nonexempt assets to extinguish one home mortgage and to reduce another four months before bankruptcy, after arranging with his creditors to be free of payment obligations until the following year, speaks for itself as a transfer of property in fraud of creditors. Asked to account for the disappearance of $19,586.83, Reed (D) could only respond that he had many business and household expenses which he paid in cash as they arose. The bankruptcy judge's finding that his did not constitute a satisfactory explanation cannot be faulted. Affirmed.

ANALYSIS

A debtor is not entitled to a discharge as a matter of right, but discharge will be granted unless challenged by the trustee or a creditor. The trustee or creditors may object to the debtor's discharge of particular debts under § 523 of the Bankruptcy Code. A § 523 denial of discharge renders only one debt nondischargeable, while under § 727 of the Code, denial of discharge renders all of the debtor's debts nondischargeable.

Quicknotes

DISCHARGE OF DEBTS In bankruptcy, the release of a debtor who is unable to pay his debts as they become due from the obligation to pay his creditors.

In re Lanza

Debtor (P) v. Creditor bank (D)

51 B.R. 125 (Bankr. E.D. Pa. 1985).

NATURE OF CASE: Debtor's objection to creditor's proofs of claim.

FACT SUMMARY: Debtor Lanza (P) objected to proofs of claim filed by a bank that had loaned the Lanzas (D) at least $300,000; neither party kept substantial records of the loan.

RULE OF LAW

The party objecting to a proof of claim, which is prima facie evidence of its validity and amount, bears the burden of going forward with proof of the claim's validity.

FACTS: When the Lanzas (P), husband and wife, filed for bankruptcy, a bank that had made three loans to them filed proofs of claim. They first claimed an initial debt of $200,000, but after $300,000 was actually advanced to the Lanzas (P) by the bank for home improvement, the loan was restructured for an amount of either $300,000 or $350,000. The second and third claimed debts were, respectively, of $40,282 and $27,689. Mr. Lanza (P) died during bankruptcy, and his widow (P) objected to the first claim. However, neither the bank nor Mrs. Lanza (P) (who professed ignorance of all her husband's financial dealings) had any evidence of the claim. The bankruptcy court held an evidentiary hearing on the validity of the claim.

ISSUE: Does the party objecting to a creditor's proof of claim, which constitutes prima facie evidence of its validity and amount, bear the burden of going forward with proof of the claim's invalidity?

HOLDING AND DECISION: (Goldhaber, J.) Yes. A creditor's proof of claim executed and filed in accordance with Bankruptcy Rule § 3001(f) constitutes prima facie evidence of the validity and amount of the claim. The burden of going forward with proof is on the objecting party, not the claimant. This burden is not met by merely filing the objection. Here, Lanza (P) was left with no financial records to disprove the bank's claim. She was not entitled to assert that the bank's own management and lack of supporting documentation for the loan alone invalidated its claim. Therefore, the claim must be upheld.

ANALYSIS

Most claims that are presented for payment are paid without question, pro rata, by the trustee. This represents ratification of the creditor's claims without the formal mechanism of adjudication. It is rare that a trustee will object to a claim and conduct an evidentiary hearing on the validity of the claim, and even rarer, as here, for a debtor to object to a claim.

Quicknotes

EVIDENTIARY HEARING Hearing pertaining to the evidence of the case.

PRIMA FACIE EVIDENCE Evidence presented by a party that is sufficient, in the absence of contradictory evidence, to support the fact or issue for which it is offered.

PRO RATA In proportion.

In re Robert W. McNamara, Debtor

Bankruptcy trustee (P) v. Debtor (D)

310 B.R. 664 (Bankr. D. Conn. 2004).

NATURE OF CASE: Petition for discharge.

FACT SUMMARY: McNamara sought discharge in bankruptcy, but had a weak explanation for the disappearance of $150,000 from his estate.

RULE OF LAW

A court must grant a debtor's discharge unless the debtor himself or someone acting on his behalf conceals, destroys, transfers, or removes debtor property within one year of the petition filing date with the intent to defraud creditors or the court.

FACTS: McNamara was the sole witness at the trial to discharge his outstanding debts. The trustee suspected McNamara of hiding money to defraud his former wife, who was a significant creditor of McNamara's estate. The trustee cross-examined McNamara on the disappearance of $150,000 from his estate. McNamara had been ordered to place that money in a state court escrow fund, but instead used approximately $11,000 to go on a Caribbean vacation. The rest was unaccounted for, and in the trustee's opinion, in offshore accounts. McNamara testified that he lost most of the money in a poker game, but he was extremely fuzzy on the details of the game or the circumstances surrounding that evening. The court did not find his testimony credible. McNamara testified that he considered the money to be rightfully his and that he could not remember details because of alcohol and poor health. McNamara did not, however, provide any medical records or other documentation to support his claims.

ISSUE: Must a court grant a debtor's discharge if the debtor himself or someone acting on his behalf conceals, destroys, transfers, or removes debtor property within one year of the petition?

HOLDING AND DECISION: (Shiff, J.) No. A court must grant a debtor's discharge unless the debtor himself or someone acting on his behalf conceals, destroys, transfers, or removes debtor property within one year of the petition. A debtor must satisfactorily explain any lost or misplaced estate assets. The plaintiff introduces evidence of the loss and the debtor must prove a reasonable explanation by a preponderance of the evidence. The Trustee introduced her evidence of the missing $150,000, but McNamara's vague, uncorroborated explanation did not meet his burden. Here, McNamara clearly believed the money was his and his creditor ex-wife had no claim to it. His excuses and explanations for removing the property from his estate and her reach are insufficient. "Bankruptcy is a privilege, not a right." Discharge denied.

ANALYSIS

The bankruptcy court has significant discretion when assessing the credibility of an explanation for missing money. A reasonable, plausible explanation will usually suffice.

Quicknotes

DISCHARGEABLE DEBTS Debts subject to discharge in a bankruptcy proceeding.

FRAUD A false representation of facts with the intent that another will rely on the misrepresentation to his detriment.

PREPONDERANCE OF THE EVIDENCE A standard of proof requiring the trier of fact to determine whether the fact sought to be established is more probable than not.

In re Sharpe

Creditor-former friend (P) v. Debtor-former friend (D)

351 B.R. 409 (Bankr. N.D. Tex. 2006).

NATURE OF CASE: Adversary proceeding against debtor objecting to the dischargeability of certain debt pursuant to 11 U.S.C.S. § 523.

FACT SUMMARY: Ms. Baker (P) contended that loans she had made to Mr. Sharpe (D) should be not be discharged in bankruptcy because Mr. Sharpe (D), who had become her close friend and whose lifestyle and demeanor indicated he was wealthy, had made various oral representations to her about his financial condition that led her to believe that he in fact was wealthy and had the ability to repay the loans, so that he had deliberately misled her so that his actions amounted to fraud.

RULE OF LAW

The trappings of wealth, demeanor, and an extravagant lifestyle, together with an oral representation by the debtor that he has sufficient funds to repay a debt, do not rise to the level of false pretenses, false representation, or actual fraud such that the debt is nondischargeable pursuant to 11 U.S.C. § 523(a)(2)(A).

FACTS: Ms. Baker (P) and Mr. Sharpe (D) had become very close friends and spent a lot of time together. Mr. Sharpe (D) seemed to be wealthy, as he dressed in very expensive clothing, ate at the most expensive restaurants, flew in a friend's private jet, and otherwise had an extravagant lifestyle and the demeanor of being wealthy. Mr. Sharpe (D) convinced Ms. Baker (P) to lend him a total of $150,000 through several loans for a business venture they were both involved in. Two of the loans were evidenced by promissory notes; the rest were not. At the same time, and unbeknownst to Ms. Baker, Mr. Sharpe (D) was actually in financial trouble and was planning to file for bankruptcy. Mr. Sharpe (D) also had apparently represented to Ms. Baker (P) at the time the loans were made that he was able to repay the loans because he was essentially hiding assets from his then-current wife to prevent her from obtaining her share of those assets as part of a then-pending divorce settlement. After Mr. Sharpe (D) filed for bankruptcy protection, Ms. Baker (P) brought an adversary proceeding to object to the discharge of her loans, claiming that they were nondischargeable under 11 U.S.C. § 523(a)(2)(A), which provides in part that a debt is not dischargeable "to the extent obtained by false pretenses, a false representation, or actual fraud, other than a statement respecting the debtor's or an insider's financial condition."

ISSUE: Do the trappings of wealth, demeanor, and an extravagant lifestyle, together with an oral representation by the debtor that he has sufficient funds to repay a debt, rise to the level of false pretenses, false representation or actual fraud such that the debt is nondischargeable pursuant to 11 U.S.C. § 523(a)(2)(A)?

HOLDING AND DECISION: (Jernigan, J.) No. The trappings of wealth, demeanor, and an extravagant lifestyle, together with an oral representation by the debtor that he has sufficient funds to repay a debt, do not rise to the level of false pretenses, false representation, or actual fraud such that the debt is nondischargeable pursuant to 11 U.S.C. § 523 (a)(2)(A). When the last part of § 523(a)(2)(A), relating to a debtor's statement of financial condition, is read in conjunction with § 523(a)(2)(B), it is clear that a statement respecting the debtor's financial condition must be in writing to result in nondischargeability. Here, Ms. Baker (P) relied only on Mr. Sharpe's (D) oral and nonverbal representations. The question thus becomes whether those rise to the level of "false pretenses, false representation, or actual fraud" under § 523 (a) (2) (A). While Mr. Sharpe's (D) representations—both verbal and nonverbal—were indeed misrepresentations, they were all about his financial condition. Therefore, they do not come within the scope of § 523 (a) (2) (A), which expressly excludes from its coverage statements concerning a debtor's financial condition. Because Ms. Baker (P) failed to protect herself by obtaining from Mr. Sharpe (D) a written statement of his financial condition, she is now not entitled to not have her debt discharged. Plaintiff's debt is dischargeable.

ANALYSIS

The Tenth Circuit has set forth succinctly the policy behind requiring that statements concerning a debtor's financial condition be in writing:

> [G]iving a statement of financial condition is a solemn part of significant credit transactions; therefore, it is only natural that solemnity be sanctified by a document which the debtor either prepares or sees and adopts. In a world where important decisions relating to the extensions of credit and service will be made upon the contents of a statement relating to financial condition, too much mischief can be done by either party to the transaction were it otherwise. Somewhere in the commercial risk allocation picture, the writing must stand as a bulwark which tends to protect both sides.
>
> A creditor who forsakes that protection, abandoning caution and sound business practices in the name of convenience, may find itself without protection.

Bellco First Federal Credit Union v. Kaspar (In re Kaspar), 125 F.3d 1358, 1361 (10th Cir. 1997).

Continued on next page.

Quicknotes

DISCHARGE OF DEBTS In bankruptcy, the release of a debtor who is unable to pay his debts as they become due from the obligation to pay his creditors.

DISCHARGEABLE DEBTS Debts subject to discharge in a bankruptcy proceeding.

In re Hill

Creditor bank (P) v. Debtor (D)

2008 WL 2227359 (Bankr. N.D. Cal. 2008).

NATURE OF CASE: Adversary proceeding against debtor in Chapter 7 objecting to the dischargeability of certain debt pursuant to 11 U.S.C. § 523.

FACT SUMMARY: National City Bank (Bank) (P), a holder of a junior deed of trust on the Hill's (Debtors') (D) home, contended that its $250,000 claim on the deed of trust, which had been foreclosed out, should not be discharged because the Debtors (D) had deliberately and knowingly misrepresented their income on loan application documents, so that the debt was nondischargeable under 11 U.S.C. § 523(a)(2)(B).

RULE OF LAW

Under 11 U.S.C. § 523(a)(2)(B), a creditor's reliance on a fraudulent written representation of a debtor's financial condition is not reasonable where the creditor's normal business practices deviate from reasonable industry standards and where the creditor ignores "red flags" concerning the misrepresentation.

FACTS: The Hills (Debtors) (D) bought a house for $220,000 pursuant to a first deed of trust. As the value of the house increased over 20 years, they refinanced the original first deed of trust to obtain additional cash. They also obtained a junior deed of trust, which they refinanced several times. Mr. Hill (D) earned around $39,000 per year, and Mrs. Hill (D), who was self-employed, earned up to $26,000. In April 2006, they contacted Ellerback, a mortgage broker, about getting more cash out of their house, and he had them apply for a $200,000 equity line of credit with National City Bank (Bank) (P). In the loan application submitted to obtain this loan, Mr. Hill's (D) monthly income was listed as $8,176, or $98,112 on an annual basis, and Mrs. Hill's (D) monthly income was listed as $3,967, or $47,604 on an annual basis for a combined monthly income of approximately $12,143, or $145,716 on an annual basis. Ellerback obtained this information from Mrs. Hill (D) on the telephone. The loan was approved. By October 2006, the Debtors (D) needed more cash. This time, Mrs. Hill (D) called the Bank (P) directly, and on the application for an increase of the line of credit to $250,000, Mr. Hill's (D) annual income was listed as $67,200 and Mrs. Hill's (D) as $123,600, for a total of $190,000 on an annual basis. The Bank's (P) guidelines for loan approval required that for a borrower who was self-employed, the Bank (P) could choose one of three types of verification: (1) a copy of the borrower's business license, (2) a copy of the most recent month's bank statement reflecting liquidity at least equal to one-tenth of the borrower's annual income, or (3) a CPA letter verifying the existence and ownership of the business. The loan was approved on the basis of a letter verifying the existence and ownership of Mrs. Hill's (D). Although the letter was written on the letterhead of a CPA, it was signed by someone other than the CPA whose name was on the letterhead. In April 2006, the house had been appraised at $785,000. In October 2006, it was appraised at $856,000. Shortly after the Debtors (D) filed for bankruptcy under Chapter 7 in April 2007, the first deed of trust holder purchased the house at its foreclosure sale for $450,000. The Bank (P) brought an adversary proceeding objecting to the discharge of $250,000 to which it had a claim, contending that the debt was nondischargeable under 11 U.S.C. § 523(a)(2)(B) because the Debtors (D) had knowingly made a material written misrepresentation as to their financial condition on which the Bank (P) reasonably relied.

ISSUE: Under 11 U.S.C. § 523(a)(2)(B), is a creditor's reliance on a fraudulent written representation of a debtor's financial condition reasonable where the creditor's normal business practices deviate from reasonable industry standards and where the creditor ignores "red flags" concerning the misrepresentation?

HOLDING AND DECISION: (Tchaikovsky, J.) No. Under 11 U.S.C. § 523(a)(2)(B), a creditor's reliance on a fraudulent written representation of a debtor's financial condition is not reasonable where the creditor's normal business practices deviate from reasonable industry standards and where the creditor ignores "red flags" concerning the misrepresentation. To establish a debt as nondischargeable under § 523(a)(2)(B), a creditor must demonstrate that: The debtor made a written representation of respecting the debtor's financial condition; the representation was material; the debtor knew at the time the representation was made that it was false; the representation was made with the intent to deceive the creditor; the creditor relied on the representation; the reliance was reasonable; and the damage suffered by the creditor proximately resulted from the representation. Although the Bank (P) meets all but one of these elements, it fails to establish nondischargeability because it fails to establish that its reliance was reasonable. The Bank (P) established that the Debtors (D) made a false representation to the Bank in writing concerning their financial condition and that the misrepresentation was material, since they overstated their income and would not have received the loan without the falsehood. The evidence also showed that the Debtors (P) knew their representation was fraudulent at the time it was made, and that the representation was made with the intent to deceive the Bank (P). However, when viewed under an objective standard of reasonableness, the Bank (P) either did

Continued on next page.

not rely on the Debtors' (D) representations concerning their income or its reliance was not reasonable. Under an objective test, a lender's reliance is usually reasonable if it follows its normal business practices, but this alone may not be enough if those practices deviate from reasonable industry standards or if the creditor ignores a "red flag" about the debtor's financial condition. Here, the Bank's (P) guidelines required an evaluation of the reasonableness of the salary listed by an employed borrower (here, Mr. Hill (D)) based on job type and geographical area, but there was no indication that the Bank (P) actually conducted such an evaluation. With regard to a self-employed borrower (here, Mrs. Hill (D)), the Bank (P) was supposed to ascertain the existence of the business by verification from a CPA. Here, the Bank (P) failed to question the verification letter supplied by Mrs. Hill (D), which, although on a CPA's letterhead, was not signed by a CPA. Further, the Bank (P) could have checked its file for the April 2006 loan against the information it received for the October 2006 loan, but failed to. If it had, it would have discovered significant discrepancies in listed incomes that purportedly occurred in just six months. The minimal verification required by the loan at issue, known as an "income stated" loan, suggests that in reality the Bank (P) made the loan principally in reliance on the value of the house as reflected by appraisals thereof. Subsequent events strongly suggest that the appraisals were inflated. Therefore, the Debtors (D) cannot be blamed for the Bank's (D) loss, and the Bank's (D) claim should be discharged notwithstanding that the Debtors (D) made a material false representation concerning their financial condition to the Bank (P) with knowledge of its falsity and the intent to deceive the Bank (P). The Bank's (P) claim is discharged.

ANALYSIS

The type of loan involved in this case, known as a "stated income" loan, does not require that the applicant's statement of income be verified by pay stubs, income tax returns, or similar documents or proof of income. As this case demonstrates, during a period of artificially inflated home values, banks were eager to make such loans, and they were widely available. However, as this case also demonstrates, because the usual verification methods are lacking with such loans (given the nickname "liar's loans" by some), having a minimally verified written finance statement may not be enough to protect the lender's claim from discharge.

Quicknotes

CHAPTER 7 BANKRUPTCY A legal proceeding whereby a debtor, who is unable to pay his debts as they become due, is relieved of his obligation to pay his creditors by liquidation and distribution of his remaining assets.

DEED OF TRUST A legal document that acts as a mortgage, placing a security interest in the deeded property with a trustee to insure the payment of a debt.

DISCHARGE OF DEBTS In bankruptcy, the release of a debtor who is unable to pay his debts as they become due from the obligation to pay his creditors.

In re Patricia M. Miller, Debtor

State agency (P) v. Student loan debtor (D)

377 F.3d 616 (6th Cir. 2004).

NATURE OF CASE: Appeal of partial discharge of student loans.

FACT SUMMARY: After taking out educational loans for her undergraduate and master's degrees and work in a doctoral program, Patricia Miller (D) filed Chapter 7 bankruptcy and sought to discharge her student loans in an adversary proceeding against the Pennsylvania Higher Education Assistance Agency (PHEAA) (P).

RULE OF LAW

A court may grant a partial student loan discharge under 11 U.S.C. § 105(a) if the Brunner criteria are met for a finding of undue hardship.

FACTS: Patricia Miller (D) received various student loans from PHEAA (P) to finance her undergraduate and master's degrees and study in a doctoral program. She did not complete the final requirements to earn her doctorate and was employed after leaving the program as a full-time administrative assistant. She had an additional part-time job at a call center. She filed a petition for Chapter 7 bankruptcy and filed an adversary proceeding against PHEAA (P) seeking a discharge of her student loans. Her loans totaled $89,832.16 and Miller (D) had repaid just $368.00. After trial, the court found that the total loan amount did not constitute an undue hardship for Miller (D) to repay, but granted Miller (D) a partial discharge. PHEAA (P) appealed and Miller (D) cross-appealed to the United States District Court for the Eastern District of Tennessee, which adopted the bankruptcy court opinion and dismissed the appeals. PHEAA (P) appeals to this court, contending that the bankruptcy court improperly partially discharged Miller's (D) loans without a finding of undue hardship.

ISSUE: May a court grant a partial student loan discharge under 11 U.S.C. § 105(a) if the Brunner criteria are met for a finding of undue hardship?

HOLDING AND DECISION: (Gibbons, J.) Yes. A court may grant a partial student loan discharge under 11 U.S.C. § 105(a) if the Brunner criteria are met for a finding of undue hardship. § 105(a) allows a court discretion to grant a partial discharge of student loans, but only upon the satisfaction of certain criteria. This court held as much in *Hornsby v. Tenn. Student Assistance Corp.*, 144 F.3d 433 (1998). The purpose of the Bankruptcy Act is met when courts may appropriately intervene in a debtor's financial burden even absent a finding of undue hardship for repayment of the student loans. A finding of undue hardship, however, must still be made for the discharged loan portion. The *Hornsby* holding is in conflict with the unpublished *DeMatteis v. Case Western Reserve University v. Case W. Reserve Univ. ([In re DeMatteis, 97 Fed. Appx. 6, 9, No. 02-3003, 2004 WL 445167, at *3 (6th Cir. 2004)])*, but this court disagrees with the conclusion that § 105(a) provides a separate equitable grounds theory. The Brunner criteria should be applied to the debtor's situation to determine if a finding of undue hardship is appropriate. The three Brunner factors include whether the debtor has made a good faith effort to repay, whether the current financial state is likely to persist, and whether repayment would prohibit a minimal standard of living. Miller (D) is underemployed and has not made a good faith effort to repay her student loans. Although Miller (D) did not satisfy the Brunner criteria, the bankruptcy court partially discharged her student loans. The discharge occurred under the bankruptcy court's own framework, which is not permissible. Reversed and remanded.

ANALYSIS

The Bankruptcy Code does not have an express provision allowing for a partial discharge of student loans. 11 U.S.C. § 105(a) states that a court "may issue any order, process, or judgment that is necessary or appropriate to carry out the provisions" of the Code. Some courts disagree that a partial discharge of student loans is allowed, but Congress allowed the Miller line of cases to stand under the 2005 amendments.

Quicknotes

CHAPTER 7 BANKRUPTCY A legal proceeding whereby a debtor, who is unable to pay his debts as they become due, is relieved of his obligation to pay his creditors by liquidation and distribution of his remaining assets.

UNDUE HARDSHIP Excessive suffering or adversity, especially referring to financial positions that are likely to continue in spite of good faith efforts to overcome the situation.

In re Milbank

Creditor wife (P) v. Debtor husband (D)

1 B.R. 150 (Bankr. S.D.N.Y. 1979).

NATURE OF CASE: Action seeking nondischargeable determination respecting claims against a bankrupt.

FACT SUMMARY: In Schulman (P) and Ann Milbank's (P) action against Mark Milbank (D), Schulman (P) and Ann Milbank (P) alleged that Mark Milbank (D), the bankrupt in this case, obtained money from them while he was having an adulterous affair with his next door neighbor, that he obtained the money under false pretenses, and that he should not be able to discharge his obligations to Schulman (P) and Ann (P) upon filing for bankruptcy.

RULE OF LAW

A bankrupt's pretenses need not be expressed in words, and a deliberately created falsehood is the same as a spoken falsehood.

FACTS: Mark Milbank (D) had been married to Ann Milbank (P) for more than ten years when they began to experience marital problems. Mark (D) left the family home for a period of five months. Upon his return, he expressed the desire to improve his marriage to Ann (P) and told her and her father, Schulman (P), that in order to spend more time with his family he wanted to relocate his custom-made furniture business closer to home. Mark (D) then requested a loan of $10,000 from Schulman (P) to relocate the business and later borrowed $12,500 from Ann (P) to purchase a car and a building for the new business. During this time, while Mark (D) was representing to Ann (P) and Schulman (P) his commitment to improve his marriage, he was also carrying on an extramarital affair with his next door neighbor. Ann (P) found out, divorced Mark (D), and Mark (D) filed for bankruptcy shortly afterwards. Mark (D) then attempted to discharge his obligations to Ann (P) and Schulman (P) under the Bankruptcy Act. Ann (P) and Schulman (P) brought an action alleging that Mark (D) had received money from them under false pretenses and that he should not be able to discharge his obligations to them.

ISSUE: Need a bankrupt's pretenses not be expressed in words, and is a deliberately created falsehood the same as a spoken falsehood?

HOLDING AND DECISION: (Schwartzberg, J.) Yes. A bankrupt's pretenses need not be expressed in words, and a deliberately created falsehood is the same as a spoken falsehood. Not every family loan made concurrently with the commission of adulterous acts can be said to be obtained as a result of fraud in the bankruptcy sense. Here, however, loans made to Mark Milbank (D) by both Ann (P) and Schulman (P) were made in reliance upon Mark's (D) representations that he and Ann (P) would make a good-faith effort to strengthen their marriage. In fact, Mark's (D) representations were a sham; his extramarital affair evidenced his false pretenses with respect to his display of marital stability. Ann (P) and Schulman (P), would not have made the loans to Mark (D) had they known he was not only not working on improving his marriage, but instead engaging in an adulterous affair. The stability of the marriage was a condition upon which Ann (P) and Schulman (P) relied to their detriment because of Mark's (D) false pretenses. Mark's (D) obligations to Ann (P) and Schulman (P) will not be discharged.

ANALYSIS

The debtor-creditor payment process may be viewed as constant balancing—a weighing and leveraging process. Ultimately, the creditor tries to decide how to influence the debtor's balancing decision. The creditor attempts to determine how, at the lowest cost to himself, he can make it more beneficial—less costly—for the debtor to pay the money owed. The creditor looks for ways to enhance his leverage with the debtor to increase the likelihood that the debtor will repay the creditor.

Quicknotes

DISCHARGE OF DEBTS In bankruptcy, the release of a debtor who is unable to pay his debts as they become due from the obligation to pay his creditors.

United States v. Cluck

Federal government (P) v. Debtor (D)

143 F.3d 174 (5th Cir. 1998).

NATURE OF CASE: Appeal from conviction for bankruptcy fraud.

FACT SUMMARY: When a tax planning attorney was convicted of bankruptcy fraud, he claimed there was insufficient evidence that he had intentionally committed fraud.

RULE OF LAW

Circumstances, which may be inconclusive if considered separately, may, by their number and joint operation, be sufficient to constitute conclusive proof.

FACTS: Cluck (D) was an attorney who specialized in legal avoidance of taxes. When a state court rendered judgment against him for $2.9 million, Cluck (D) filed for bankruptcy. Before filing for Chapter 7 liquidation, Cluck (D) had disposed of property by signing a promissory note and pawning some assets. Cluck (D) did not disclose these and other transfers to the bankruptcy court. When the bankruptcy court found Cluck (D) had engaged in intentional concealment, the U.S. Attorney charged Cluck (D) with eight counts of bankruptcy fraud. A jury found Cluck (D) guilty on seven counts, and Cluck (D) appealed.

ISSUE: May circumstances, which may be inconclusive if considered separately by their number and joint operation, be sufficient to constitute conclusive proof?

HOLDING AND DECISION: (Jolly, J.) Yes. Circumstances, which may be inconclusive if considered separately, may, by their number and joint operation, be sufficient to constitute conclusive proof. Cluck's (D) repeated omissions and questionable transfers formed the kind of circumstances that could constitute conclusive proof. A rational jury could have inferred the existence of an intentional plan to defraud from the bare facts of Cluck's (D) systematic concealment and false statements. Affirmed.

ANALYSIS

The denial of discharge in bankruptcy may lead to criminal prosecution, as well. False oaths, false claims, concealment of assets, and fee fixing may be punishable as crimes. The attorney in this case had some of his accounts paid directly to a Nevada corporation owned by his wife.

Quicknotes

CHAPTER 7 BANKRUPTCY A legal proceeding whereby a debtor, who is unable to pay his debts as they become due, is relieved of his obligation to pay his creditors by liquidation and distribution of his remaining assets.

INTENTIONAL CONCEALMENT A false representation of facts with the intent that another will rely on the misrepresentation to his detriment.

INTENTIONAL FRAUD A false representation of facts with the intent that another will rely on the misrepresentation to his detriment.

In re Pendlebury

Debtors (P) v. Creditor savings and loan (D)

94 B.R. 120 (Bankr. E.D. Pa. 1988).

NATURE OF CASE: Motion to strike attorney fees clause in reaffirmation agreement.

FACT SUMMARY: Four Chapter 7 debtors (P) eager to retain possession of their mobile homes, which constituted security for pre-petition loans from a savings and loan association (D), negotiated reaffirmation agreements with the savings and loan association (D) that contained clauses requiring that they pay attorney fees.

RULE OF LAW

The bankruptcy court will make an independent inquiry as to whether a voluntary post-petition reaffirmation agreement between debtor and creditor is in the best interests of the debtor only when the debtor is unrepresented by counsel.

FACTS: Four Chapter 7 debtors (P) had pre-petition loans secured by their mobile homes. The Creditor (D), a savings and loan association, negotiated reaffirmation agreements with the debtors under which they could keep their homes and continue loan payments. The proposed reaffirmation agreements contained a clause requiring the Debtors (P) to pay attorney fees in the amount of $250. The debtors (P) filed a motion to strike the fees clause, and the bankruptcy court postponed granting discharge of the debtors (P) until the motion was considered.

ISSUE: Will a bankruptcy court make an independent inquiry into whether a voluntary post-petition reaffirmation agreement between the debtor and creditor is in the best interest of the debtor when the debtor is represented by counsel?

HOLDING AND DECISION: (Stair, J.) No. Reforms to the Bankruptcy Act in 1984 abrogated the previous requirement that the bankruptcy court independently inquire into the fairness of reaffirmation agreements between the debtor and creditor; now, 11 U.S.C. § 524 (c) requires the debtor's attorney to file an affidavit that the reaffirmation agreement he helped the debtor negotiate with the creditor does not pose an undue hardship on the debtor. Only when the debtor appears pro se will a court step in to approve reaffirmation agreements. Reaffirmation agreements are viable alternatives to redemption because they do not require lump-sum payments by the debtor, they are negotiated voluntarily between the debtor and creditor, and they allow the debtor to retain the secured collateral. Although the allowance of reaffirmation is somewhat at odds with the purpose of Chapter 7 to provide debtors a "fresh start," debtors in fact have leverage in negotiating reaffirmation agreements, and creditors can avoid having their loans discharged and can avoid the expenses of repossession and foreclosure. Here, the court will not shift the burden of examining the fairness of reaffirmation agreements from the attorneys back to the court. Motion denied.

ANALYSIS

Reaffirmation agreements were wholly informal and unsupervised until the 1978 Code required court examination of their fairness. However, the burden placed on the courts prompted the 1984 reform, leaving the task of supervision to the debtor's attorney. Some, but not all, courts also allow a debtor to retain his security interest in the absence of a reaffirmation agreement if he keeps up his payments after filing of the petition. Especially creative debtors today also engage in "lien stripping," whereby they keep up payments until the fair market value of the collateral is paid to the creditor, at which time they stop payments entirely.

Quicknotes

CHAPTER 7 BANKRUPTCY A legal proceeding whereby a debtor, who is unable to pay his debts as they become due, is relieved of his obligation to pay his creditors by liquidation and distribution of his remaining assets.

REAFFIRMATION An agreement after the filing of the bankruptcy petition to repay obligations that arose prior to its filing.

UNDUE HARDSHIP Excessive suffering or adversity, especially referring to financial positions that are likely to continue in spite of good faith efforts to overcome the situation.

In re Paglia, Debtor

Debtor (P) v. Lending bank (D)

302 B.R. 162 (Bankr. W.D. Pa. 2003).

NATURE OF CASE: Adversary proceeding in bankruptcy.

FACT SUMMARY: Paglia (P) filed a Chapter 7 bankruptcy petition and received a discharge of his outstanding debts, including a promissory note in favor of First National Bank (D) and guaranteed by his mother. Prior to receiving his discharge and in exchange for First National Bank (D) forgoing litigation against his mother to collect on her pledge of payment, Paglia (P) executed a second promissory note. Paglia (P) seeks to discharge that second note.

RULE OF LAW

(1) Creditors may not "act to collect" discharged debts from debtors.
(2) Creditors may accept voluntary repayment from debtors.

FACTS: Paglia (P) executed a promissory note in favor of First National Bank (D), and Irene Paglia, his mother, assigned her interest in an annuity as pledge for payment. Paglia (P) defaulted on the note and then sought Chapter 7 bankruptcy protection and a discharge of his obligations. First National (D) moved to enforce Irene Paglia's pledge of payment and demanded that she liquidate her annuity to satisfy the note obligation. In exchange for not moving forward with litigation against his mother, Paglia (P) executed a second promissory note in favor of First National Bank (D) for the full amount of the prior debt. Irene Paglia executed a second pledge of her annuity interest to secure the payment of the second note. Paglia (P) then received a discharge of his pre-petition obligations. Paglia (P) made ten years of payments on the second promissory note and then defaulted once again. He moved to reopen his bankruptcy case so that he might file an adversary proceeding seeking to discharge the second promissory note. Paglia (P) contended that First National Bank (D) violated the discharge injunction and automatic stay sections of the Bankruptcy Code. The motion to reopen was granted.

ISSUE:

(1) May creditors "act to collect" discharged debts from debtors?
(2) May creditors accept voluntary repayment from debtors?

HOLDING AND DECISION: (Markovitz, J.)

(1) No. Creditors may not "act to collect" discharged debts from debtors. A secured creditor may not "act to collect" a debt of a personally liable debtor once a discharge has issued. The same secured creditor may, however, move forward in rem against the collateral securing the original debt. First National Bank (D) permissibly sought to move forward against Irene Paglia's annuity pledged as security for Paglia's (P) debt. Paglia (P) signed the second promissory note in exchange for First National Bank (D) agreeing not to move forward against Irene Paglia's annuity interest. The second promissory note was also not a "reaffirmation" of the first note because of the new consideration (i.e., agreement to forgo collection efforts against Irene Paglia).
(2) Yes. Creditors may accept voluntary repayment from debtors. First National Bank (D) did not coerce Paglia (P) into executing the second note, but merely accepted his offer of voluntary repayment. Active collection efforts are required to demonstrate a violation of the prohibition against acting to collect found in § 524(a)(2). For the same reasons that First National Bank (D) did not violate the collection prohibition, it did not violate the automatic stay provision of the Code.

ANALYSIS

Creditors cannot openly seek to collect a debt once the debtor is under bankruptcy protection. Creditors can, however, seek to collect the same debt through "encouragement" tactics such as that used in *Paglia*. Such a tactic is completely permissible when the prior debt is secured by collateral and is not considered coercive.

Quicknotes

AUTOMATIC STAY Upon the filing of a voluntary bankruptcy petition, creditors are prohibited from attempting to recover payment from the debtor or his property.

CHAPTER 7 BANKRUPTCY A legal proceeding whereby a debtor, who is unable to pay his debts as they become due, is relieved of his obligation to pay his creditors by liquidation and distribution of his remaining assets.

REAFFIRMATION An agreement after the filing of the bankruptcy petition to repay obligations that arose prior to its filing.

UNSECURED CREDITOR A creditor whose loan is not backed by specified collateral or a security agreement.

CHAPTER **6**

Chapter 13 Bankruptcy

Quick Reference Rules of Law

1. **Payments to Secured Creditors.** A debtor may retain property under § 362 of the Bankruptcy Code if that property is necessary for an effective reorganization. (In re Radden) *44*

2. **Payments to Secured Creditors.** Where a debtor exercises the cramdown option of Bankruptcy Code § 1325(a)(5)(B), seeking to retain and utilize a secured creditor's collateral pursuant to a Chapter 13 plan, the value of that collateral is to be determined in accordance with a replacement-value standard. (Associates Commercial Corp. v. Rash) *45*

3. **Payments to Secured Creditors.** The formula approach is the proper method to calculate the appropriate discount interest rate under Chapter 13 reorganization. (Till v. SCS Credit Corporation) *47*

4. **Payments on the Home Mortgage.** The power granted to debtors under Chapter 13 that allows the debtor to cure defaults encompasses the power to allow debtor mortgagors to "de-accelerate" their mortgages and to reinstate their original payment schedules. (In re Taddeo) *49*

5. **Payments to Unsecured Creditors.** Where a spouse is filing for bankruptcy individually, the other spouse's income must be considered in calculating the bankrupt spouse's disposable income. (In re Carter) *51*

6. **Payments to Unsecured Creditors.** Only those expenses that are reasonably necessary may be deducted from a debtor's repayment plan. (In the Matter of Wyant) *52*

7. **Payments to Unsecured Creditors.** (1) "Projected disposable income" under 11 U.S.C. § 1325 means "disposable income," as defined by § 1325(b)(2), projected over the "applicable commitment period." (2) The "applicable commitment period" requirement of 11 U.S.C. § 1325 is inapplicable to a plan submitted voluntarily by a debtor with no "projected disposable income." (In re Kagenveama) *53*

8. **Payments to Unsecured Creditors.** A Chapter 13 bankruptcy case will not be dismissed on bad faith grounds where above-median income debtors have allegedly claimed an improper housing allowance deduction and have refused to amend their proposed plan. (In re Farrar-Johnson) *55*

9. **Threshold Eligibility for Chapter 13.** To be eligible for Chapter 13 bankruptcy, an individual with regular income may include funding from diverse and nontraditional sources. (In re Murphy) *56*

10. **Threshold Eligibility for Chapter 13.** The issue of the debtor's liability should not be taken into account when determining the liquidity of a claim. (In re Huelbig) *57*

11. **The Consumer Bankruptcy System.** One of the express congressional purposes of Chapter 13 is the repayment of creditors. (In re San Miguel) *58*

In re Radden

Debtor (P) v. GMAC creditor (D)

35 B.R. 821 (Bankr. E.D. Va. 1983).

NATURE OF CASE: Action to recover repossessed property.

FACT SUMMARY: In Radden's (P) action against GMAC (D), to recover an auto that GMAC (D) repossessed when Radden (P) failed to make payments required by the auto sales contract, Radden (P) contended that the auto was necessary for his reorganization under a Chapter 13 bankruptcy, and thus it should be returned to him.

RULE OF LAW

A debtor may retain property under § 362 of the Bankruptcy Code if that property is necessary for an effective reorganization.

FACTS: Radden (P) purchased an automobile and financed the purchase by a retail sales contract secured by the vehicle. The installment sales agreement was assigned to GMAC (D) pursuant to its agreement with the dealer from whom Radden (P) purchased the car. Radden (P) fell behind on his payments, and GMAC (D) repossessed the car. Radden (P) then filed for relief under Chapter 13 of the Bankruptcy Code. The Chapter 13 plan proposed to pay GMAC (D) in full to the extent of the value of the collateral plus interest. GMAC (D) contended that Radden (P) did not have any equity in the car and that the car was not necessary for Radden's (P) effective reorganization. Radden (P) contended that the car was necessary for his reorganization and that it should be returned to him.

ISSUE: May a debtor retain property under § 362 of the Bankruptcy Code if that property is necessary for an effective reorganization?

HOLDING AND DECISION: (Shelley, J.) Yes. A debtor may retain property under § 362 of the Bankruptcy Code if that property is necessary for an effective reorganization. The debtor bears the burden of proving that the property is necessary for his effective reorganization under § 362. Here, it is obvious that an automobile is necessary for an individual's effective reorganization in today's society. Radden (P) testified that he needed the auto to get to and from his job as well as to obtain medical and other necessary services. GMAC (D) will, therefore, have to return the repossessed auto to Radden (P).

ANALYSIS

The secured creditor in a Chapter 13 bankruptcy case is better protected than the unsecured creditor. The debtor's Chapter 13 plan to retain property subject to a security interest often provokes a dispute with the secured party who declares the debtor in default and wants the property back. Whether the creditor can exercise its right to repossession and sale, realizing the value of the collateral and ending the contract with the debtor, depends on the debtor's ability to comply with the provisions of Chapter 13, which are designed to protect secured creditors.

Quicknotes

CHAPTER 13 BANKRUPTCY Debtor may modify plan at any time before the completion of the payments under such plan.

REPOSSESSION The taking back of an item paid for under an installment contract when payment of an installment is not made.

SECURED CREDITOR A creditor, the repayment of whose loan is secured by collateral sufficient to repay the debt owed.

UNSECURED CREDITOR A creditor whose loan is not backed by specified collateral or a security agreement.

Associates Commercial Corp. v. Rash

Lien holder (P) v. Debtor (D)

520 U.S. 953 (1997).

NATURE OF CASE: Review of judgment approving bankruptcy plan and limiting secured claim to net foreclosure value of collateral.

FACT SUMMARY: Associates Commercial Corporation (P) filed an objection to the Rashes' (D) Chapter 13 reorganization plan, seeking repossession of their tractor truck and alleging a secured interest of $47,171 constituting the replacement value of the truck.

RULE OF LAW

Where a debtor exercises the cramdown option of Bankruptcy Code § 1325(a)(5)(B), seeking to retain and utilize a secured creditor's collateral pursuant to a Chapter 13 plan, the value of that collateral is to be determined in accordance with a replacement-value standard.

FACTS: Rash (D) purchased a tractor truck for use in his freight-hauling business for $73,700. He made a down payment on the truck and agreed to pay the seller the balance in sixty monthly installments. The seller assigned the loan and lien to Associates Commercial Corporation (ACC) (P). The Rashes (D) subsequently filed a petition in bankruptcy under Chapter 13. ACC (P) was listed as a secured creditor. Under Bankruptcy Code § 506(a), ACC's (P) claim was only secured to the extent of the value of the collateral, and any amount of the claim above the value of the truck was unsecured. In order for the Rashes' (D) plan to be confirmed, it had to satisfy the requirements of § 1324 (a). Pursuant to this section, the plan may be confirmed if the secured creditor accepts the plan, the debtor surrenders the secured property to the creditor, or the debtor selects the cramdown option. Under the cramdown option, the debtor retains the secured property in which the creditor still has a lien, and the debtor tenders payments to the creditor in conformity with the plan amounting to the value of the secured interest in the collateral, equal to its present value. The Rashes (D) selected the cramdown option. Their plan proposed their continued use of the truck for business purposes and payment to ACC (P) of the present value of the truck in fifty-eight monthly installments totaling $28,500. ACC (P) filed an objection seeking to remove the application of the automatic stay to the truck, alleging a secured interest of $47,171. The bankruptcy court held that the proper valuation of the claim was the net amount ACC (P) would obtain from a foreclosure sale of the property, determined to equal $31,875. The bankruptcy court approved the plan, and the district court affirmed. The court of appeals reversed, then affirmed upon a rehearing en banc. The Supreme Court granted review.

ISSUE: Where a debtor exercises the cramdown option of Bankruptcy Code § 1325(a)(5)(B), seeking to retain and utilize a creditor's collateral pursuant to a Chapter 13 plan, is the value of that collateral to be determined in accordance with a replacement-value standard?

HOLDING AND DECISION: (Ginsburg, J.) Yes. Where a debtor exercises the cramdown option of Bankruptcy Code § 1325(a)(5)(B), seeking to retain and utilize a creditor's collateral pursuant to a Chapter 13 plan, the value of that collateral is to be determined in accordance with a replacement-value standard. Bankruptcy Code § 506(a) provides that a creditor's claim is secured to the extent of the bankruptcy estate's interest in the property. Therefore, in a cramdown context, the value of the collateral is to be ascertained in accordance with the price a buyer in the debtor's business would pay to obtain similar property for a comparable use. The creditor's secured claim is limited by this section to the value of the collateral. In order to determine this amount, the court must compare the creditor's claim with the value of the collateral. The section requires such value to be determined in accordance with the proposed use of the property and the purposes of the valuation. Where, as in the present case, the Debtor (D) retains the property and uses it for business purposes, the proper valuation method is in accordance with the cost the debtor would incur in obtaining similar property for a comparable use. Reversed and remanded.

DISSENT: (Stevens, J.) Foreclosure is the proper valuation method here under 11 U.S.C. § 506(a), although the section is not clear. The value should be determined from the creditor's perspective because the section's purpose is to put the creditor in that position he would occupy if able to foreclose upon his lien. The debtor's secured property cannot be in the creditor's hands, but its value should be. Foreclosure valuation maintains the respective recoveries of secured and unsecured creditors throughout the Code chapters.

ANALYSIS

Note that the determinative issue in evaluating the amount of the creditor's secured claim is the proposed use or disposition of the collateral. Where a secured creditor rejects a debtor's Chapter 13 reorganization plan, the debtor has two options regarding the proposed use of the collateral. First, the debtor can relinquish possession of the collateral to the creditor. Alternatively, the debtor can retain possession of the collateral and tender payments

Continued on next page.

equaling the collateral's present value. The conflict among the Circuit courts was in reference to the determination of the present value of the collateral for cramdown purposes. Where the debtor chooses to surrender the collateral, the creditor obtains immediate possession and may sell the property at a foreclosure sale. However, where the debtor elects to retain the property and make continued business use of the collateral, the Court determines that a foreclosure sale valuation is inappropriate and the replacement-value standard is more in conformity with the requirement that such valuation be made consistent with the proposed use of the property.

Quicknotes

CHAPTER 13 BANKRUPTCY Debtor may modify plan at any time before the completion of the payments under such plan.

CRAMDOWN Refers to a court's confirmation of a reorganization plan in a bankruptcy proceeding despite the opposition of creditors.

EN BANC The hearing of a matter by all the judges of the court, rather than only the necessary quorum.

FORECLOSURE VALUE The amount realized when a property is sold either by court order or by power of sale contained in a mortgage.

REPLACEMENT VALUE The monetary amount necessary in order to replace property or improvements.

SECURED CREDITOR A creditor, the repayment of whose loan is secured by collateral sufficient to repay the debt owed.

Till v. SCS Credit Corporation

Debtors (P) v. Subprime lender (D)

541 U.S. 465 (2004).

NATURE OF CASE: Challenge to rate of interest in proposed plan.

FACT SUMMARY: Congress did not specify a particular method to determine an appropriate interest rate under the Bankruptcy Code's cramdown provision. Four judicial opinions offered four separate methods.

RULE OF LAW

The formula approach is the proper method to calculate the appropriate discount interest rate under Chapter 13 reorganization.

FACTS: Lee and Amy Till (P) financed a used truck through Instant Auto, which assigned the loan to SCS Credit Corporation (SCS) (D), a subprime lender. The loan's interest rate was 21 percent and the Tills (P) were to make 68 payments. The Tills (P) defaulted and filed for Chapter 13 reorganization. Their proposed plan used the "formula" approach to offer to pay the secured auto loan at 9.5 percent interest—the prime rate of 8 percent plus a 1½ percent adjustment to account for the risk of their default. The bankruptcy court approved the cramdown interest rate and confirmed the plan. SCS (D) appealed, arguing that 21 percent interest was the standard in the subprime lending market. The district court reversed based on the "coerced loan" approach, which applies the interest rate at the foreclosure and similar re-investment level. Based on SCS's (D) unrebutted testimony, 21 percent was that rate. On appeal, the Seventh Circuit applied the "presumptive contract rate" approach, which set the 21 percent interest rate as a rebuttable presumption. The Seventh Circuit remanded to allow the Tills (P) the opportunity to rebut the presumptive 21 percent. The dissenting judge on the Seventh Circuit opinion would have applied the "cost of funds" approach, which seeks to avoid overcompensating secured creditors by discounting rates for costs associated with issuing a new loan. This Court granted certiorari review to determine the appropriate method from among the four proffered in this case.

ISSUE: Is the formula approach the proper method to calculate the appropriate discount interest rate under Chapter 13 reorganization?

HOLDING AND DECISION: (Stevens, J.) Yes. The formula approach is the proper method to calculate the appropriate discount interest rate under Chapter 13 reorganization. Creditors must be adequately compensated for a debtor's promise of future payment because the money is not immediately available to the creditor, inflation may occur, and the debtor could default. The interest rate is used to compensate for these factors. The approach to determine that interest rate should be a familiar financial approach, ensuring the creditor receives present-day value of its claim, and the inquiry into the terms of the cramdown loan should be an objective one. The bankruptcy court unambiguously has the right to modify the terms of the original loan to secure the most appropriate outcome for both debtor and secured creditors. Keeping these considerations in mind, the formula approach is straightforward, minimizes the need for expensive evidentiary proceedings, and ensures present value to the creditors. The formula approach simply takes the national prime rate and adjusts it to account for a risk of nonpayment. This approach differs from the dissent's approach in determining where the burden should lie, on the debtor or the creditor, to rebut the presumptive rate, whether prime or contract. Bankruptcy courts may determine the adjustment rate for risk to ensure compensation to the creditor without dooming the debtor to failure. Reversed and remanded.

CONCURRENCE: (Thomas, J.) The plurality and the dissent ignore the express language of the statute, which requires the "value . . . of property to be distributed under the plan" be at least the amount of the secured creditor's claim. The value of the "promise" under the plan does not have to be at least the claim amount. The judgment of the plurality is correct, however. If the prime rate is the risk-free rate and the proposed plan rate is higher than that amount, the proposed rate will sufficiently compensate the creditor.

DISSENT: (Scalia, J.) The prime rate is objectively known to be too low to sufficiently compensate creditors, so the contract rate is more appropriate as a presumptive rate rebuttable by either party by motion. The contract rate approach is supported by the assumptions that the subprime lending market is competitive and efficient and that the costs of default under Chapter 13 equal the costs of default under the original loan. Both assumptions are reasonable and supported by data. Justice Thomas proposes only the risk-free interest rate but the property right secured by confirmation of the plan requires accounting for risk of nonpayment. Compensation for risk is required by most jurisdictions to adequately protect creditors.

ANALYSIS

The difference among the plurality, concurrence, and dissent hinged less on the approaches to determine the appropriate interest rate and more on the appropriate level of compensation to the creditors. Justice Thomas

Continued on next page.

did not believe that the risk of default should enter into the analysis, while the other two opinions strongly believed that it should but differed on the starting point (i.e., high contract rate or low prime rate). The likely result from this opinion is that creditors will now face the burden of proving the low prime rate is too low.

Quicknotes

CERTIORARI A discretionary writ issued by a superior court to an inferior court in order to review the lower court's decisions; the Supreme Court's writ ordering such review.

CHAPTER 13 BANKRUPTCY Debtor may modify plan at any time before the completion of the payments under such plan.

CRAMDOWN Refers to a court's confirmation of a reorganization plan in a bankruptcy proceeding despite the opposition of creditors.

In re Taddeo

Mortgagor (P) v. Mortgagee (D)

685 F.2d 24 (2d Cir. 1982).

NATURE OF CASE: Appeal from order allowing debtor to cure default and reinstate mortgage.

FACT SUMMARY: DiPierro (D) appealed from a district court decision affirming the bankruptcy court's decision allowing Taddeo (P) to cure a default on his mortgage to DiPierro (D) and to allow Taddeo (P) to reinstate the mortgage pursuant to a plan filed under Chapter 13.

RULE OF LAW

The power granted to debtors under Chapter 13 that allows the debtor to cure defaults encompasses the power to allow debtor mortgagors to "de-accelerate" their mortgages and to reinstate their original payment schedules.

FACTS: DiPierro (D) sold a house to Taddeo (P) on June 14, 1979, taking in return a purchase-money second mortgage to secure a principal balance of $13,000. This mortgage was payable over fifteen years in monthly installments of $128.05. After taking occupancy, Taddeo (P) notified DiPierro (D) of defects in the property and told DiPierro (D) that they would withhold mortgage payments, depositing the payments with their attorney. Several months went by without resolution of the problem, and on October 5, 1979, pursuant to an acceleration clause in the mortgage, DiPierro (D) notified Taddeo (P) that she was accelerating the mortgage, declaring the entire balance due immediately. DiPierro (D) commenced foreclosure proceedings in state court on October 19, 1979. Taddeo (P) tendered full payment of the arrears by check on October 31, 1979, but DiPierro (D) refused the payment. The state court granted summary judgment to DiPierro (D) and on June 30, 1980, a referee found Taddeo (P) liable for $14,153.48 in principal and interest. Before DiPierro (D) could obtain final judgment and sale of the property, Taddeo (P) filed a petition in bankruptcy under Chapter 13, which stayed the foreclosure action. DiPierro (D) was listed as the only creditor, and the plan submitted by Taddeo (P) proposed to pay off the arrears of the mortgage in monthly installments of $100 and would also restore the mortgage and its original payment schedule. DiPierro (D) objected to the plan, contending that her rights as a mortgagee could not be affected by a Chapter 13 plan. The bankruptcy court allowed the plan, notwithstanding DiPierro's (D) acceleration, and denied her relief from the automatic stay. The district court affirmed, and from this affirmation, DiPierro (D) appealed.

ISSUE: Does the power granted to debtors under Chapter 13 that allows the debtor to cure defaults encompass the power to allow debtor mortgagors to "de-accelerate" their mortgages and to reinstate their original payment schedules?

HOLDING AND DECISION: (Lumbard, J.) Yes. The power granted to debtors under Chapter 13 that allows the debtor to cure defaults encompasses the power to allow debtor mortgagors to "de-accelerate" their mortgages and to reinstate their original payment schedules. A default is an event that triggers certain consequences, in the present case, acceleration. Curing a default under the Code commonly means taking care of the triggering event and returning to pre-default conditions; this means that consequences are nullified. The scant legislative history on the subject supports this conclusion with respect to the cure and de-acceleration of mortgages. Policy considerations also counsel a reading of this power into the power to cure default in that it will encourage parties to negotiate in good faith rather than promoting races to the courthouse to postpone foreclosure proceedings. The ban against modifying claims does not limit the power to cure since under the Code curing defaults and maintaining payments does not constitute a modification of the claim. The legislature in enacting the Code provisions distinguished between the modification of claims and the curing of defaults, indicating that the two powers were different. In short then, curing a default Chapter 11 means that the default is remedied and the consequences are nullified. In the present case, this means that the mortgage is de-accelerated and it is returned to its original fifteen-year maturity period. Any state law that would require otherwise would emasculate the "cure remedy" under Chapter 13 and would be at odds with its rehabilitative purpose, and therefore it must fail. Affirmed.

ANALYSIS

Note the very limited nature of the Code provision at work in the present case. Claims secured by a security interest in real property serving as the debtor's principal place of residence may not be modified by a Chapter 13 plan. Claims secured by other property of the debtor may be modified, and claims in the debtor's principal place of residence secured by a lien other than a security interest may be modified.

Quicknotes

ACCELERATION CLAUSE A contract provision that provides an interest will vest immediately upon the happening of a specified event.

Continued on next page.

AUTOMATIC STAY Upon the filing of a voluntary bankruptcy petition, creditors are prohibited from attempting to recover payment from the debtor or his property.

CHAPTER 11 BANKRUPTCY A legal proceeding whereby a debtor, who is unable to pay his debts as they become due, is relieved of his obligation to pay his creditors through reorganization and payment from future income.

LIEN A claim against the property of another in order to secure the payment of a debt.

MORTGAGEE Party to whom an interest in property is given in order to secure a loan.

SUMMARY JUDGMENT Judgment rendered by a court in response to a motion made by one of the parties, claiming that the lack of a question of material fact in respect to an issue warrants disposition of the issue without consideration by the jury.

In re Carter

Debtor (P) v. Creditors (D)

205 B.R. 733 (Bankr. E.D. Pa. 1996).

NATURE OF CASE: Objection to debtor's plan.

FACT SUMMARY: When a married woman filed for bankruptcy and failed to include her husband's income, a creditor filed an objection.

RULE OF LAW

Where a spouse is filing for bankruptcy individually, the other spouse's income must be considered in calculating the bankrupt spouse's disposable income.

FACTS: Mrs. Carter (P) filed for bankruptcy alone, without including her husband. A creditor who had obtained a foreign judgment against the couple objected to Mrs. Carter's (P) plan, alleging it was not filed in good faith because it failed to provide full disclosure of her family's financial status.

ISSUE: Where a spouse is filing for bankruptcy individually, must the other spouse's income be considered in calculating the bankrupt spouse's disposable income?

HOLDING AND DECISION: (Sigmund, J.) Yes. Where a spouse is filing for bankruptcy individually, the other spouse's income must be considered in calculating the bankrupt spouse's disposable income. This results from the reality that married couples live as a unit and pool their resources. Honesty and full disclosure are the hallmarks of good faith. Here, Mrs. Carter (P) may have misunderstood her obligations and did not seemingly act in bad faith. Confirmation is denied without prejudice.

ANALYSIS

Chapter 12 debtors must devote all their disposable income to the Chapter 13 plans. Courts are left to determine a debtor's disposable income. Generally, the debtor's income and expenses are considered in making that determination. This problem would not arise in community property states.

Quicknotes

CHAPTER 12 BANKRUPTCY Refers to that chapter of the bankruptcy code that applies to family farmers.

CHAPTER 13 BANKRUPTCY Debtor may modify plan at any time before the completion of the payments under such plan.

GOOD FAITH An honest intention to abstain from taking advantage of another.

In the Matter of Wyant

Debtor (P) v. Bankruptcy trustee (D)

217 B.R. 585 (Bankr. D. Neb. 1998).

NATURE OF CASE: Objection to confirmation of a debtor's plan.

FACT SUMMARY: When a debtor increased his projected monthly expenses after his ex-wife died and he no longer had to pay alimony, the bankruptcy trustee claimed that the increases were not reasonable.

RULE OF LAW

Only those expenses that are reasonably necessary may be deducted from a debtor's repayment plan.

FACTS: Wyant (P) filed for Chapter 13 bankruptcy after borrowing money from his employer in return for a security interest in several vehicles he owned. When obliged to pay alimony of $1,100 per month, Wyant (P) appealed the divorce decree. His wife died shortly thereafter, and Wyant (P) filed an amended schedule, excluding the alimony. The court considered whether to confirm the proposed plan.

ISSUE: May only those expenses that are reasonably necessary be deducted from a debtor's repayment plan?

HOLDING AND DECISION: (Minahan, J.) Yes. Only those expenses that are reasonably necessary may be deducted from a debtor's repayment plan. Wyant (P) attempted to preserve assets through extensive pre-bankruptcy planning, to manipulate expenses to minimize payments to unsecured creditors, and to provide for payment of excessive attorney fees. The majority of the increase in projected monthly expenditures were discretionary and not reasonable. Wyant's (P) proposed expenses on veterinary expenses and livestock feed were unreasonable. As between the debtor's elderly horses and dogs and his creditors, the creditors should be paid first. Confirmation is denied, trustee's objection is sustained and application for attorney fees is denied.

ANALYSIS

The court decided that only $100 per month should be allowed for feed and veterinary expenses. The court disallowed $375 of the proposed increase in monthly expenditures. The proposed expenses for the animals were found to be excessive, unreasonable, and not necessary for the maintenance or support of the debtor or his dependents.

Quicknotes

BANKRUPTCY TRUSTEE Individual charged with the administration of the bankruptcy estate.

CHAPTER 13 BANKRUPTCY Debtor may modify plan at any time before the completion of the payments under such plan.

CONFIRMATION Court approval of a bankruptcy reorganization plan.

SECURITY INTEREST An interest in property that may be sold upon a default in payment of the debt.

In re Kagenveama

Trustee (P) v. Debtor (D)

2008 U.S. App. Lexis 13299 (9th Cir.).

NATURE OF CASE: Appeal from order confirming Chapter 13 plan.

FACT SUMMARY: After Kagenveama (D) determined that her "projected disposable income" was negative and voluntarily proposed a plan under which she would make payments to unsecured creditor for three years, the Trustee (P) objected to the confirmation of the plan because the plan extended only three years, not the five-year "applicable commitment period" under § 1325(b)(4)(A)(ii). The parties disputed the meaning of "projected disposable income" and "applicable commitment period."

RULE OF LAW

(1) "Projected disposable income" under 11 U.S.C. § 1325 means "disposable income," as defined by § 1325(b)(2), projected over the "applicable commitment period."
(2) The "applicable commitment period" requirement of 11 U.S.C. § 1325 is inapplicable to a plan submitted voluntarily by a debtor with no "projected disposable income."

FACTS: Kagenveama (D) was an above-median income debtor in Chapter 13 bankruptcy. Therefore, in determining her disposable income, she was required to recalculate her expenses pursuant to § 707(b)(2). This recalculation produced a negative number. Based on this negative number, she determined that her "projected disposable income" was also a negative number. Although, because her "projected disposable income" was a negative number and she would not be subject to the "applicable commitment period," she nonetheless voluntarily proposed a plan in which she would pay $1,000 per month with a commitment period of three years. Although this plan yielded an estimated dividend of $9,444.38 to her unsecured creditors, the Trustee (P) still objected because the plan extended only three years, not the five-year "applicable commitment period" under § 1325(b)(4)(A)(ii). The bankruptcy court held that because Kagenveama (D) had no "projected disposable income," she was not required to propose a plan with an "applicable commitment period" of five years, and it confirmed the plan. The Trustee (P) appealed the confirmation order, and the court of appeals granted review.

ISSUE:

(1) Does "projected disposable income" under 11 U.S.C. § 1325 mean "disposable income," as defined by § 1325(b)(2), projected over the "applicable commitment period?"
(2) Is the "applicable commitment period" requirement of 11 U.S.C. § 1325 inapplicable to a plan submitted voluntarily by a debtor with no "projected disposable income?"

HOLDING AND DECISION: (Siler, J.)

(1) Yes. "Projected disposable income" under 11 U.S.C. § 1325 means "disposable income," as defined by § 1325(b)(2), projected over the "applicable commitment period." Kagenveama (D) contends that the term "disposable income," as used in § 1325(b)(1)(B), is specifically defined in § 1325(b)(2) and accordingly asserts that the word "projected" is a modifier of "disposable income" that requires multiplying "disposable income" out over the "applicable commitment period." The Trustee (P) contends that "projected" necessarily implies a forward-looking concept of "disposable income," which would allow a court to depart from the § 1325(b)(2) "disposable income" calculation and consider other evidence to derive "projected disposable income." Looking at the statute, one notices that "projected disposable income" is not defined, but "disposable income" is. Because courts must give meaning to every clause and word of a statute, the definition of "disposable income" would become mere surplusage if the meaning of "projected disposable income" was not linked to the definition of "disposable income," since then it would have no apparent purpose in the statute. "Projected" is simply a modifier of the defined term "disposable income;" it does not imply additional data that must be added to the calculation. Therefore, to give meaning to every word of § 1325(b), "disposable income" must be "projected" in order to derive "projected disposable income." This reading is supported by the statute's history. Before the amendments to the Bankruptcy Code effected by the Bankruptcy Abuse Prevention and Consumer Protection Act of 2005 (BAPCPA), "projected disposable income" was linked to the definition of "disposable income." Post-amendments, what has changed is not this linkage, but the new "disposable income" calculation itself. Further, a line of cases that the Trustee (P) argues is controlling views data from Form B22C as creating a presumptively correct definition of "disposable income" that can be rebutted. This line of authority is not persuasive because the language of the Bankruptcy Code does not create a presumptively correct definition of "disposable income" subject to modification based on anticipated changes in income or expenses. The revised "disposable income" test uses a formula and deliberately departs

Continued on next page.

from the pre-amendments approach that accounted for the facts and circumstances of the debtor's financial affairs. Had Congress instead wanted to create a presumption, it could have done so, but chose not to. Merely because the results for unsecured creditors of above-median income debtors is less favorable than under the pre-amendment Code, that is not a reason to override the statutory definition and process for calculating disposable income under the amended statute. Congress was made aware of the impacts these changes would have, but declined to act. If the results of BAPCPA reflect poor policy choices, it is up to Congress to amend the Code, not the courts. Affirmed as to this issue.

(2) Yes. The "applicable commitment period" requirement of 11 U.S.C. § 1325 is inapplicable to a plan submitted voluntarily by a debtor with no "projected disposable income." Although the Trustee (P) correctly argues that "applicable commitment period" mandates a temporal measurement—based on the retention of the word "period" and its temporal connotations—his proffered definition is inapplicable to the voluntary plan proposed by Kagenveama (D). That is because the "applicable commitment period" must be applied to the payment of "projected disposable income." Here, however, there is no "projected disposable income." Finally, "applicable commitment period" does not mean the minimum plan duration, but instead represents the period over which payments of projected disposable income must be made to unsecured creditors. Affirmed as to this issue.

ANALYSIS

BAPCPA significantly changed the definition of "disposable income." Before BAPCPA, "disposable income" was defined as income "received by the debtor and which is not reasonably necessary to be expended for the maintenance or support of the debtor. . . . " Determining what was "reasonably necessary" for the maintenance or support of the debtor was dependent on each debtor's individual facts and circumstances. This amorphous standard produced determinations of a debtor's "disposable income" that varied widely among debtors in similar circumstances. BAPCPA replaced the old definition of what was "reasonably necessary" with a formulaic approach for above-median debtors. 11 U.S.C. § 1325(b)(3). This formula significantly changed the way in which "disposable income" is calculated. However, as demonstrated in this case, "disposable income" has always been—and continues to be—linked to "projected disposable income."

Quicknotes

CHAPTER 13 BANKRUPTCY Debtor may modify plan at any time before the completion of the payments under such plan.

UNSECURED CREDITOR A creditor whose loan is not backed by specified collateral or a security agreement.

In re Farrar-Johnson

Trustee (P) v. Debtors (D)

353 B.R. 224 (Bankr. N.D. Ill. 2006).

NATURE OF CASE: Motion to dismiss a Chapter 13 bankruptcy case.

FACT SUMMARY: The Trustee (P) in a Chapter 13 bankruptcy contended that the above-median income Debtors' (D) case should be dismissed because they had acted in bad faith by claiming an improper housing allowance deduction and refusing to amend their proposed plan.

RULE OF LAW

A Chapter 13 bankruptcy case will not be dismissed on bad faith grounds where above-median income debtors have allegedly claimed an improper housing allowance deduction and have refused to amend their proposed plan.

FACTS: The Debtors (D), who were above-median income debtors, took a housing allowance under the Internal Revenue Service (IRS) National and Local Standards even though they lived rent-free in military housing. The bankruptcy court held they were entitled to this deduction. The Trustee (P) then moved to dismiss their case, arguing that they had acted in bad faith by claiming the deduction and by refusing to amend their proposed plan.

ISSUE: Will a Chapter 13 bankruptcy case be dismissed on bad faith grounds where above-median income debtors have allegedly claimed an improper housing allowance deduction and have refused to amend their proposed plan?

HOLDING AND DECISION: (Goldgar, J.) No. A Chapter 13 bankruptcy case will not be dismissed on bad faith grounds where above-median income debtors have allegedly claimed an improper housing allowance deduction and have refused to amend their proposed plan. Neither inflated expenses on a Schedule J, nor an improper housing allowance deduction, establish bad faith. The 1984 amendments to the Code essentially eliminated a good faith inquiry by adding 11 U.S.C. § 1325(b) and its disposable income test, which determined whether a debtor's expenses were "reasonably necessary" or not. If the expenses were reasonably necessary, the plan would be confirmed, assuming all other requirements were met. Thus, good faith was no longer tied to economic considerations. The 2005 amendments to the Code further eroded the relevance of a good faith analysis, at least in the case of debtors with above-median income. For those debtors, the determination of disposable income has become an arithmetic calculation. Debtors may claim applicable expenses under the IRS National and Local Standards, and may also claim actual Other Necessary Expenses. The courts do not have discretion to determine whether those expenses are in fact "reasonably necessary." As a matter of logic, if the reasonable necessity of a debtor's expenses is no longer relevant, then the debtor's good faith in claiming them also cannot be relevant. Instead, improper expenses must be challenged as failing to comply with § 1325(b), not that the plan was proposed in bad faith. Here, the disposable income amount must be accepted because the Debtors (D) in fact did not claim an improper housing expense on their Form B22C. Moreover, because the Debtors (D) had above-median income, the expenses on their Schedule J are irrelevant. Even assuming the debtors here had below-median income, thus permitting review of their Schedule J, the Trustee's (P) objections would still fail because the disposable income a debtor decides to commit to his plan is not a measure of his good faith in proposing the plan. For these reasons, the case will not be dismissed. Motion denied.

ANALYSIS

As this case demonstrates, debtors are permitted by § 1325 (b)(3) under the current Code to deduct amounts allowed by the means test even if they seem excessive to a trustee or creditor. Under such an approach, which apparently was sanctioned by Congress, it is feasible that certain debtors will pay nothing to their unsecured creditors.

Quicknotes

BAD FAITH Conduct that is intentionally misleading or deceptive.

CHAPTER 13 BANKRUPTCY Debtor may modify plan at any time before the completion of the payments under such plan.

In re Murphy

Debtor (P) v. Creditor (D)

226 B.R. 601 (Bankr. M.D. Tenn. 1998).

NATURE OF CASE: Petition for Chapter 13 bankruptcy.

FACT SUMMARY: When Murphy (P) filed for bankruptcy, a Creditor (D) objected that Murphy (P) did not qualify because she had no regular income.

RULE OF LAW

To be eligible for Chapter 13 bankruptcy, an individual with regular income may include funding from diverse and nontraditional sources.

FACTS: Murphy (P) lived with a man and his two children whom she cared for. Murphy (P) filed for Chapter 13 bankruptcy after her car was seized by the Sheriff. The man she was living with signed an affidavit that he would make Murphy's (P) Chapter 13 plan payments. Murphy (P) filed a motion to get her car back and the Creditor (D) objected that Murphy (P) was not eligible for Chapter 13 because she did not have regular income. Murphy (P) claimed that her boyfriend's written promise to make payments for her was a formal commitment that was just as concrete as an employer's promises of work.

ISSUE: To be eligible for Chapter 13 bankruptcy, may an individual with regular income include funding from diverse and nontraditional sources?

HOLDING AND DECISION: (Lundin, J.) Yes. To be eligible for Chapter 13 bankruptcy, an individual with regular income may include funding from diverse and nontraditional sources. The Code does not restrict the notion of income to wages, salary, return on investment or any other restrictions. Self-employed individuals are eligible to use Chapter 13 if they have regular income. Unmarried individuals sharing a household may enforce financial commitments by their significant others. The promise to fund this plan may generate rights and obligations that are every bit as enforceable as any employment contract. Petition granted.

ANALYSIS

The court here referred to cases involving enforcement of contract rights of unmarried couples. Other courts have been more traditional. Some courts have narrowed the definition of regular income to require that the debtor have a legal right to the funding.

Quicknotes

AFFIDAVIT A declaration of facts written and affirmed before a witness.

CHAPTER 13 BANKRUPTCY Debtor may modify plan at any time before the completion of the payments under such plan.

In re Huelbig

Creditor (P) v. Debtor (D)

299 B.R. 721 (Bankr. D.R.I. 2003).

NATURE OF CASE: Motion to dismiss Chapter 13 petition.

FACT SUMMARY: Mr. Huelbig (D), previously an operator of an auto body repair shop, pleaded nolo contendere to state criminal charges related to fraudulent insurance claims and was the defendant in a civil suit initiated by Allstate Insurance Company (Allstate) (P). The Huelbigs (D) filed for Chapter 13 reorganization, but Allstate (P) contested the petition on the grounds that the Huelbigs' (D) unsecured debt exceeded the statutory limits.

RULE OF LAW

The issue of the debtor's liability should not be taken into account when determining the liquidity of a claim.

FACTS: Mr. Huelbig (D) operated an auto body repair shop that did business with Allstate (P). Allstate (P) filed a civil complaint against the Huelbigs (D) and others alleging insurance fraud among other counts, seeking $330,505 in damages. Mr. Huelbig (D) pleaded nolo contendere to criminal charges arising out of the fraudulent insurance claims, and he and Mrs. Huelbig filed a petition for Chapter 13 reorganization on the same day of the plea. Allstate (P) filed a motion to dismiss the petition on the grounds that the Huelbigs' (D) unsecured debt exceeded the Chapter 13 limits. The Huelbigs (D) countered that Allstate's (P) claim is unliquidated, therefore could not be considered to determine their eligibility under Chapter 13.

ISSUE: Should the issue of the debtor's liability be taken into account when determining the liquidity of a claim?

HOLDING AND DECISION: (Votolato, J.) No. The issue of the debtor's liability should not be taken into account when determining the liquidity of a claim. The Huelbigs (D) assert that the Allstate (P) claim should not be included in the determination of their eligibility under Chapter 13 because it is not a liquidated claim. The Huelbigs (D) also weakly argue that the Allstate (P) claim is contingent to their petition filing and not includable in their eligibility determination. Clearly all of the events in this case arose prior to the petition filing date, so the claim is noncontingent. The question before this court is the liquidity determination. A liquidated claim is subject to "ready determination and precision in computation of the amount due." An unliquidated claim has the amount of the debt in dispute. The Huelbigs (D) argue that they are vigorously contesting liability for the Allstate (P) claim, therefore, it is not subject to precise computation as of the petition-filing date. This is the stance adopted by the Ninth Circuit in determining the liquidity of a claim. That stance has been widely criticized, however, and is only employed in a minority of jurisdictions. A dispute over the amount of the debt owed differs from a dispute over liability for the debt at all. The far better approach is simply to determine whether the claim is readily calculable. This is true even in the face of vigorous denial as to liability. In this case, Allstate (P) has included a list of checks that can be easily added together to arrive at a determinable claim. Such a ready computation demonstrates that the Allstate (P) claim is liquidated and therefore includable in the Huelbigs' (D) Chapter 13 eligibility. The Allstate (P) claim puts the Debtors' (D) debt in excess of $269,250, and they are therefore ineligible for Chapter 13 reorganization. Motion granted.

ANALYSIS

It is important to note the difference between a debt amount in dispute and the liability for that debt in dispute. A liquidated claim is ascertainable, computable, and readily determined at the time of the claim. The liability for that claim, as in the Huelbigs' (D) case, can be in dispute, but the dollar amount of the claim itself can be determined. The debt amount could be in dispute when the final figures for medical treatment are not before the court, for example. That case could involve parties stipulating as to liability but unable to provide a sum certain for the claim. That uncertain sum means that claim is unliquidated and not considered in the eligibility determination for Chapter 13.

Quicknotes

CHAPTER 13 BANKRUPTCY Debtor may modify plan at any time before the completion of the payments under such plan.

UNLIQUIDATED CLAIM Disputed claim; one not finally determined as to damages or liability.

In re San Miguel

Debtors (P) v. Bankruptcy court (D)

40 B.R. 481 (Bankr. D. Colo. 1984).

NATURE OF CASE: Consolidated action for hearing respecting good faith of proposed Chapter 13 plans.

FACT SUMMARY: The Bankruptcy court (D) questioned the good faith of the San Miguels' (P) Chapter 13 payment plan to creditors because of the short duration of each plan and the minimal payment afforded to unsecured creditors.

RULE OF LAW

One of the express congressional purposes of Chapter 13 is the repayment of creditors.

FACTS: The San Miguels (P) proposed a Chapter 13 payment plan proposing to pay unsecured creditors minimal payments of $1.00 each over a period of sixteen months. The primary reason that the San Miguels (P) selected Chapter 13 instead of Chapter 7 was to spread attorney's fees over the 16-month period. No creditor objected to the proposed plans. However, the Court (D), sua sponte, raised the issue of good faith due to the very short duration of each plan and the minimal payment afforded to unsecured creditors. The San Miguels, et al. (P) responded that the proposed plans were necessitated so that attorney fees could be paid over the period of the plan, rather than in advance, as is customarily required by lawyers who accept Chapter 7 debtors.

ISSUE: Is one of the express congressional purposes of Chapter 13 repayment of creditors?

HOLDING AND DECISION: (Gueck, J.) Yes. One of the express congressional purposes of Chapter 13 is repayment of creditors. Here, the basic question to be determined is whether the plans constitute an abuse of the provision, purpose, or spirit of Chapter 13. The San Miguels' (P) plan demonstrates no malevolent motive in the selection of a sixteen-month plan. However, no desire for repayment of creditors is demonstrated either. If a debtor simply desires relief from debt, Chapter 7 provides an adequate remedy in most cases. The San Miguels (P) would also achieve a fresh start sooner in Chapter 7 as attorney fees are usually smaller and the debtor's financial affairs are resolved much earlier. The real purpose of the sixteen-month plan, here, is to avail the San Miguels, et al. (P) of the opportunity to defer attorney fees since it seems difficult to obtain counsel in Chapter 7 without payment of fees in advance. The congressional intent of Chapter 13 cannot be modified, however, because of the local practice of attorneys regarding fees. These proposed plans do not promote the purpose of repayment of creditors. Therefore, they must be denied.

ANALYSIS

Many debtors are not solely influenced by the statutory consequences of their decisions. Demographic, social, and psychological factors may be more compelling in individual debtor decisions about bankruptcy than simple economic analysis would reveal. The impact of a bankruptcy on the debtor's family, career, and social standing may be foremost in a debtor's mind. That is why many debtors might choose Chapter 13, which even avoids the label "bankruptcy" and allows an honorable alternative to liquidation in Chapter 7 bankruptcy.

Quicknotes

CHAPTER 13 BANKRUPTCY Debtor may modify plan at any time before the completion of the payments under such plan.

GOOD FAITH An honest intention to abstain from taking advantage of another.

LIQUIDATION The reduction to cash of all assets for distribution to creditors.

SUA SPONTE An action taken by the court by its own motion and without the suggestion of one of the parties.

UNSECURED CREDITOR A creditor whose loan is not backed by specified collateral or a security agreement.

CHAPTER 7

Chapter 7 Liquidation

Quick Reference Rules of Law

1. **Involuntary Bankruptcy.** The courts have long evinced a disposition to honor the separate corporate entity in bankruptcy matters. (In re Gibraltor Amusements) *60*

2. **Involuntary Bankruptcy.** Post-petition payments will not deprive the court of jurisdiction or require dismissal of the bankruptcy petition. (In re Faberge Restaurant of Florida, Inc.) *61*

3. **Involuntary Bankruptcy.** A creditor does not have standing to file an involuntary bankruptcy petition if his claim is the subject of a bona fide dispute. (In re Silverman) *62*

In re Gibraltor Amusements

Creditor (P) v. Debtor (D)

291 F.2d 22 (2d Cir.), *cert. denied,* 368 U.S. 925 (1961).

NATURE OF CASE: Appeal from granting of involuntary bankruptcy.

FACT SUMMARY: In the Wurlitzer Company's (P) action for involuntary bankruptcy against Gibraltor Amusements (D), Gibraltor (D) contended that it had more than twelve creditors, that Wurlitzer (P) therefore must be joined by two other creditors for a proper involuntary petition, and that Wurlitzer Acceptance Corporation, a wholly owned subsidiary of Wurlitzer (P), could not be a separate petitioning creditor.

RULE OF LAW

The courts have long evinced a disposition to honor the separate corporate entity in bankruptcy matters.

FACTS: Wurlitzer Company (P), principal creditor of Gibraltor Amusements (D), filed an involuntary bankruptcy petition against Gibraltor (D), alleging insolvency, bankruptcy, and that Gibraltor (D) had fewer than twelve creditors. Gibraltor (D) contended that it had more than twelve creditors and that Wurlitzer (P) must be joined by two other creditors for a successful involuntary petition. Gibraltor (D) also contended that Wurlitzer Acceptance Corporation, a wholly owned subsidiary of Wurlitzer (P), which was joined as a petitioning creditor, was not a separate entity from Wurlitzer (P) and could not be joined as a separate petitioning creditor. The lower court judged Wurlitzer Acceptance to be a separate entity and allowed it to join Wurlitzer (P) as a petitioning creditor. Gibraltor (D) appealed.

ISSUE: Have the courts long evinced a disposition to honor the separate corporate entity in bankruptcy matters?

HOLDING AND DECISION: (Smith, J.) Yes. The courts have long evinced a disposition to honor the separate corporate entity in bankruptcy matters. Here, the evidence shows that both parent, Wurlitzer (P), and subsidiary, Wurlitzer Acceptance, have scrupulously honored Wurlitzer Acceptance's separate corporate form. Here, Wurlitzer Acceptance has not been used as a "front" or "mere conduit" or so-called alter ego of Wurlitzer (P). There has been strict honoring of corporate form as to assets and intercorporate transactions and complete absence of fraud. There has been no showing that Wurlitzer (P) has abused distinct corporate form nor that it has used it fraudulently to subvert the Bankruptcy Act. Wurlitzer Acceptance is a separate corporate entity, which may be joined as a separate petitioning creditor in this involuntary petition against Gibraltor Amusement (D). Affirmed.

DISSENT: (Friendly, J.) It is not consistent with Bankruptcy Code policy to hold that a single creditor corporation may ensure its ability to initiate involuntary bankruptcy by the simple expedient of organizing two financing subsidiaries—perhaps with independent creditors—and seeing to it that claims against each debtor are parceled out in advance of bankruptcy.

ANALYSIS

Traditionally, an involuntary bankruptcy was always a Chapter 7 case. The Code permits a creditor to put a debtor into an involuntary Chapter 11, as well, pursuant to § 303(b). A creditor might decide to put a debtor into Chapter 11 to obtain disclosure and court supervision of the debtor's activities while allowing the business to continue operations.

Quicknotes

INSOLVENT One's liabilities exceed one's assets; inability to pay one's debts.

INVOLUNTARY PETITION A bankruptcy petition that is filed by the debtor's creditors forcing him into bankruptcy.

In re Faberge Restaurant of Florida, Inc.

Debtor (P) v. Creditors (D)

222 B.R. 385 (Bankr. S.D. Fla. 1997).

NATURE OF CASE: Debtor's motion to dismiss involuntary bankruptcy proceedings.

FACT SUMMARY: When Faberge (P) paid its creditors, it sought to dismiss the pending bankruptcy petition.

RULE OF LAW

Post-petition payments will not deprive the court of jurisdiction or require dismissal of the bankruptcy petition.

FACTS: Three creditors of Faberge (P) petitioned for involuntary Chapter 7 bankruptcy. Three more creditors then joined the petition. Faberge (P) paid three of the creditors and filed a motion to dismiss.

ISSUE: Will post-petition payments deprive the court of jurisdiction or require dismissal of the bankruptcy petition?

HOLDING AND DECISION: (Cristol, C.J.) No. Post-petition payments will not deprive the court of jurisdiction or require dismissal of the bankruptcy petition. There was an existing debt on the date of the filing of the involuntary petition. A panel trustee will be set up to handle the affairs of the restaurant. Motion denied.

ANALYSIS

The panel trustee may be appointed from the standing panel of persons qualified to act as trustees. There was a possibility that the restaurant could continue to operate while in Chapter 7. Section 303 of the Bankruptcy Code governs the filing of involuntary petitions.

Quicknotes

BANKRUPTCY A legal proceeding whereby a debtor, who is unable to pay his debts as they become due, is relieved of his obligation to pay his creditors either by liquidation and distribution of his remaining assets or through reorganization and payment from future.

CHAPTER 7 BANKRUPTCY A legal proceeding whereby a debtor, who is unable to pay his debts as they become due, is relieved of his obligation to pay his creditors by liquidation and distribution of his remaining assets.

INVOLUNTARY PETITION A bankruptcy petition that is filed by the debtor's creditors forcing him into bankruptcy.

In re Silverman

Creditor (P) v. Debtor (D)

230 B.R. 46 (Bankr. D.N.J. 1998).

NATURE OF CASE: Motion for punitive damages after involuntary bankruptcy petition.

FACT SUMMARY: A creditor sought to file an involuntary bankruptcy case against Silverman (D) over a disputed debt.

RULE OF LAW

A creditor does not have standing to file an involuntary bankruptcy petition if his claim is the subject of a bona fide dispute.

FACTS: Cantor (P) sued Silverman (D) on a $200,000 promissory note in state court. While that case continued, Cantor (P) filed an involuntary bankruptcy case against Silverman (D) as well. Silverman (D) moved to dismiss and for sanctions, alleging that there was a bona fide dispute over the claim and that Cantor (P) had exhibited bad faith.

ISSUE: Does a creditor have standing to file an involuntary bankruptcy petition if his claim is the subject of a bona fide dispute?

HOLDING AND DECISION: (Stripp, J.) No. A creditor does not have standing to file an involuntary bankruptcy petition if his claim is the subject of a bona fide dispute. Cantor (P) did not obtain a credit report on Silverman (D) before filing. If he had done so, he would have seen that Silverman (D) had been paying his debts on time and had good credit. In order to file an involuntary case against a debtor, the debtor must not be paying his bills as they come due. Cantor's (P) bad faith in filing an involuntary bankruptcy shortly after the superior court ruled that genuine issues of material fact existed with respect to the existence and amount of the alleged debt was exacerbated by his denial that partial summary judgment had been requested in the state court proceeding. Attorney's fees, costs and $50,000 in punitive damages are awarded. Motion granted.

ANALYSIS

Cantor (P) also claimed that he had acted on advice of counsel. The court did not mention sanctions against the attorney. The court did say that Cantor (P) might have a cause of action against his attorney if he was telling the truth about his reliance on his attorney's bad advice.

Quicknotes

INVOLUNTARY BANKRUPTCY Proceedings brought against a debtor by his creditors thereby forcing him into bankruptcy.

PUNITIVE DAMAGES Damages exceeding the actual injury suffered for the purposes of punishment, deterrence and comfort to plaintiff.

SANCTIONS A penalty imposed in order to ensure compliance with a statute or regulation.

SUMMARY JUDGMENT Judgment rendered by a court in response to a motion by one of the parties, claiming that the lack of a question of material fact in respect to an issue warrants disposition of the issue without consideration by the jury.

CHAPTER 8

Chapter 11 Reorganization

Quick Reference Rules of Law

PAGE

1. **Scope of the Stay.** A debtor cannot unilaterally waive the automatic stay provision in Chapter 11 bankruptcy when it protects the interests of the creditors as well as the interests of the debtors. (Farm Credit of Central Florida, ACA v. Polk) *67*
2. **Scope of the Stay.** The automatic stay will not be lifted in a government action where the government's primary focus is pecuniary. (United States v. Seitles) *68*
3. **Lifting the Stay.** A benchmark in determining adequate protection is the liquidation value of the collateral at the date of the bankruptcy petition, and the standard of valuation approximating fair market value is the "commercially reasonable" standard. (In re Rogers Development Corp.) *69*
4. **Good Faith.** A Chapter 11 petition is filed in bad faith, and therefore must be dismissed for cause, where the corporation filing the petition is not near insolvency and merely anticipates extensive potential liability stemming from litigation. (In re SGL Carbon Corporation) *70*
5. **Who's Running the Show?** A court may appoint a bankruptcy trustee if a debtor-in-possession shows serious mismanagement. (In re Sharon Steel Corp.) *71*
6. **What Happens to the Cash?** If a debtor can show that a creditor is adequately protected, the debtor may use its cash collateral. (In re Earth Lite) *72*
7. **What Happens to the Cash?** Federal government agencies are a single entity for purposes of setoff under bankruptcy laws. (In re HAL, Inc.) *73*
8. **Post-petition Financing.** Unsecured creditors need not be given "adequate protection" before a post-petition security interest may become operative. (In re Garland Corp.) *74*
9. **Post-petition Financing.** A creditor's claim is secured only to the extent of the value of the property on which the lien is fixed. (In re Hubbard Power & Light, Inc.) *75*
10. **Post-petition Financing.** The right to incur debt as part of a Chapter 11 reorganization does not include the right to grant liens to secure pre-petition loans. (Shapiro v. Saybrook Manufacuring Co., Inc.) *76*
11. **The Strong Arm Clause, Section 544(a).** A defectively executed mortgage can be avoided under a Chapter 7 trustee's strong-arm powers under § 544(a)(3) of the Bankruptcy Code. (In re Bowling) *77*
12. **Preferences.** A judicial lien will be avoided as a preference under 11 U.S.C. § 547(b) where the debtor was insolvent at the time of the post-judgment attachment that was the basis for the lien, where the lienholder would receive more with the lien than he would without the lien, and where all other elements of § 547(b) are met. (In re Pysz) *78*
13. **Preferences.** (1) A refinanced mortgage lien does not fall within the grace period of 11 U.S.C. § 547(e) where it is not perfected within the grace period, even where the same mortgagee holds both the new mortgage and prior mortgage and the discharge of the prior mortgage is not recorded until after the new mortgage is recorded. (2) The earmarking doctrine does not apply to a refinanced mortgage interest where the mortgagee holds both the old and new mortgages and where the mortgagee perfects late, so that the debtor's bankruptcy estate is diminished. (Chase Manhattan Mortgage Corp. v. Shapiro) *80*

CHAPTER 8

14. **Preferences.** A bankruptcy trustee can avoid as a preference, and recover from guarantors of a loan, debtor's payments on the loan. (In re Denochick) *82*

15. **Exceptions.** Neither the contemporaneous exchange for new value exception nor the ordinary course of business exception to Code § 547 apply to a preferential transfer made by cashier's check for an antecedent debt where the cashier's check was used after a personal check made in payment of the debt was dishonored for lack of sufficient funds and payment by cashier's check is not typical in the industry. (In re Stewart) *83*

16. **Exceptions.** The "substantially contemporaneous exchange" exception, and the earmarking doctrine, are not defenses to the preferential avoidance of a security interest in a refinancing loan that is perfected after the relation-back period required in Code § 547(e)(2)(B), but during the preference period. (In re Shreves) *85*

17. **The "Floating Lien."** For purposes of determining a secured creditor's "improvement in position" pursuant to 11 U.S.C. § 547(c)(5), interest, late charges, and other fees may be considered in arriving at a value of "debt." (In re QMECT, Inc.) *87*

18. **The "Floating Lien."** More increases in the value of crops do not by themselves constitute a voidable preference. (In re Nivens) *89*

19. **The "Floating Lien."** A creditor has a valid right to a pre-petition setoff. (In re Wild Bills, Inc.) *90*

20. **Executory Contracts: The Statute.** Where a franchise agreement was in force on the date the bankruptcy petition was filed, the franchise agreement was an asset of the bankruptcy estate. (In re Krystal Cadillac-Oldsmobile-GMC Truck, Inc.) *91*

21. **Executory Contracts: The Statute.** Provisions restricting, conditioning, or prohibiting a debtor's right to assign a subject lease are invalid. (In re Jamesway Corp.) *92*

22. **Extra-Statutory Constraints on the Trustee's Right to Assume or Reject.** A contract is executory if each side must render performance, on account of an existing legal duty or to fulfill a condition, to obtain the benefit of the counterparty's performance. (In re Riodizio, Inc.) *93*

23. **Statutory Liens.** Where a statute requires that a statutory lien be recorded to render it valid against a bona fide purchaser, the lien is avoidable in a Chapter 11 bankruptcy proceeding if it has not been recorded pursuant to the statute. (In re TWA Inc. Post Confirmation Estate) *94*

24. **Fraudulent Conveyances and Other State Avoidance Laws in Bankruptcy.** Indirect benefits to a guarantor may be considered when determining whether a corporation receives reasonably equivalent value for a guarantee. (In re Image Worldwide, Ltd.) *96*

25. **Fraudulent Conveyances and Other State Avoidance Laws in Bankruptcy.** A trustee may not recover from a subsequent transferee if the subsequent transferee accepted the transfer for value, in good faith, and without knowledge of the transfer's voidability. (In re Video Depot, Ltd.) *97*

26. **Fraudulent Conveyances and Other State Avoidance Laws in Bankruptcy.** A debtor's pre-petition right to revoke its election to be treated as a subchapter S corporation under I.R.C. § 1362, n.10 has value to a debtor's estate and is therefore properly characterized as property. (In re Bakersfield Westar, Inc.) *98*

27. **Equitable Subordination.** Where one creditor improperly moves ahead of others, equitable subordination may be used to void the preference. (In re Carolee's Combine) *99*

28. **Equitable Subordination.** A secured claim belonging to a corporate debtor's insider creditors will not be equitably subordinated where there is no showing either that the creditors' conduct was inequitable, or that there was injury to the debtor or its other creditors. (In re SI Restructuring) *100*

29. **Best Interests of the Creditors and Feasibility.** A Chapter 11 plan of reorganization will not be confirmed where it is not feasible, as demonstrated by debtor's past performance. (In re Malkus, Inc., Debtor) *102*

30. **Best Interests of the Creditors and Feasibility.** A Chapter 11 plan of reorganization will not be confirmed where it is not feasible, as demonstrated by conditional financing and a lack of exit financing. (In re Made in Detroit, Inc., Debtor) *103*

31. **Best Interests of the Creditors and Feasibility.** A joint plan of reorganization under Chapter 11 will be confirmed where an objecting creditor cannot prove its claim that the plan is not in the creditor's best interests. (SK-Palladin Partners, L.P. v. Platinum Entertainment, Inc.) *105*

32. **Classification and Voting.** Excluding a creditor in a Chapter 11 reorganization from a class of similarly situated creditors for the sole purpose of plan approval may be invalid. (In re U.S. Truck Co., Inc.) *107*

33. **Classification and Voting.** Under a Chapter 11 plan of reorganization, unsecured consignment creditors may be classified separately from general unsecured creditors where there are good business reasons to do so. (In re Bernhard Steiner Pianos USA, Inc.) *108*

34. **Classification and Voting.** A creditor is not impaired for purposes of voting on a reorganization plan where the creditor is subject to the statutory cap of Code § 502(b)(6). (In re PPI Enterprises (U.S.), Inc.) *110*

35. **Claims Trading.** On request of a party in interest, and after notice and a hearing, the court may designate (disqualify from voting) any entity whose acceptance or rejection of a plan was not in good faith. (In re Figter Ltd.) *112*

36. **Claims Trading.** An ad hoc committee represented by counsel must disclose "the amounts of claims or interests owned by the members of the committee, the times when acquired, the amounts paid therefor, and any sales or other disposition thereof," as required by Bankruptcy Rule 2019. (In re Northwest Airlines Corp.) *113*

37. **Solicitation and Discourse.** A debtor must provide a disclosure statement in conformity with the letter and spirit of the Code. (In re Malek) *114*

38. **Cramdown.** Plans providing junior interest holders with exclusive opportunities free from competition and without benefit of market valuation are prohibited under the Bankruptcy Code. (Bank of America National Trust & Savings Assn. v. 203 North LaSalle Street Partnership) *115*

39. **Small Business Reorganization.** A Chapter 11 plan of reorganization is not confirmable where an impaired class does not accept the plan and the plan violates the absolute priority rule, even if no creditor raises the rule as an issue. (In re MJ Metal Products, Inc.) *116*

40. **Reorganization of Public Companies Control.** (1) A cap on professional fees in an approved financing order does not preclude a court from approving any fees that are in excess of the cap. (2) A court may reduce requested professional fees that are based on unnecessary services or necessary services that are overvalued. (In re Channel Master Holdings, Inc.) *117*

41. **Reorganization of Public Companies Control.** Where an insider compensation plan mostly has compensation elements that effectively serve to retain insiders regardless of performance and that provide severance pay, the plan must comply with the provisions of 11 U.S.C. § 503(c) before the plan will be approved. (In re Dana Corp.) *119*

42. **Reorganization of Public Companies Control.** Where an insider compensation plan mostly has compensation elements that incentivize insiders to increase the debtor's value, with only incidental retentive features, and that provide severance pay in accordance with limits set forth in 11 U.S.C. § 503(c), the plan will be approved if it otherwise is within the debtor's business judgment. (In re Dana Corp.) *121*

43. **Reorganization of Public Companies Control.** A bankruptcy court does not have discretion to deny appointment of an examiner where the $5,000,000 debt threshold is met under Code § 1104(c)(2) and shareholders of a public company have moved for the appointment of an examiner. (In re Loral Space & Communications, Ltd.) *123*

CHAPTER 8

44. Environmental Claims. Post-reorganization environmental claims brought against a debtor under the Comprehensive Environmental Response, Compensation and Liability Act have not been previously discharged in Chapter 11 where the Environmental Protection Agency could not have fairly contemplated the debtor's potential liability prior to its reorganization. (Signature Combs, Inc. v. United States) *124*

45. Mass Torts. Corporations faced with "mass tort" litigation may attempt to resolve liability through a Chapter 11 reorganization plan so long as the plan is submitted in good faith in an attempt to accomplish a successful reorganization of the corporation and creditors are at least assured of receiving what they would have received had the corporation undergone a liquidation pursuant to Chapter 7 of the Bankruptcy Code. (Kane v. Johns-Manville Corp.) *126*

46. Mass Torts. Where a debtor has not made any provision for the interests of tort claimants in its financial restructuring plan, those interests cannot be said to have been discharged in the bankruptcy. (In re Fairchild Aircraft Corp.) *128*

47. Regulatory Claimants. Bankruptcy Code § 525 prohibits the Federal Communications Commission (FCC) from revoking licenses held by a debtor in bankruptcy upon the debtor's failure to make timely payments owed to the FCC for purchase of the license. (FCC v. NextWave Personal Communications, Inc.) *129*

48. After Chapter 11. Pre-petition claims are barred where the claimants are unknown creditors and the bankruptcy proceedings were published in accordance with law. (In re U.S.H. Corp.) *131*

49. After Chapter 11. Claims that could have been brought in reorganization plan confirmation proceedings are barred by res judicata where these subsequent claims are based on the same nucleus of operative facts and were discoverable during the bankruptcy proceedings. (In re Howe) *133*

50. After Chapter 11. A nondebtor's release in a plan of reorganization will not be approved where there is no finding of unique circumstances that would make the release important to the success of the plan. (In re Metromedia Fiber Network, Inc.) *135*

51. After Chapter 11. A Chapter 11 plan of reorganization may be confirmed where it provides a temporary injunction against enforcement of claims against a third-party guarantor where the third party enjoys an identity of interest with the debtor such that the claims against the third party are essentially claims against the debtor, and where the third-party claims would have an adverse effect on the debtor's ability to accomplish reorganization. (In re Bernhard Steiner Pianos USA, Inc.) *136*

52. Compensation and Disclosure. A single attorney or law firm will be disqualified from representing two or more Chapter 11 debtors when the lawyer has failed to disclose a retainer or the existence of parallel employment applications or when the joint representation gives rise to an actual conflict of interest. (In re Lee) *138*

53. Compensation and Disclosure. (1) Where debtor's counsel has failed to disclose a material conflict of interest, it is in the creditors' best interest to disqualify counsel and to have counsel replaced by a Chapter 11 trustee. (2) Conversion of a Chapter 11 case to a Chapter 7 case is not preferable to appointing a Chapter 11 trustee and in the creditors' best interest where the committee of unsecured creditors and its counsel may not be fulfilling their duties to the creditor class. (In re SONICblue Inc.) *139*

54. Compensation and Disclosure. Whether a mortgage given to an attorney to secure the payment of his fees by a Chapter 11 debtor-client gives rise to an actual, perceived, or potential conflict of interest necessitating its invalidation is to be determined on a case-by-case basis. (In re Martin) *141*

55. Privilege and Conflict of Interest. A bankruptcy trustee may waive the attorney-client privilege for prefiling corporate communications. (Commodity Futures Trading Commission v. Weintraub) *142*

Farm Credit of Central Florida, ACA v. Polk

Creditor (P) v. Debtor (D)

160 B.R. 870 (Bankr. M.D. Fla. 1993).

NATURE OF CASE: Appeal from denial of motion for relief from automatic stay under Chapter 11 bankruptcy.

FACT SUMMARY: Although Polk (D) and Farm Credit (P) had entered into a pre-petition agreement that Polk (D) would not contest Farm Credit's (P) motion for relief from an automatic stay, Polk (D) contested the motion.

RULE OF LAW

A debtor cannot unilaterally waive the automatic stay provision in Chapter 11 bankruptcy when it protects the interests of the creditors as well as the interests of the debtors.

FACTS: Polk (D) had significant and long-standing business operations and many secured and unsecured creditors. Polk (D), threatened with a foreclosure sale of his property, entered into a foreclosure agreement with Farm Credit (P). Under that agreement, Farm Credit (P) would delay the foreclosure sale in exchange for an agreement by Polk (D) not to contest Farm Credit's (P) motion for relief from the automatic stay of all judicial proceedings against Polk (D) in the event Polk (D) filed bankruptcy. Polk (D) subsequently did file for Chapter 11 bankruptcy and contested Farm Credit's (P) motion. Farm Credit (P) claimed that Polk's (D) protest was barred by the parties' previous agreement. The bankruptcy court found that Farm Credit (P) was not entitled to an immediate lifting of the stay, and Farm Credit (P) appealed.

ISSUE: Can a debtor unilaterally waive the automatic stay provision in Chapter 11 bankruptcy when it protects the interests of the creditors as well as the interests of the debtors?

HOLDING AND DECISION: (Kovachevich, J.) No. A debtor cannot unilaterally waive the automatic stay provision in Chapter 11 bankruptcy when it protects the interests of the creditors as well as the interests of the debtors. The automatic stay is intended to protect the claims of creditors during the reorganization of the debtor's assets by preventing the dissipation of the assets of the estate. Bankruptcy courts have upheld agreements such as this one in cases where bad faith existed and there was a single asset. However, such waivers are not appropriate where there are substantial assets that need to be reorganized. Polk (D) in effect gave Farm Credit (P) priority over all other creditors by granting the waiver. Polk (D) did not have the right to waive the interests of the other creditors in the bankruptcy proceedings. Affirmed.

ANALYSIS

There are numerous statutory exceptions to the stay under § 362(b) of the Bankruptcy Code, including protection of public health and safety. However, courts have construed these exceptions narrowly. As well as narrow construction of the exceptions, the courts may also use their broad power under § 105 to extend the scope of the stay.

Quicknotes

AUTOMATIC STAY Upon the filing of a voluntary bankruptcy petition, creditors are prohibited from attempting to recover payment from the debtor or his property.

CHAPTER 11 BANKRUPTCY A legal proceeding whereby a debtor, who is unable to pay his debts as they become due, is relieved of his obligation to pay his creditors through reorganization and payment from future income.

United States v. Seitles

Federal government (P) v. Debtor (D)

106 B.R. 36 (Bankr. S.D.N.Y. 1989).

NATURE OF CASE: Motion to stay action for damages under the False Claims Act.

FACT SUMMARY: Bankrupt Seitles (D) sought a stay in an action for damages and restitution brought against him by the Government (P) under the False Claims Act.

RULE OF LAW

The automatic stay will not be lifted in a government action where the government's primary focus is pecuniary.

FACTS: Alleging that Seitles (D) had bribed certain U.S. officials, the Government (P) commenced an action against him. The nature of the relief sought consisted of damages and restitution. Seitles (D) filed for bankruptcy under Chapter 11 and moved to stay this proceeding under the automatic stay provisions of Chapter 11. The Government (P) opposed this.

ISSUE: Will the automatic stay be lifted in a governmental action where the government's primary focus is pecuniary?

HOLDING AND DECISION: (Kram, J.) No. The automatic stay will not be lifted in a governmental action where the government's primary focus is pecuniary. The automatic stay provisions of Chapter 11 are as applicable to the government as any other creditor. Sections 362(b)(4) and (5) permit the government to avoid the stay in actions "to protect the public health and safety." This exception has been narrowly construed. Actions that in some way may affect public health or safety, but whose focuses are principally pecuniary, have been held inapplicable. Here, the Government's (P) focus was unquestionably pecuniary. The nature of relief sought was damages and/or restitution. An action to protect the public health will usually involve, at least in part, some sort of injunctive relief. Since the Government's (P) focus was pecuniary, the automatic stay applies to this action. Motion granted.

ANALYSIS

The ruling above was directed to Seitles's (D) company, Westbrook Publishing Co. (D). Under § 362, a bankruptcy stay does not automatically flow to a bankrupt's principals. However, § 105 of the Code permits a court to do this, based on equity principles. The court in this instance elected to extend the stay to Seitles (D).

Quicknotes

AUTOMATIC STAY Upon the filing of a voluntary bankruptcy petition, creditors are prohibited from attempting to recover payment from the debtor or his property.

CHAPTER 11 BANKRUPTCY A legal proceeding whereby a debtor, who is unable to pay his debts as they become due, is relieved of his obligation to pay his creditors through reorganization and payment from future income.

PECUNIARY Consisting of, or pertaining to, money.

In re Rogers Development Corp.

Creditor savings and loan (P) v. Debtor (D)

2 B.R. 679 (Bankr. E.D. Va. 1980).

NATURE OF CASE: Creditor's action seeking relief from Chapter 11 automatic stay.

FACT SUMMARY: In Heritage Savings & Loan Association's (P) action against Rogers Development Corp. (D), seeking relief from the automatic stay that went into effect when Rogers (D) filed for bankruptcy under Chapter 11, Heritage (P) alleged that the stay should be lifted because there was a lack of adequate protection of its interest in a property development, that Rogers (D) did not have equity in the property, and that the property was not necessary to Rogers's (D) effective reorganization.

RULE OF LAW

A benchmark in determining adequate protection is the liquidation value of the collateral at the date of the bankruptcy petition, and the standard of valuation approximating fair market value is the "commercially reasonable" standard.

FACTS: Rogers (D), a real estate developer, formulated a plan for development of 89.7 acres to be developed for single and multifamily dwellings. Heritage (P) made a $520,000 acquisition and development loan to Rogers (D) and a $360,000 line of credit construction loan. Rogers (D) went into default on the acquisition and development loan, advances were made by Heritage (P) under the construction loan, and construction at the site continued until the homes were completed and sold. Rogers (D) then went into default on the construction loan and filed for Chapter 11 protection. Heritage (P) alleged that the Chapter 11 automatic stay should be lifted because there was a lack of adequate protection of its interest in the property development, that Rogers (D) did not have equity in the property, and that the property was not necessary to Rogers's (D) effective reorganization.

ISSUE: Is a benchmark in determining adequate protection the liquidation value of the collateral at the date of the bankruptcy petition, and is the standard of valuation approximating fair market value the "commercially reasonable" standard?

HOLDING AND DECISION: (Shelley, J.) Yes. A benchmark in determining adequate protection is the liquidation value of the collateral at the date of the bankruptcy petition, and the standard of valuation approximating fair market value is the "commercially reasonable" standard. In this case, the collateral is primarily real property, which by all testimony is appreciating in value. There was some evidence that the partially completed houses were suffering some deterioration; the impact of this deterioration in value loses significance when measured against the value of the property as a whole. While there is no guarantee that real property will sell, this property should sell at or near the fair market value. Here, the standard of valuation approximating fair market value is the "commercially reasonable" standard. This standard is the most commercially reasonable disposition practicable in the circumstances and encompasses the nature of the debtor's business, prospects for rehabilitation, and nature of the collateral. According to expert testimony, the value of the property is between $704,000 and $801,000; the court finds valuation of $750,000 for the purposes of this proceeding reasonable. Thus, Heritage (P) is adequately protected as Rogers's (D) total debt to Heritage (P) is $548,188.41. Here, Rogers (D) has no equity in the property as claims of over $1 million are outstanding against the property valued at $750,000. However, Heritage (P) has not shown that the property is not needed by Rogers (D) for an effective reorganization, and Rogers (D) has shown that without the property there can be no reorganization. Therefore, Heritage (P) will not be granted relief from the stay pursuant to § 362(d)(2).

ANALYSIS

All Chapter 11 negotiations are held in the shadow of Chapter 7. The debtor generally has an absolute right to convert the case to Chapter 7 under Code § 1112(a), and the creditor can do so on a proper showing pursuant to § 1112(b). Also, conversion will be necessary if creditors do not approve a debtor's plan by the majorities specified in § 1126(c). For this reason, each side often threatens the other with Chapter 7 even though both really wish to avoid it.

Quicknotes

AUTOMATIC STAY Upon the filing of a voluntary bankruptcy petition, creditors are prohibited from attempting to recover payment from the debtor or his property.

CHAPTER 11 BANKRUPTCY A legal proceeding whereby a debtor, who is unable to pay his debts as they become due, is relieved of his obligation to pay his creditors through reorganization and payment from future income.

FAIR MARKET VALUE The price of particular property or goods that a buyer would offer and a seller would accept in the open market following full disclosure.

In re SGL Carbon Corporation

Debtor (P) v. Creditors (D)

200 F.3d 154 (3d Cir. 1999).

NATURE OF CASE: Appeal from denial of motion to dismiss Chapter 11 petition on bad faith grounds.

FACT SUMMARY: Certain of SGL Carbon Corporation's (SGL Carbon) (P) creditors (D), plaintiffs in an antitrust action against SGL Carbon, contended that SGL Carbon's (P) Chapter 11 petition was filed prematurely and in bad faith.

RULE OF LAW

A Chapter 11 petition is filed in bad faith, and therefore must be dismissed for cause, where the corporation filing the petition is not near insolvency and merely anticipates extensive potential liability stemming from litigation.

FACTS: Criminal and civil antitrust actions were brought against SGL Carbon Corporation (SGL Carbon) (P), and, at the direction of its parent company, it filed a voluntary Chapter 11 bankruptcy petition. The filing only discussed the antitrust litigation, and proposed a reorganization plan whereby only the litigation plaintiffs (D) who obtained judgments against SGL Carbon (P) would be required to accept less than full cash payments on their judgments. SGL Carbon (P) asserted that its filing was necessary to avoid financial ruin. The potential judgment creditors (D) moved to dismiss the Chapter 11 petition on the ground that it had been filed in bad faith. The district court denied this motion, finding that the petition had not been filed in bad faith because the distractions of the litigation posed a serious threat to the continued SGL Carbon's (P) successful operations and because the potential liability faced by the corporation could force it out of business. At the time the petition was filed, SGL Carbon (P) was in good financial health. The court of appeals granted review.

ISSUE: Is a Chapter 11 petition filed in bad faith, and therefore must be dismissed for cause, where the corporation filing the petition is not near insolvency and merely anticipates extensive potential liability stemming from litigation?

HOLDING AND DECISION: (Scirica, J.) Yes. A Chapter 11 petition is filed in bad faith, and therefore must be dismissed for cause, where the corporation filing the petition is not near insolvency and merely anticipates extensive potential liability stemming from litigation. A Chapter 11 petition is subject to dismissal if not filed in good faith. Although there was some evidence that defending against the antitrust litigation occupied some officers' time, there was no evidence this "distraction" posed a "serious threat" to the company's operational well-being. Moreover, there was no evidence that the possible antitrust judgments might force SGL Carbon (P) out of business. To the contrary, the record was replete with evidence of SGL Carbon's (P) economic strength. Thus, whether or not the corporation faced a potentially crippling antitrust judgment, it was incorrect to conclude that it had to file when it did. Although the Bankruptcy Code encourages early filing, and a debtor need not be insolvent before filing, it is also clear that the Code does not permit premature filing, nor permits the filing of a bankruptcy petition that lacks a valid reorganizational purpose. SGL Carbon's (P) ability to meet its debts, its net worth of $124 million, its unimpaired business relationships with the antitrust plaintiffs, and its unimpaired ability to access the capital markets prevented it from entering Chapter 11 with a valid reorganizational purpose. This does not mean that a company must wait to file until after a massive judgment has been entered against it, but, as here, where the possibility of becoming insolvent is merely an attenuated possibility standing alone, that is insufficient to establish the good faith of a Chapter 11 petition. Accordingly, the petition lacks good faith, making it subject to dismissal for cause. Reversed and remanded.

ANALYSIS

Although a debtor does not have to be insolvent to file a Chapter 11 petition, this case demonstrates that neither may a debtor use such a petition to merely frustrate the prosecution of pending litigation or to preserve a debtor's equity from legal claims. As this case essentially rules, filing a petition for such ends is an abuse of the bankruptcy system. As the court in this case noted, while SGL Carbon (P) might have had to file a Chapter 11 petition after judgment had been entered against it, doing so before that time, while it was still healthy, served no valid reorganizational purpose.

Quicknotes

ANTITRUST Body of federal law prohibiting business conduct that constitutes a restraint on trade.

BAD FAITH Conduct that is intentionally misleading or deceptive.

CHAPTER 11 BANKRUPTCY A legal proceeding whereby a debtor, who is unable to pay his debts as they become due, is relieved of his obligation to pay his creditors through reorganization and payment from future income.

GOOD FAITH An honest intention to abstain from taking advantage of another.

In re Sharon Steel Corp.

Creditors (P) v. Debtor corporation (D)

871 F.2d 1217 (3d Cir. 1989).

NATURE OF CASE: Review of order granting petition for appointment of trustee in bankruptcy.

FACT SUMMARY: Creditors (P) of Sharon Steel (D) petitioned for a trustee to be appointed for bankrupt Sharon Steel (D) on the grounds that it was being mismanaged.

RULE OF LAW

A court may appoint a bankruptcy trustee if a debtor-in-possession shows serious mismanagement.

FACTS: Faced with debts of $742 million and only $478 million in assets, Sharon Steel Corp. (D) filed for bankruptcy under Chapter 11. During the pendency of the bankruptcy, it became clear that Sharon's (D) management had made several improper pre-petition transfers, kept poor records, and made several questionable financial transactions. Creditors (P) petitioned for the appointment of a bankruptcy trustee. The bankruptcy court granted the petition, and the district court affirmed. Sharon Steel (D) appealed.

ISSUE: May a court appoint a bankruptcy trustee if a debtor-in-possession shows serious mismanagement?

HOLDING AND DECISION: (Gibbons, C.J.) Yes. A court may appoint a bankruptcy trustee if a debtor-in-possession shows serious mismanagement. Under normal circumstances, a debtor is permitted to remain in charge of the bankrupt estate. This is because the debtor itself usually has the best expertise in running the business. However, under Code § 1104, a trustee may be appointed to manage the estate under certain conditions. When distilled, these conditions amount to a situation where various acts of mis- or nonfeasance endanger the estate. Essentially, mismanagement legitimizes the appointment of a trustee. Here, the management of Sharon Steel (D) made questionable real and personal property transactions, kept poor records, and made poor financial transactions. This was sufficient to justify the appointment of a trustee. Affirmed.

ANALYSIS

As noted in the opinion, the most common situation in a bankruptcy is for a debtor to remain in charge of the bankrupt estate. However, at this point the debtor becomes a fiduciary to the creditors. Since the debtor's and creditors' interests are often divergent, the temptation for abuse is strong.

Quicknotes

BANKRUPTCY TRUSTEE Individual charged with the administration of the bankruptcy estate.

DEBTOR-IN-POSSESSION In a Chapter 11 proceeding, refers to a debtor who retains control of assets or property pursuant to a plan of reorganization.

In re Earth Lite

Creditor bank (P) v. Debtor (D)

9 B.R. 440 (Bankr. M.D. Fla. 1981).

NATURE OF CASE: Application for relief from a Chapter 11 automatic stay.

FACT SUMMARY: Sun Bank (P), creditor of Earth Lite (D), sought to prevent Earth Lite (D) from access to its account receivable receipts.

RULE OF LAW

If a debtor can show that a creditor is adequately protected, the debtor may use its cash collateral.

FACTS: Sun Bank (P) made certain loans to Earth Lite (D) for the purpose of Earth Lite (D) starting a decorated glass wholesaling business. Inventory and accounts receivable acted as security. Earth Lite (D) subsequently filed under Chapter 11. Earth Lite (D) was allowed to remain in business. Sun Bank (P) advanced more funds under a provision that insiders personally guarantee the loan and that a designated third party collect the accounts receivable. These conditions were met. Earth Lite (D) subsequently defaulted on the post-petition financing agreement. However, the inventory and accounts receivable of Earth Lite (D) well exceeded the amounts owed to Sun Bank (P). Sun Bank (P) filed a motion for relief from the automatic stay to obtain access to the inventory and accounts receivable, and Earth Lite (D) filed a petition to allow it to use its accounts receivable as cash collateral.

ISSUE: If a debtor can show that a creditor is adequately protected, may the debtor use its cash collateral?

HOLDING AND DECISION: (Paskay, J.) Yes. If a debtor can show that a creditor is adequately protected, the debtor may use its cash collateral. Liquid assets present a problem in bankruptcy. On the one hand, without access to such assets, the debtor is unlikely to successfully reorganize; on the other hand, such assets easily are dissipated. Congress compromised between these concerns by enacting 11 U.S.C. § 363 and related sections. To use the cash proceeds, the debtor must show adequate security for the creditors. The cash cannot be used without the bankruptcy court's permission. Here, the record shows that Earth Lite (D) had sufficient assets to protect Sun Bank (P), as well as the personal guarantees of the insiders. Request for relief from the automatic stay denied; permission for use of cash receivables granted.

ANALYSIS

The present action summarizes well the special nature of liquid assets. A company in reorganization often has a great need for cash as sources of working capital quickly dry up. To permit its liquid assets to be frozen would certainly spell the end of the company. Section 363 is an attempt to permit, through court supervision, proper use of cash assets.

Quicknotes

AUTOMATIC STAY Upon the filing of a voluntary bankruptcy petition, creditors are prohibited from attempting to recover payment from the debtor or his property.

COLLATERAL Property that secures the payment of a debt.

In re HAL, Inc.

Federal agency (P) v. Debtors (D)

196 B.R. 159 (B.A.P. 9th Cir. 1996).

NATURE OF CASE: Appeal from decision to allow a setoff.

FACT SUMMARY: The bankruptcy court allowed the Internal Revenue Service (IRS) to apply overpayments to offset other debts owed the government.

RULE OF LAW

Federal government agencies are a single entity for purposes of setoff under bankruptcy laws.

FACTS: When Hawaiian Airlines, along with related entities HAL, Inc. and West Maui Airport, Inc. (collectively, the "Debtors") (D) filed for Chapter 11 bankruptcy, the IRS conducted an audit and found that Hawaiian Airlines (D) had overpaid its excise taxes. The United States (P) sought relief from the automatic stay and an order allowing it to use the overpayment to offset the claims of other agencies. The bankruptcy court held that the United States (P) and its agencies were a single entity for purposes of the mutuality requirement for setoff under 11 U.S.C. § 553(a). The Debtors (D) appealed, alleging that the court had abused its discretion in allowing the setoff.

ISSUE: Are federal government agencies a single entity for purposes of setoff under bankruptcy laws?

HOLDING AND DECISION: (Jones, J.) Yes. Federal government agencies are a single entity for purposes of setoff under bankruptcy laws. The principal element of setoff is mutuality, requiring that the debts be in the same right and between the same parties. Since all relevant debts arose pre-petition, the United States (P) had a nonbankruptcy right to setoff. Affirmed.

ANALYSIS

There is a split of authority on this issue. The majority holds that the governmental agencies satisfy the mutuality requirement. A minority of courts have held that government agencies are not entitled to setoff because the mutuality requirement should be more strictly construed in bankruptcy.

Quicknotes

AUTOMATIC STAY Upon the filing of a voluntary bankruptcy petition, creditors are prohibited from attempting to recover payment from the debtor or his property.

FEDERAL AGENCY Any department of the executive branch of government.

MUTUALITY Reciprocal actions of two parties; in a contract context, refers to mutual promises between two parties to perform an action in exchange for performance on the part of the other party.

SETOFF A claim made pursuant to a counter-claim, arising from a cause of action unrelated to the underlying suit, in which the defendant seeks to have the plaintiff's claim of damages reduced.

In re Garland Corp.

Unsecured creditors (P) v. Debtor (D)

6 B.R. 456 (Bankr. D. Mass. 1980).

NATURE OF CASE: Appeal of bankruptcy order.

FACT SUMMARY: Debtor Garland Corp. (D) obtained post-bankruptcy financing by permitting liens to be filed upon heretofore unsecured property.

RULE OF LAW

Unsecured creditors need not be given "adequate protection" before a post-petition security interest may become operative.

FACTS: Garland Corp. (D) petitioned for bankruptcy. Desperately in need of working capital to remain in operation, Garland Corp. (D) made a deal with a bank that additional capital would be supplied. Part of the arrangement was that liens would be placed on unsecured property. After a hearing in which it was shown that Garland Corp. (D) had a fair chance of survival and that no possibility of an unsecured loan existed, the bankruptcy court granted the security interest. Various unsecured creditors (P) appealed.

ISSUE: Need unsecured creditors be given "adequate protection" before a post-petition security interest may become operative?

HOLDING AND DECISION: (Cyr, C.J.) No. Unsecured creditors need not be given adequate protection before a post-petition security interest may become operative. Post-petition security interests are controlled by U.S.C. § 364. Adequate protection for unsecured creditors is a consideration in various parts of the Bankruptcy Code, but is not mentioned in the relevant part of § 364, this being § 364(c)(2). Where a realistic opportunity for rehabilitation exists and no source of unsecured credit can be found, a legitimate basis for allowing a post-petition security interest exists. Affirmed.

ANALYSIS

Section 364(c)(2) deals with the necessity for post-petition loans. Since a bankruptcy petitioner usually is in dire need of capital and the likelihood of unsecured loans borders on zero, some provision for a post-petition security interest must be made. Section 364 allows some finality to be placed on such security interests as the threat of lengthy appeals of bankruptcy orders would drive away most lenders.

Quicknotes

SECURITY INTEREST An interest in property that may be sold upon a default in payment of the debt.

UNSECURED CREDITOR A creditor whose loan is not backed by specified collateral or a security agreement.

In re Hubbard Power & Light, Inc.

Debtor (P) v. Creditors (D)

202 B.R. 680 (Bankr. E.D.N.Y. 1996).

NATURE OF CASE: Debtor's motion to obtain priority financing.

FACT SUMMARY: When Hubbard Power & Light (P) was unable to obtain financing to clean up its site, it sought the court's approval to prime its senior liens.

RULE OF LAW

A creditor's claim is secured only to the extent of the value of the property on which the lien is fixed.

FACTS: Hubbard Power & Light (HPL) (P) was engaged in the production of electrical power by burning wood debris to produce steam. The New York State Department of Environmental Conservation (DEC) found that HPL (P) had been violating conditions of its operating permit and obtained a temporary restraining order that effectively shut down HPL's (P) plant. After a fire, HPL (P) filed a Chapter 11 bankruptcy petition. As part of its reorganization plan, HPL (P) sought authorization for post-petition financing to clean up its site. HPL (P) sought senior priority financing because it had been unable to obtain credit since all of its property was already subject to a lien. One creditor (D), Suffolk County, opposed the plan because it would not be adequately protected.

ISSUE: Is a creditor's claim secured only to the extent of the value of the property on which the lien is fixed?

HOLDING AND DECISION: (Eisenberg, J.) Yes. A creditor's claim is secured only to the extent of the value of the property on which the lien is fixed. The secured lien of Suffolk County (D) at the present time has zero value. The property will be improved by a clean-up and all secured creditors will benefit. Motion granted.

ANALYSIS

The court found that any improvement would greatly improve the value of the collateral. The site had to be cleaned up to satisfy the DEC. The DEC's injunction would have to be removed first.

Quicknotes

CHAPTER 11 BANKRUPTCY A legal proceeding whereby a debtor, who is unable to pay his debts as they become due, is relieved of his obligation to pay his creditors through reorganization and payment from future income.

COLLATERAL Property that secures the payment of a debt.

INJUNCTION A court order requiring a person to do or prohibiting that person from doing a specific act.

LIEN A claim against the property of another in order to secure the payment of a debt.

Shapiro v. Saybrook Manufacturing Co., Inc.

Unsecured creditor (P) v. Debtor (D)

963 F.2d 1490 (11th Cir. 1992).

NATURE OF CASE: Appeal from district court dismissal of appeal of cross-collateralization order as moot.

FACT SUMMARY: Shapiro (P), an unsecured creditor, opposed the bankruptcy court's authorization of cross-collateralization of post-petition debt to secure pre-petition debt with property subsequently acquired.

RULE OF LAW
The right to incur debt as part of a Chapter 11 reorganization does not include the right to grant liens to secure pre-petition loans.

FACTS: Saybrook Manufacturing (D) owed Manufacturers Hanover $34 million dollars, which was secured by collateral worth only $10 million. The bankruptcy court approved Saybrook's (D) motion to incur an additional $3 million in debt to facilitate its reorganization. Manufacturers lent Saybrook (D) the money and in turn received a security interest securing both the post-petition debt and the unsecured pre-petition debt. Seymour and Jeffrey Shapiro (P), unsecured creditors, opposed the court's authorization of the subsequent debt and requested the court to issue a stay pending appeal. The court refused to grant either the objection or the stay. The Shapiros (P) appealed to the district court, which dismissed the case finding that the motion was moot because the Shapiros (P) had not obtained a stay. The Shapiros (P) appealed.

ISSUE: Does the right to incur debt, as part of a Chapter 11 reorganization, include the right to grant liens to secure pre-petition loans?

HOLDING AND DECISION: (Cox, J.) No. The right to incur debt, as part of a Chapter 11 reorganization, does not include the right to grant liens to secure pre-petition loans. Cross-collateralization is not specifically allowed or prohibited by the Bankruptcy Code or the court precedence. Cross-collateralization goes against the Bankruptcy Code's policy of imposing a priority scheme on the reorganization of debts. Debtors may not discriminate among classes of creditors, yet by securing a previously nonsecured debt via cross-collateralization, Manufacturers is given a priority it normally would not have enjoyed. Further, the cross-collateralization reduces the assets from which the other unsecured creditors can recoup their losses. Section 364 of the Code does not authorize cross-collateralization as a method of post-petition financing. Reversed and remanded.

ANALYSIS

Clearly, the prospect of cross-collateralization of a significant debt was a sufficient incentive to Manufacturers to lend the money. Another financing option for companies in bankruptcy is to borrow from old equity holders who wish to keep the company running. Many times these equity holders seek an ownership interest in the post-bankruptcy company. However, such ownership is governed by the Absolute Priority Rule.

Quicknotes

CHAPTER 11 REORGANIZATION A plan formulated pursuant to Chapter 11 of the Bankruptcy Code whereby a debtor, who is unable to pay his debts as they become due, is relieved of his obligation to pay his creditors through reorganization and payment from future income.

In re Bowling

Mortgagor-debtor (P) v. Mortgagee-creditor (D)

314 B.R. 127 (Bankr. S.D. Ohio 2004).

NATURE OF CASE: Cross-motions for summary judgment in trustee's bankruptcy action to avoid a mortgage.

FACT SUMMARY: The bankruptcy trustee for the Bowling's (P) estate contended that a defectively executed mortgage (because a notary had not witnessed it) could be avoided under the trustee's strong-arm powers under § 544(a)(3) of the Bankruptcy Code.

RULE OF LAW

A defectively executed mortgage can be avoided under a Chapter 7 trustee's strong-arm powers under § 544(a)(3) of the Bankruptcy Code.

FACTS: Mr. Bowling (P) was the sole owner of real estate. Although the deed conveying the property to Bowling (P) reflected that he was married, it did not include Mrs. Bowling (P) as a grantee. Subsequently, Mr. Bowling (P) executed a mortgage in favor of a mortgage company (predecessor to the Mortgage Registration System (MERS)) (D), conveying the property as security. On its face, the mortgage reflected that Mr. Bowling's (P) signature was notarized by Ms. Eisenhut, a notary. By her certificate, Eisenhut certified that Mr. Bowling (P) had executed the mortgage in her presence. The Bowlings (P) filed a Chapter 7 petition, and the trustee sought to avoid the mortgage on the ground that in fact Eisenhut was not present when Mr. Bowling (P) executed the mortgage. Mrs. Bowling (P) did not sign the promissory note or the mortgage. Mr. Bowling (P) testified that Eisenhut had not been present at the closing, and that in addition to himself and his wife, only another man had been present.

ISSUE: Can a defectively executed mortgage be avoided under a Chapter 7 trustee's strong-arm powers under § 544 (a)(3) of the Bankruptcy Code?

HOLDING AND DECISION: (Aug, J.) Yes. A defectively executed mortgage can be avoided under a Chapter 7 trustee's strong-arm powers under § 544(a)(3) of the Bankruptcy Code. The trustee must show by clear and convincing evidence that the mortgage was not signed and notarized as purported. MERS (D) contests Mr. Bowling's (P) assertion that Eisenhut was not present when Mr. Bowling (P) signed the mortgage. However, MERS (D) has presented no evidence that Eisenhut was present. On the other hand, Mr. Bowling (P) testified that the refinancing was done at his home and that there was only one other person besides Mr. and Mrs. Bowling (P) present at the closing, that being a male. A refinancing is an extraordinary event for a consumer, so it would stick out in Mr. Bowling's (P) mind. In particular, it seems that Mr. Bowling (P) would remember whether the person coming to close the loan was male or female. Given that there is no per se state rule that Mr. Bowling's (P) testimony alone is insufficient to overcome the notary's certification, in the absence of MERS's (D) presentation of any evidence to the contrary, the trustee has met his burden and presented clear and convincing evidence that a notary was not present at the time Mr. Bowling (P) executed the mortgage. Summary judgment is granted.

ANALYSIS

The court also held that given that the trustee had avoided the mortgage pursuant to the trustee's strong-arm powers, MERS (D) would not be entitled to a replacement lien in the real estate pursuant to Code § 550. In reaching this conclusion, the court relied on the Sixth Circuit's determination that where the trustee has avoided a mortgage pursuant to its strong-arm powers, the mortgagee's interest is preserved and becomes a part of the bankruptcy estate without the need for the trustee to resort to the recovery process pursuant to § 550(a). Therefore, the court reasoned, the statutory provisions of § 550(e) providing for a replacement lien for the creditor are not triggered for the benefit of the mortgagee.

Quicknotes

CHAPTER 7 BANKRUPTCY A legal proceeding whereby a debtor, who is unable to pay his debts as they become due, is relieved of his obligation to pay his creditors by liquidation and distribution of his remaining assets.

MORTGAGEE Party to whom an interest in property is given in order to secure a loan.

MORTGAGOR Party who grants an interest in property in order to secure a loan.

In re Pysz

Debtor (P) v. Lienholder (D)

2008 WL 2001753 (Bankr. D.N.H. 2008).

NATURE OF CASE: Motion for summary judgment in action to avoid a judicial lien as a preference.

FACT SUMMARY: The Debtor (P) sought to avoid as a preference the Defendant's (D) judicial lien that arose from a post-judgment attachment for unpaid professional services, claiming that the Debtor (P) had been insolvent at the time of the attachment and that the Defendant (D) would receive more with the judicial lien than he would without the lien, thus satisfying all the requirements for avoiding the lien as a preference.

RULE OF LAW

A judicial lien will be avoided as a preference under 11 U.S.C. § 547(b) where the debtor was insolvent at the time of the post-judgment attachment that was the basis for the lien, where the lienholder would receive more with the lien than he would without the lien, and where all other elements of § 547(b) are met.

FACTS: The Defendant (D) obtained a judgment for unpaid professional services against the Debtor (P), and then issued a writ of attachment on the Debtor's (P) property (Newport Property) on January 18, 2007, and recorded it the following day. The Debtor (P) filed for bankruptcy protection under Chapter 13 on April 5, 2007. The Debtor (P) listed the Newport Property's fair market value as $300,000, but the Defendant (D) offered a separate appraisal report that valued it at $443,000. Even using the Defendant's (D) appraised value for the Newton Property, along with some unscheduled property, the Debtor's (P) liabilities exceeded his assets. The Debtor (P) moved for summary judgment seeking to avoid the Defendant's (D) judicial lien as a preference under 11 U.S.C. § 547(b).

ISSUE: Will a judicial lien be avoided as a preference under 11 U.S.C. § 547(b) where the debtor was insolvent at the time of the post-judgment attachment that was the basis for the lien, where the lienholder would receive more with the lien than he would without the lien, and where all other elements of § 547(b) are met?

HOLDING AND DECISION: (Vaughn, C.J.) Yes. A judicial lien will be avoided as a preference under 11 U.S.C. § 547(b) where the debtor was insolvent at the time of the post-judgment attachment that was the basis for the lien, where the lienholder would receive more with the lien than he would without the lien, and where all other elements of § 547(b) are met. There is no issue that the obtainment of the attachment was a transfer of the Debtor's (P) interest in property, as required by 11 U.S.C. § 547(b). This section also sets forth five elements that must be met. It is clear from the record, without further discussion, that three of those elements are satisfied here. They are: the subject lien was for the benefit of a creditor; the subject lien was for or on account of an antecedent debt; and the attachment occurred during the 90-day preference period. The two other elements—whether the Debtor (P) was insolvent at the time of the attachment (§ 547(b)(3)) and whether the Defendant (D) would receive more with the lien than he would without the lien (§ 547(b)(5))—merit further discussion. As to the insolvency issue, the Defendant (D), as creditor, bears the burden of proving that the Debtor (P) was not insolvent, i.e., there is a presumption that the Debtor (P) was insolvent during the 90 days immediately preceding the date of the filing of the petition. Even reading the record most favorably to the Defendant (D) (using the Defendant's (D) higher appraised value for the Newton Property and adding some non-exempt property that had not been scheduled), it is clear that the Debtor's (P) liabilities exceeded his assets when he filed his petition, so that there is no genuine issue regarding the Debtor's (P) insolvency during the preference period. Thus, the Defendant (D) failed to rebut the presumption of insolvency. As to the "receive more" element, there are three sub-elements that must be met, showing that the judicial lien would enable the creditor to receive more than such creditor would receive if: (1) the case were a liquidation case under Chapter 7; (2) the transfer had not been made; and (3) the creditor received payment of such debt to the extent provided by Chapter 13. Where, as here, the creditor is a general unsecured creditor absent the attachment, if the distribution in bankruptcy is less than 100 percent, any payment "on account" to the creditor during the preference period will enable that creditor to receive more than he would have received in liquidation had the payment not been made. Also, as a matter of law, whenever a general unsecured creditor obtains within the preference period a judicial lien against a debtor who cannot fully repay his unsecured creditors, he has received a preference. Finally, because the Debtor's (P) liabilities exceed his assets, under a hypothetical Chapter 7 liquidation analysis, the Debtor (P) would not be able to repay his general unsecured creditors 100 percent. Thus, since the Defendant (D) converted an otherwise unsecured claim to a secured one, the lien would enable the Defendant (D) to receive more than he would without the lien in a Chapter 7 case. For these reasons, the "receive more" element is satisfied, and, consequently, all the elements of § 547(b) are met. Summary judgment is granted to the Debtor (P).

Continued on next page.

ANALYSIS

Section 547 serves two primary purposes. First, it fosters equality of distribution among creditors, which is one of the primary goals of the Bankruptcy Code. Second, it discourages "secret liens" upon the debtor's collateral that are not perfected until just before the debtor files for bankruptcy.

Quicknotes

ATTACHMENT The seizing of the property of one party in anticipation of, or in order to satisfy, a favorable judgment obtained by another party.

LIEN A claim against the property of another in order to secure the payment of a debt.

SUMMARY JUDGMENT Judgment rendered by a court in response to a motion made by one of the parties, claiming that the lack of a question of material fact in respect to an issue warrants disposition of the issue without consideration by the jury.

Chase Manhattan Mortgage Corp. v. Shapiro

Mortgagee (P) v. Trustee (D)

2008 U.S. App. Lexis 13455 (6th Cir. 2008).

NATURE OF CASE: Appeal from reversal of order avoiding a refinanced mortgage as a preferential transfer.

FACT SUMMARY: The Trustee (D) of Lee's bankruptcy estate contended that a residential mortgage loan that Lee obtained in a refinance transaction from Chase Manhattan Mortgage Corporation (Chase) (P), which was both the holder of the original mortgage and the refinanced mortgage, should be avoided as a preferential transfer under 11 U.S.C. § 547 because Chase (P) had failed to perfect its interest in the new loan within the grace period under § 547(e) that would take the transfer in Lee's property out of being made on account of an antecedent debt, and because Chase (P) was not a "new creditor," so that it was precluded from invoking the earmarking doctrine.

RULE OF LAW

(1) A refinanced mortgage lien does not fall within the grace period of 11 U.S.C. § 547(e) where it is not perfected within the grace period, even where the same mortgagee holds both the new mortgage and prior mortgage and the discharge of the prior mortgage is not recorded until after the new mortgage is recorded.

(2) The earmarking doctrine does not apply to a refinanced mortgage interest where the mortgagee holds both the old and new mortgages and where the mortgagee perfects late, so that the debtor's bankruptcy estate is diminished.

FACTS: Lee refinanced his residential mortgage with Chase Manhattan Mortgage Corporation (Chase) (P), which was both the holder of the original mortgage and the refinanced mortgage. About six months later, Lee filed a voluntary Chapter 7 bankruptcy petition. Seventy-seven days before Lee filed his bankruptcy case, and 72 days after Chase (P) had distributed the funds that were used to discharge the original mortgage, the new mortgage was recorded in favor of Chase (P) to secure Lee's obligation to repay the new loan. The discharge was then recorded. The Trustee (D) sought to avoid Chase's (P) new mortgage lien as a preferential transfer under 11 U.S.C. § 547. The bankruptcy court ordered the avoidance of the new mortgage lien, the district court reversed, and the court of appeals granted review.

ISSUE:

(1) Does a refinanced mortgage lien fall within the grace period of 11 U.S.C. § 547(e) where it is not perfected within the grace period, even where the same mortgagee holds both the new mortgage and prior mortgage and the discharge of the prior mortgage is not recorded until after the new mortgage is recorded?

(2) Does the earmarking doctrine apply to a refinanced mortgage interest where the mortgagee holds both the old and new mortgages and where the mortgagee perfects late, so that the debtor's bankruptcy estate is diminished?

HOLDING AND DECISION: (Cole, J.)

(1) No. A refinanced mortgage lien does not fall within the grace period of 11 U.S.C. § 547(e) where it is not perfected within the grace period, even where the same mortgagee holds both the new mortgage and prior mortgage and the discharge of the prior mortgage is not recorded until after the new mortgage is recorded. The applicable, pre-BAPCPA, grace period is 10 days. As long as the mortgage is perfected within the 10-day time period, the associated mortgage debt is not deemed antecedent. To fall within the grace period, the lender must perfect its security interest within the grace period. To determine when perfection has occurred, § 547(e)(1)(A) states that perfection has occurred "when a bona fide purchaser of [the Property] from the debtor against whom applicable law permits such transfer to be perfected cannot acquire an interest that is superior to the interest of the transferee." Here, the "applicable law" is state law, under which perfection occurs upon recording. It is clear that Chase (P) recorded the new mortgage lien 72 days after it disbursed the loan proceeds to Lee; therefore, Chase (P) did not perfect its interest within the 10-day grace period. Accordingly, the transfer of Lee's property must be deemed to have been made on account of an antecedent debt. Moreover, it does not matter, as Chase (P) argues, that the discharge was recorded after the new mortgage was recorded, so that third parties were on notice of Chase's (P) secured interest in the property. The fact that third parties may have been on notice of Chase's (P) original mortgage is irrelevant to the requirements of § 547(e)(1)(A), which is not couched in terms of third-party notice. Accordingly, the transfer occurred when Chase (P) perfected its security interest—72 days after disbursing the loan proceeds—and cannot be deemed not to have been made on account of an antecedent debt. Because it occurred within the 90-day preferential transfer period, it must be avoided. Reversed as to this issue.

(2) No. The earmarking doctrine does not apply to a refinanced mortgage interest where the mortgagee holds both the old and new mortgages and where the mortgagee perfects late, so that the debtor's bankruptcy estate is

Continued on next page.

diminished. The earmarking doctrine is an exception to the general rule that the use of borrowed funds to discharge a debt constitutes a transfer of property of the debtor. To satisfy the doctrine, the lender must show that the borrowed funds have been specifically earmarked by the lender for payment to a designated creditor, regardless of whether the funds pass through the debtor's hands in getting to the selected creditor. If the doctrine is satisfied, it will be deemed that a transfer of an interest of the debtor in property has not occurred, thus negating the threshold requirement for preference treatment. It has been held that for the doctrine to apply, the agreement must be between a new creditor and the debtor for the payment of a specific antecedent debt; the agreement must be performed according to its terms; and the transaction may not diminish the debtor's estate. Because Chase (P) is not a "new creditor," it is precluded for that reason alone from invoking the earmarking doctrine. Even if it were a "new creditor," however, it would still not be able to use that doctrine as a defense. While a minority of courts characterize a refinancing transaction such as the one at issue here as a single unitary transaction, the majority find that a refinancing involves multiple transfers. The latter approach is the better one. A unitary-transaction theory ignores the Code's plain meaning because it ignores the definition of "transfer" set forth in § 101(54), as supplemented by § 547(e). Under this definition, it is clear that Lee's refinancing transaction was comprised of two transfers by him—first, a transfer of the proceeds of the new loan to Chase (P) to pay off the original mortgage, and second, the grant of the new mortgage to Chase (P) to secure his obligation to repay the new loan. Moreover, to apply the earmarking doctrine to the transfer of a lien interest would extend the doctrine beyond its logical limits, which were intended to encompass transfers of funds. A debtor's grant of a mortgage lien in a refinancing transaction does not involve a transfer of "earmarked" property because the debtor is not serving as a conduit for the transfer of property from a third party. As here, the grant of a mortgage to the mortgagee is a transfer of a property interest owned and controlled by the debtor. In addition, the earmarking doctrine is inapplicable here because Chase's (P) perfection of the new mortgage resulted in diminution of Lee's bankruptcy estate. During the period from when the new loan was made and the original mortgage was discharged up until Chase's (P) recording of the new mortgage, Chase (P) did not hold a perfected lien interest. Thus, Chase's (P) subsequent perfection of the new mortgage diminished Lee's estate because the non-exempt equity in the property that otherwise would have been available for distribution to Lee's unsecured creditors became encumbered, and unavailable to unsecured creditors, by the new mortgage that Chase (P) received. Finally, applying principles of equity here, as Chase (P) requests—on the grounds that the refinancing lowered Lee's monthly mortgage payments, thus making more money available to him to pay his other creditors—is inappropriate. Even if Chase (P) is correct that equitable considerations would favor it, the bankruptcy courts have only those equitable powers that they are granted by the Bankruptcy Code. The courts cannot substitute their judgment for that of Congress, which in this case clearly indicated that the appropriate length of time between a creditor's transfer of value and perfection was 10 days (subsequently expanded to 30 days by BAPCPA). By giving effect to Congress' plain meaning, the courts foster predictability in the law of preferences. Also, it is not clear that equity should extend to Chase (P)—a sophisticated lender well aware of the consequences of failing to perfect its security interest within the grace period afforded by § 547(e)(2). Chase (P) could easily have avoided the harsh results it brought on itself by recording the new mortgage within the grace period; there is no equitable ground here for protecting a late-perfecting secured creditor. Reversed as to this issue.

DISSENT: (Merritt, J.) As opposed to the majority, which focuses only on the time of recording by Chase (P) of the new mortgage, the inquiry should be broadened to consider the purpose, consequences, details, and common sense of the complete financing transaction at issue, and whether anyone was misled or if any congressional policies were violated.

ANALYSIS

As the court here also indicated, it believed that applying the earmarking doctrine to insulate a late-perfecting secured creditor from preference liability would essentially write § 547(e) out of the Code and, in the process, defeat the policy the statute was intended to promote—the discouragement of secret liens, which that section's grace period (previously 10 days, now 30 days) was intended to inhibit. For these and other reasons, the court, in another case, also declined to apply the earmarking doctrine where the mortgagee failed to record an original mortgage within the grace period. See *Moyer v. RBC Mortgage Co (In re Maracle)*, 159 F. App'x 692 (6th Cir. 2005).

Quicknotes

CHAPTER 7 BANKRUPTCY A legal proceeding whereby a debtor, who is unable to pay his debts as they become due, is relieved of his obligation to pay his creditors by liquidation and distribution of his remaining assets.

EARMARK To distinguish certain property from other property.

PERFECT Execute; enforce; to make marketable.

In re Denochick

Guarantors (D) v. Trustee (P)

287 B.R. 632 (Bankr. W.D. Pa. 2003).

NATURE OF CASE: Appeal from judgment for trustee in adversary action to avoid a preference.

FACT SUMMARY: Guarantors (D) on Denochick's (debtor) debt consolidation loan argued that payments made by Denochick could not be recovered from them as a preference by the Bankruptcy trustee (P).

RULE OF LAW

A bankruptcy trustee can avoid as a preference, and recover from guarantors of a loan, debtor's payments on the loan.

FACTS: Guarantors (D) agreed to guarantee a debt consolidation loan from NBOC to Denochick (debtor). Denochick made $1,713.35 in loan payments to NBOC in the year prior to filing bankruptcy. The Guarantors (D) received none of this money, but the payments had the indirect effect of reducing their exposure on the guarantee they gave to NBOC. The Trustee (P) commenced an adversary action to avoid as a preference and recover from the Guarantors (D) the money Denochick paid to NBOC. The bankruptcy court concluded that the Guarantors (D) fell within the definition of "creditors" and that they had failed to establish the applicability of the "ordinary course of business" exception. Thus, the court concluded that the Trustee (P) could avoid the $1,713.35 and recover that amount from the Guarantors (D). The district court granted review.

ISSUE: Can a bankruptcy trustee avoid as a preference, and recover from guarantors of a loan, debtor's payments on the loan?

HOLDING AND DECISION: (Cindrich, J.) Yes. A bankruptcy trustee can avoid as a preference, and recover from guarantors of a loan, debtor's payments on the loan. The definition of a "creditor" under the bankruptcy code and state law is very broad and encompasses a guarantor of a debt. Thus, the Guarantors (D) were "creditors," even though their claim was derivative of NBOC's and was contingent upon Denochick's default. Denochick's payments to NBOC conferred a benefit upon the Guarantors (D), to the detriment of her other creditors. Affirmed.

ANALYSIS

This case illustrates the problem of the "indirect preference," which arises from Code § 547(b)(2). The Code thus helps the lender, but not the guarantor, even though the lender already received the payment that is being sought, via the preference, from the guarantor. Thus, there may be two or more persons potentially liable for a preferential transfer: the transferee and others who benefit indirectly from the transfer.

Quicknotes

PREFERENCE A transfer made by the insolvent debtor to a creditor prior to filing the bankruptcy petition, giving a priority to one creditor over others in respect to the debtor's assets.

PREFERENTIAL TRANSFER A transfer made by the insolvent debtor to a creditor prior to filing the bankruptcy petition, giving a priority to one creditor over others with respect to the debtor's assets.

In re Stewart

Trustee (P) v. Unsecured creditor (D)

274 B.R. 503 (Bankr. W.D. Ark. 2002).

NATURE OF CASE: Action under Chapter 13 alleging an avoidable preferential transfer.

FACT SUMMARY: Barry County Livestock Auction, Inc. (Barry County) (D) argued that either the contemporaneous exchange for new value exception or the ordinary course of business exception to Code § 547 applied to relieve it from preferential transfer liability for payments made by Stewart (debtor) by cashier's checks for livestock purchased two weeks earlier where the cashier's checks were used after Stewart's personal checks made at the time of purchase were returned for insufficient funds.

RULE OF LAW

Neither the contemporaneous exchange for new value exception nor the ordinary course of business exception to Code § 547 apply to a preferential transfer made by cashier's check for an antecedent debt where the cashier's check was used after a personal check made in payment of the debt was dishonored for lack of sufficient funds and payment by cashier's check is not typical in the industry.

FACTS: Stewart purchased cattle from Barry County Livestock Auction, Inc. (Barry County) (D) and paid by personal checks, both of which were later returned for insufficient funds. Two weeks later, Stewart paid with cashier's checks the amount he owed Barry County (D). Within 90 days of the purchase, Stewart filed a Chapter 13 bankruptcy petition, and the Trustee (P) brought an action claiming that the payments to Barry County (D) were avoidable preferential transfers. The payments made with the cashier's checks enabled Barry County (D) to receive more than it would have received if the case had been a Chapter 7 case. It was also stipulated that at the time he made the payments, Stewart was insolvent. The court found that the Trustee (P) met her burden of proof as to the preferential transfer of the two cashier's checks, and Barry County (D) argued that either the contemporaneous exchange for new value exception or the ordinary course of business exception to Code § 547 applied to relieve it of preferential transfer liability.

ISSUE: Do either the contemporaneous exchange for new value exception or the ordinary course of business exception to Code § 547 apply to a preferential transfer made by cashier's check for an antecedent debt where the cashier's check was used after a personal check made in payment of the debt was dishonored for lack of sufficient funds and payment by cashier's check is not typical in the industry?

HOLDING AND DECISION: (Fussell, J.) No. Neither the contemporaneous exchange for new value exception nor the ordinary course of business exception to Code § 547 apply to a preferential transfer made by cashier's check for an antecedent debt where the cashier's check was used after a personal check made in payment of the debt was dishonored for lack of sufficient funds and payment by cashier's check is not typical in the industry. First, the debt here was an antecedent debt because it was incurred prior to the allegedly preferential transfer—all buyers at the auction were required to pay for their purchases on the date of sale. Therefore, the debts were incurred two weeks before the delivery of the cashier's checks. Here, too, Barry County (D) is a creditor. Because the Trustee (P) met her burden of proving preferential transfers, Barry County (D) may avoid preference liability only if it can prove that if falls within one of the exceptions set forth in § 547(c).

To qualify for the contemporaneous exchange for new value exception under § 547(c)(1), a creditor must prove that an otherwise preferential transfer was (A) intended by the debtor and the creditor to be a contemporaneous exchange for new value given to the debtor; and (B) in fact a substantially contemporaneous exchange. "New value" is defined as "money or money's worth in goods, services, or new credit, or release by a transferee of property previously transferred to such transferee in a transaction that is neither void nor voidable by the debtor or the trustee under any applicable law, including proceeds of such property, but does not include an obligation substituted for an existing obligation." Here, if the transfer of the cattle did not occur until the cashier's checks were presented to Barry County (D), the transactions may have been contemporaneous exchanges for new value. If, on the other hand, the transfer of the cattle occurred on the day of the sale, two weeks before Stewart presented the cashier's checks to Barry County (D), the court must determine whether the subsequent delivery of the cashier's checks to replace the insufficient funds checks constituted contemporaneous exchanges for new value. Under the UCC, title to the cattle passed to Stewart on the day of the sales. Thus, had Stewart's personal checks cleared, a contemporaneous exchange for value would have occurred. But the bank's dishonor of the personal checks changed the nature of the transactions, so that they became credit transactions and created an antecedent debt. Any subsequent payment, no matter how quickly made, would satisfy that antecedent debt. Thus, here, the cashier's checks satisfied the antecedent debt, and were not contemporaneous exchanges for new value. Hence, Barry County's (D) contemporaneous exchange for new value exception fails.

Continued on next page.

To qualify for the ordinary course of business exception, a creditor must prove that the transfer was "(A) in payment of a debt incurred by the debtor in the ordinary course of business or financial affairs of the debtor and the transferee; (B) made in the ordinary course of business or financial affairs of the debtor and the transferee; and (C) made according to ordinary business terms." Stewart and Barry County (D) had ongoing business relationships for several years. In the course of their business relationship, Stewart purchased cattle from Barry County (D) and was required to pay for the cattle purchased the same day of the purchases. Because the payments were made to satisfy debts that Stewart incurred in the ordinary course of his business dealings with Barry County (D), the elements of subsection (c)(2)(A) are satisfied. The second factor deals with the way the parties actually conducted their business dealings. During the course of their several-year relationship, Stewart paid Barry County (D) by personal check at the time of sale. It was only right before and during the preference period that those personal checks were dishonored. Thus, the payments by personal checks made during the preference period that were dishonored by the bank when presented for payment, but later paid with cashier's checks, were not sufficiently consistent with the payments made during the prior 12 months. Therefore, Barry County (D) has failed to meet the elements of subsection (c)(2)(B). Finally, the general practice in the industry was that cattle purchases were always paid on the day of purchase. Again, because payment by cashier's check two weeks after the date of sale was not typical in the industry, Barry County (D) failed to meet the elements of subsection (c)(2)(C).
Because Barry County (D) has not proven any exceptions to the preferential transfers, it is liable for them.

ANALYSIS

After this case was decided, the Bankruptcy Code was amended in 2005 as to what a creditor must show to keep an otherwise avoidable transfer under the 547(c)(2) exception. While the first element remains the same (i.e., that the debt was incurred in the debtor's ordinary course of business), the creditor only needs to prove either the second or the third element, not both. Since Barry County (D) failed to prove both these elements, the outcome in this case would have been the same even after the amendments.

Quicknotes

ANTECEDENT DEBT For the purposes of bankruptcy law, refers to a debt incurred more than four months prior to the filing of a petition in bankruptcy, and which does not constitute a preferential transfer.

PREFERENTIAL TRANSFER A transfer made by the insolvent debtor to a creditor prior to filing the bankruptcy petition, giving a priority to one creditor over others with respect to the debtor's assets.

In re Shreves

Trustee (P) v. Secured interest holder (D)

272 B.R. 614 (Bankr. N.D. W.Va. 2001).

NATURE OF CASE: Adversary proceeding under Chapter 7 to set aside security interest as a preference.

FACT SUMMARY: The bankruptcy trustee for the Shreves' (debtors) Chapter 7 estate sought to set aside Valley National Bank's (Valley) (D) security interest in an automobile as preferential on the grounds that Valley (D) failed to timely perfect its interest, so it could not relate back to the initial loan date. Among Valley's (D) defenses were the "substantially contemporaneous exchange" exception, and the earmarking doctrine.

RULE OF LAW

The "substantially contemporaneous exchange" exception, and the earmarking doctrine, are not defenses to the preferential avoidance of a security interest in a refinancing loan that is perfected after the relation-back period required in Code § 547(e)(2)(B), but during the preference period.

FACTS: The Shreves (debtors) purchased a vehicle financed by United National Bank (United) and granted United a security interest in the vehicle. However, before United perfected its interest, the Shreves refinanced the loan through Valley National Bank (Valley) (D) on April 3. On April 5, Valley (D) executed and sent a check to United. United recorded its lien on the motor vehicle title on April 21. Ten days later, on May 1, United released the lien. Valley's (D) lien was not recorded until August 11, so no lien was recorded for over three months. The perfection of the security interest thus occurred more than four months after the security agreement. The Shreves filed a Chapter 7 petition on October 18. The Bankruptcy trustee (P) sought to set aside Valley's (D) security interest as preferential under Code § 547(b). Among Valley's (D) defenses were the "substantially contemporaneous exchange" exception, and the earmarking doctrine.

ISSUE: Are the "substantially contemporaneous exchange" exception, and the earmarking doctrine, defenses to the preferential avoidance of a security interest in a refinancing loan that is perfected after the relation-back period required in Code § 547(e)(2)(B), but during the preference period?

HOLDING AND DECISION: (Friend, J.) No. The "substantially contemporaneous exchange" exception, and the earmarking doctrine, are not defenses to the preferential avoidance of a security interest in a refinancing loan that is perfected after the relation-back period required in Code § 547(e)(2)(B), but during the preference period. Under the substantially contemporaneous exchange defense, Valley (D) must first prove that the transfer was intended by the parties to be a contemporaneous exchange for new value given to the debtor, and further, that the transfer was in fact a substantially contemporaneous exchange. The first requirement is satisfied, but the fact that the perfection of the security interest occurred later than the security agreement is problematic. Prior case law held that purchase money security interests perfected outside the statutory period for the enabling loan exception did not qualify for the contemporaneous exchange exception. In a non-bankruptcy context, state law often allows for a longer relation-back or grace period than bankruptcy law (here, the non-bankruptcy relation back period was 60 days). The U.S. Supreme Court held in *Fidelity Financial Services, Inc. v. Fink*, 522 U.S. 211 (1998), that a security interest is "perfected" under § 547 (c)(3) on the date the necessary state law perfection steps are taken, but that a creditor may invoke the enabling loan exception only by satisfying the state law perfection requirements within the enabling loan exception period provided by the Bankruptcy Code. Here, Valley (D) did not make an enabling loan, but rather refinanced a previous loan. Since the enabling loan exception is applicable only to purchase money security transactions, this defense is not available to Valley (D). Valley (D) is essentially requesting that a more lenient standard be applied for the perfection of non-purchase money liens than the one clearly established for purchase money security loans under the enabling loan defense. If a more flexible standard were adopted, as requested by Valley (D), it would result in non-purchase money security interests having more flexibility than purchase-money security interests. Accordingly, Valley's (D) perfection of its security interest was not "in fact substantially contemporaneous" with the transfer as required by § 547(c)(1)(B). Therefore, Valley (D) may not invoke the § 547(c) defense to the trustee's avoidance power.

Under the earmarking doctrine, Valley (D) asserts it lent money specifically to pay off United, so that it should step into United's secured position. Under the facts of this case, however, the earmarking doctrine is inapplicable. The earmarking doctrine "is clearly applicable in a refinancing situation to determine whether the debtor's payment of an existing creditor with funds borrowed from a new creditor constitutes a preferential transfer—that is, whether such payment is a transfer of the debtor's 'interest in property' to pay the debt owed to the first creditor." However, where, as here, the "transfer" at issue is not the transfer of funds to the initial creditor, but the transfer that occurs when the new creditor perfects its lien more than ten days after the parties' loan agreement, as required by § 547(e)(2)(B), it does not

Continued on next page.

involve the payment of funds by a third party, or the payment of borrowed funds at all. For this reason, the earmarking doctrine has no logical relevance to such transfer. Valley's (D) failure to timely perfect its interest within ten days as required by § 547 (e)(2)(B) precludes the relation-back of the transfer to the initial loan date. Since the lien perfection is a transfer occurring during the preference period, and because Valley (D) has no valid defenses, its lien is void.

ANALYSIS

Valley (D) could have protected itself by having United transfer its security interest to Valley (D) at the time of payment. If United had made such a transfer, the debtors would not be considered to have transferred their interest, so no preference would be at issue. Instead, the transfer would have been of United's perfected security interest.

Quicknotes

EARMARK To distinguish certain property from other property.

PERFECTED SECURITY INTEREST A security interest that is safeguarded against other claims to the collateral; perfection is generally accomplished by legal steps necessary to give other creditors notice of the interest.

In re QMECT, Inc.

Debtor (P) v. Junior secured creditor (D)

2007 Bankr. Lexis 4172 (2007).

NATURE OF CASE: Motions for reconsideration and summary judgment in adversary proceeding to avoid security interests as preferential transfers.

FACT SUMMARY: The Trustee (P) for the Debtor's (P) Chapter 11 bankruptcy estate contended that the security interests of its undersecured junior secured creditor, Burlingame (D), should be avoided as preferential transfers because its debt had not increased during the preference period. Burlingame (D) asserted that its debt, which it claimed should include the accrual of interest and late fees, had increased even more than the value of its collateral had increased during the preference period, so that it had a complete "improvement in position" defense under 11 U.S.C. § 547(c)(5) to its interest being avoided as preferences.

RULE OF LAW

For purposes of determining a secured creditor's "improvement in position" pursuant to 11 U.S.C. § 547(c)(5), interest, late charges, and other fees may be considered in arriving at a value of "debt."

FACTS: Burlingame (D), a junior creditor of the debtor, had a security interest in virtually all of the Debtor's (P) assets, including accounts receivable and inventory. Burlingame (D) was undersecured throughout the Chapter 11 preference period, meaning that the value of its collateral, taking into account the amount of the senior secured debt, was less than the amount of Burlingame's (D) debt. During this period, the Debtor's (P) accounts receivable and inventory increased by $156,939, and Burlingame's (D) security interest likewise automatically increased by this amount. The Trustee (P) sought to avoid Burlingame's (D) security interests as preferential transfers. Burlingame (D) asserted the "improvement in position" defense under 11 U.S.C. § 547 (c)(5), which provides that transfers during the preference period are only avoidable to the extent that its undersecured position on the beginning of the preference period is greater than its undersecured position on the petition date. Burlingame (D) argued that its "position" had not "improved" because its debt had increased during the preference period, due to the accrual of interest and late fees, even more than the value of its collateral had increased—to $165,184. Burlingame (D) moved for summary judgment (as well as reconsideration). The bankruptcy court granted review.

ISSUE: For purposes of determining a secured creditor's "improvement in position" pursuant to 11 U.S.C. § 547(c)(5), may interest, late charges, and other fees be considered in arriving at a value of "debt?"

HOLDING AND DECISION: (Tchaikovsky, J.) Yes. For purposes of determining a secured creditor's "improvement in position" pursuant to 11 U.S.C. § 547(c)(5), interest, late charges, and other fees may be considered in arriving at a value of "debt." The Trustee (P) argued, on policy grounds, that under § 547(c)(5) the only changes in the "debt" during the preference period that should be considered are increases due to additional "advances" or decreases pursuant to additional "payments." However, there is no support for this position in the Code. Instead, the Trustee (P) notes that this position is supported by the fact that if the transfers attacked as preferences had been payments rather than transfers of security interests and Burlingame (D) were asserting a "new value" defense pursuant to 11 U.S.C. § 547(c)(3), increases due to interest, late charges, and attorneys' fees would not qualify as "new value." He also observes that 11 U.S.C. § 506(b) excludes post-petition interest and attorneys' fees from an undersecured creditor's secured claim. Section 547(c)(3) refers only to "debt," not to "advances" or "new value." Also, unless otherwise indicated, the definition of terms used in the Code are governed by state law, under which additional interest, late fees, and attorneys' fees incurred during the preference period are clearly considered part of "debt." Debt is defined as "liability on a claim," and "claim" is defined broadly enough to encompass interest, late fees, and attorney fees. Finally, 11 U.S.C. § 506(b) excludes only "post-petition" interest and attorneys' fees from an undersecured creditor's secured debt—not during the prepetition preference period—and therefore has no bearing on the creditor's "debt." For these reasons, Burlingame (D) has a complete defense. Motions for rehearing and summary judgment granted to Burlingame (D).

ANALYSIS

It should be noted that the Trustee (P) was able to establish all the elements of a preference claim, so that barring Burlingame's (D) "improvement in position" defense, its interests would have been avoidable. Burlingame (D) had contended that the Trustee (P) would be unable, as a matter of law, to establish the fifth element of a preference claim, i.e., that the transfers of security interests in the accounts receivable generated and inventory acquired during the preference period permitted it to receive more than if the transfers had not been made and the assets of the debtor had been liquidated in accordance with bankruptcy law. The court rejected this contention, reasoning that the "proceeds" of Burlingame's (D) security interest did not include new accounts receivable although the "floating lien" contained in its security agreement did cause its security interest to attach to them. The court further reasoned that even if its construction of the term

Continued on next page.

"proceeds" was incorrect, the result still had to be the same, since the transfer of a security interest in an account receivable created during the preference period is subject to avoidance as a preference even if the account receivable in question is the "proceeds" of inventory in existence prior to the beginning of the preference period. Thus, without the legal fiction that a different asset is really not a different asset, but merely a change in description, the result is a potentially avoidable transfer.

Quicknotes

PREFERENCE A transfer made by the insolvent debtor to a creditor prior to filing the bankruptcy petition, giving a priority to one creditor over others in respect to the debtor's assets.

SECURED CREDITOR A creditor, the repayment of whose loan is secured by collateral sufficient to repay the debt owed.

SUMMARY JUDGMENT Judgment rendered by a court in response to a motion made by one of the parties, claiming that the lack of a question of material fact in respect to an issue warrants disposition of the issue without consideration by the jury.

In re Nivens

Trustee (P) v. Secured creditor bank (D)

22 B.R. 287 (Bankr. N.D. Tex. 1982).

NATURE OF CASE: Action to set aside a preference.

FACT SUMMARY: The Trustee (P) contended that the holder of a security interest in Nivens's crop was benefited by post-petition increases in the value of such crops, and such benefits were voidable preferences.

RULE OF LAW

More increases in the value of crops do not by themselves constitute a voidable preference.

FACTS: The Bank (D) owned a security interest in Nivens's crops. Nivens filed for bankruptcy, and the crops increased in value. The government paid increased support payments, and the Bank (D) laid claim as the secured creditor. The Trustee (P) contended the increased value was a voidable preference and sought to recover the value for the estate.

ISSUE: Are increases in crop value voidable preferences?

HOLDING AND DECISION: (Brister, J.) No. Mere increases in the value of crops do not by themselves constitute a voidable preference. Crops are unique items of inventory in that their value increases and decreases based upon a continued cycle of maturity. The crop exists from germination and only fluctuations in quantity will give rise to voidable preferences. In this case, the natural progression of development gave greater value to the crops. Thus, no quantitative increase was shown, and no preference existed.

ANALYSIS

Commentators have pointed out that the increased value of crops due to growth cannot be viewed in a vacuum. The owner clearly expends time and money cultivating, feeding, and watering. Thus, this value should be considered in analyzing voidable preferences.

Quicknotes

PREFERENCE A transfer made by the insolvent debtor to a creditor prior to filing the bankruptcy petition, giving a priority to one creditor over others in respect to the debtor's assets.

In re Wild Bills, Inc.

Trustee (P) v. Company (D)

206 B.R. 8 (Bankr. D. Conn. 1997).

NATURE OF CASE: Claim that a borrower made preferential transfers to creditor after filing Chapter 11.

FACT SUMMARY: A company (D) filed a petition for Chapter 11 and the lender exercised its right of setoff. The Trustee (P) sought to recover those funds.

RULE OF LAW

A creditor has a valid right to a pre-petition setoff.

FACTS: Union Trust made a number of loans to Wild Bills, Inc. (D). Before Wild Bills (D) filed a petition for Chapter 11, Union Trust declared the loans in default and exercised its right of setoff. The Trustee (P) sought to recover over $100,000 from Union Trust alleging that Wild Bills (D) made preferential transfers to Union Trust in violation of 11 U.C.S. § 547(b). Union Trust argued that it had a valid right of setoff under 11 U.C.S. § 553.

ISSUE: Does a creditor have a right to a pre-petition setoff?

HOLDING AND DECISION: (Shiff, C.J.) Yes. Some courts have concluded that a setoff is not a "transfer" therefore transfer avoidance issues are properly analyzed under 11 U.C.S. § 553. We agree with Union Trust that it had a valid right of setoff and therefore analyze the Trustee's (P) right to recover funds set off by Union Trust under 11 U.C.S. § 553(b). Under state law, all of the accounts were subject to setoff. Further, the court must assess those accounts for the entire ninetieth day prior to the filing of the petition in order to arrive at the correct setoff amount. After analyzing the amounts involved, Union Trust did not improve its position as a result of the setoff and the Trustee (P) may not recover those setoff amounts. Judgment entered.

ANALYSIS

The right to setoff must be exercised before bankruptcy in order for the avoidance power to apply. If the creditor waits and exercises its right of setoff after bankruptcy after obtaining court permission, then that creditor will not have to surrender any improvement in setoff position it obtains during the 90-day period.

Quicknotes

CHAPTER 11 BANKRUPTCY A legal proceeding whereby a debtor, who is unable to pay his debts as they become due, is relieved of his obligation to pay his creditors through reorganization and payment from future income.

PRE-PETITION Before bankruptcy petition has been filed.

In re Krystal Cadillac-Oldsmobile-GMC Truck, Inc.

Debtor (P) v. Creditor (D)

142 F.3d 631 (3d Cir. 1998).

NATURE OF CASE: Appeal from order affirming bankruptcy court.

FACT SUMMARY: When the General Motors Acceptance Corporation (D) withdrew its line of credit, Krystal Cadillac (P) was forced into bankruptcy and claimed that the vehicle franchise was an asset of its bankruptcy estate.

RULE OF LAW

Where a franchise agreement was in force on the date the bankruptcy petition was filed, the franchise agreement was an asset of the bankruptcy estate.

FACTS: Krystal Cadillac (P) lost its line of credit and was unable to purchase new vehicles under an agreement with General Motors (GM) (D). GM (D) gave 60 days notice that it would terminate its franchise agreement and Krystal (P) filed an appeal with the Pennsylvania Vehicle Board, requesting a hearing. Before the hearing, Krystal (P) filed for bankruptcy. The Vehicle Board allowed GM (D) to terminate the agreement. The bankruptcy trustee moved to sell Krystal's (P) assets, including the franchise. GM (D) filed an objection to the plan, alleging that the franchise had been validly terminated and was no longer an asset of the corporation. The district court affirmed the bankruptcy court's decision that the proceeding before the Vehicle Board did not fall within the scope of the automatic stay and was valid. Krystal (P) and the trustee appealed.

ISSUE: Where a franchise agreement was in force on the date the bankruptcy petition was filed, was the franchise agreement an asset of the bankruptcy estate?

HOLDING AND DECISION: (Mansmann, J.) Yes. Where a franchise agreement was in force on the date the bankruptcy petition was filed, the franchise agreement was an asset of the bankruptcy estate. Once a dealer has filed an appeal with the Vehicle Board, the termination does not become effective until the Vehicle Board issues its decision. The subsequent determinations of the Vehicle Board violated the automatic stay provisions of the Bankruptcy Code. Reversed.

ANALYSIS

The debtor fought for the right to sell the franchise himself. Real estate leases are also frequently hotly contested. Once a debtor files for bankruptcy, all his property is included in the bankruptcy estate.

Quicknotes

AUTOMATIC STAY Upon the filing of a voluntary bankruptcy petition, creditors are prohibited from attempting to recover payment from the debtor or his property.

BANKRUPTCY ESTATE Created by the filing of a petition in bankruptcy and includes all legal and equitable interests of the debtor in property as of that time.

CONTRACT An agreement pursuant to which a party agrees to act, or to forbear from acting, in exchange for performance on the part of the other party.

FRANCHISE AGREEMENT A contract pursuant to which a supplier of goods or services agrees to permit a re-seller to sell the good or service or to otherwise conduct business on behalf of the franchise.

In re Jamesway Corp.

Debtor (P) v. Landlord (D)

201 B.R. 73 (Bankr. S.D.N.Y. 1996).

NATURE OF CASE: Motion requesting an order declaring lease provisions unenforceable.

FACT SUMMARY: Jamesway (P), a debtor in bankruptcy, claimed that certain lease provisions limited his ability to realize the full economic value of the leases, and asked the court find them void and unenforceable.

RULE OF LAW

Provisions restricting, conditioning, or prohibiting a debtor's right to assign a subject lease are invalid.

FACTS: Jamesway (P) operated a business in a mall and filed for relief under Chapter 11 of the Bankruptcy Code. Jamesway (P) alleged that lease provisions conditioning his right to assignment upon the payment of a portion of the profit limited his ability to realize the intrinsic value of the lease. Jamesway (P) requested an order declaring the profit sharing provisions of the leases unenforceable and asked the court for permission to assume and assign a lease over the landlord's (D) objection.

ISSUE: Are provisions restricting, conditioning, or prohibiting a debtor's right to assign a subject lease invalid?

HOLDING AND DECISION: (Garrity, J.) Yes. Provisions restricting, conditioning, or prohibiting a debtor's right to assign a subject lease are invalid. The statute must be read in light of the congressional policy favoring the assumption and assignment of unexpired leases as a means of assisting the debtor in its reorganization or liquidation efforts. Motion granted.

ANALYSIS

The landlord's (D) proposed reading of the statute was held to be very narrow. The landlord (D) claimed that the court did not have the power to nullify the lease provisions. The court ruled that all provisions of a contract were subject to court scrutiny regarding their anti-assignment effect.

Quicknotes

ASSIGNMENT A transaction in which a party conveys his or her entire interest in property to another.

ASSUMPTION Laying claim to or taking possession of.

CHAPTER 11 BANKRUPTCY A legal proceeding whereby a debtor, who is unable to pay his debts as they become due, is relieved of his obligation to pay his creditors through reorganization and payment from future income.

LEASE An agreement or contract that creates a relationship between a landlord and tenant (real property) or lessor and lessee (real or personal property).

In re Riodizio, Inc.

Debtor (P) v. Creditor (D)

204 B.R. 417 (Bankr. S.D.N.Y. 1997).

NATURE OF CASE: Debtor's motion to reject stock option agreement.

FACT SUMMARY: When a Debtor (P) sought to reject a stock option agreement, the Creditor (D) claimed the contract was not executory.

RULE OF LAW

A contract is executory if each side must render performance, on account of an existing legal duty or to fulfill a condition, to obtain the benefit of the counterparty's performance.

FACTS: Riodizio (P) owned and operated a restaurant and had borrowed money from Riodizio Company, LLC (LLC) (D) in exchange for a stock option contract. When Riodizio (P) filed for Chapter 11 bankruptcy and sought to reject the agreement, LLC (D) claimed that the stock option contract was not executory and therefore could not be rejected by the trustee.

ISSUE: Is a contract executory if each side must render performance, on account of an existing legal duty or to fulfill a condition, to obtain the benefit of the counterparty's performance?

HOLDING AND DECISION: (Bernstein, J.) Yes. A contract is executory if each side must render performance, on account of an existing legal duty or to fulfill a condition, to obtain the benefit of the counterparty's performance. Here the contract is executory and the court must decide whether its rejection will benefit the estate. Since the Debtor's (P) management has an interest in preventing the exercise of the option by LLC (D), the court will not defer to the business judgment of the debtor's management. Breaching the contract through rejection produces a minimal, adverse effect on the estate. Motion granted.

ANALYSIS

In order for a bankruptcy trustee to accept or reject a contract, the contract must be executory. Most courts apply the material breach test to determine whether a contract is executory. If both parties have material obligations to perform at the time of filing, the contract is executory.

Quicknotes

CHAPTER 11 BANKRUPTCY A legal proceeding whereby a debtor, who is unable to pay his debts as they become due, is relieved of his obligation to pay his creditors through reorganization and payment from future income.

CONTRACT An agreement pursuant to which a party agrees to act, or to forbear from acting, in exchange for performance on the part of the other party.

EXECUTORY Something that has not been fully completed or performed.

OPTION CONTRACT A contract pursuant to which a seller agrees that property will be available for the buyer to purchase at a specified price and within a certain time period.

TRUSTEE A person who is entrusted to keep or administer something.

In re TWA Inc. Post Confirmation Estate

Debtor (P) v. Federal agency (D)

312 B.R. 759 (Bankr. D. Del. 2004).

NATURE OF CASE: Motion for summary judgment in proceeding to reclassify a proof of claim, allegedly secured by a statutory lien, as an unsecured claim.

FACT SUMMARY: The post-confirmation bankruptcy estate of TWA Inc. (TWA) (P) contended that the U.S. Department of Agriculture's (USDA's) (D) proof of claim, allegedly secured by a statutory lien, should be reclassified as an unsecured claim because the USDA (D) had failed to record the lien with the Federal Aviation Administration (FAA).

RULE OF LAW

Where a statute requires that a statutory lien be recorded to render it valid against a bona fide purchaser, the lien is avoidable in a Chapter 11 bankruptcy proceeding if it has not been recorded pursuant to the statute.

FACTS: The U.S. Department of Agriculture (USDA) (D) conducted inspections on TWA Inc.'s (TWA) (P) airplanes for about nine months before TWA (P) and its subsidiaries filed for Chapter 11 bankruptcy protection. The USDA (D) filed a proof of claim for the amount owed for aircraft inspection services, reimbursable overtime inspections, and violations of animal welfare regulations. The proof of claim asserted that it was secured by a statutory lien pursuant to 21 U.S.C.S. § 136a, which authorizes the Secretary of Agriculture to collect fees sufficient to cover the inspection services of the type provided by the USDA (D). TWA's (P) post-confirmation estate argued that the proof of claim should be reclassified as unsecured, because, it claimed, USDA (D) had to record its statutory liens pursuant to the Federal Aviation Administration Act (Act) to render them unavoidable, and USDA (D) had not so recorded the liens. Act § 44107 (49 U.S.C. § 44107) provides for the establishment of a recording system to record conveyances (including liens) that affect an interest in U.S. civil aircraft. Act § 44108 (49 U.S.C. § 44108) gives a statutory lien only limited effect until it is recorded, so that until recorded it is valid only against the person making it, that person's successors, or a person having actual notice of it. TWA (P) moved for summary judgment.

ISSUE: Where a statute requires that a statutory lien be recorded to render it valid against a bona fide purchaser, is the lien avoidable in a Chapter 11 bankruptcy proceeding if it has not been recorded pursuant to the statute?

HOLDING AND DECISION: (Walsh, J.) Yes. Where a statute requires that a statutory lien be recorded to render it valid against a bona fide purchaser, the lien is avoidable in a Chapter 11 bankruptcy proceeding if it has not been recorded pursuant to the statute. Code § 545(2) permits a trustee or debtor in possession to avoid a statutory lien if it "is not perfected or enforceable at the time of the commencement of the case against a bona fide purchaser. . . . " This means that the trustee's or debtor in possession's power is that of a bona fide purchaser, which is generally understood to mean one who has purchased property for value without notice of any defects in the title of the seller. Because the USDA (D) had not recorded its lien, there was no public notice of it, and, hence, a bona fide purchaser would not have had notice of it. Therefore, the lien is avoidable. USDA (D) is incorrect that merely because its lien is set forth in the statute (21 U.S.C.S. § 136a), and the statute's plain words do not require USDA (D) to take any additional steps to prefect its lien or enforce its rights, the statutory lien was automatically perfected. It is also incorrect that neither 21 U.S.C.S. § 136a nor the Act requires that the USDA's (D) statutory liens be recorded in the FAA registry system to render them unavoidable. That is because Congress is presumed to have been aware of the Code at the time it enacted § 136a, and, since Congress did not provide a recording requirement in § 136a, it may be presumed that the lien was not meant to be enforceable against a bona fide purchaser. The intent of the Act, on the other hand, was to create a central clearinghouse for recording aircraft titles so that the public would have ready access to the claims against, or liens, or other legal interests in an aircraft. Therefore, liens, such as the one at issue, must be recorded to be valid against third parties. Because TWA's (P) estate does not fall within any of the three enumerated exceptions in Act § 44108, it is deemed a bona fide purchaser with power to avoid the lien. Finally, contrary to USDA's (D) assertion, giving effect to the Act's recordation requirement will not nullify the lien. The Act is not in direct conflict with § 136a, since § 136a does not address recordation or perfection. When a debtor fails to pay the inspection fees, a § 136a statutory lien is still created, albeit with limited application, until it is recorded under the Act. Summary judgment granted to TWA's (P) estate.

ANALYSIS

As this case demonstrates, the trustee or debtor in possession in a Chapter 11 case may take on the powers of a bona fide purchaser in the case of a statutory lien. This power is applicable to liens that have a perfection requirement, but not where perfection arises automatically.

Quicknotes

LIEN A claim against the property of another in order to secure the payment of a debt.

Continued on next page.

PERFECT Execute; enforce; to make marketable.

SUMMARY JUDGMENT Judgment rendered by a court in response to a motion made by one of the parties, claiming that the lack of a question of material fact in respect to an issue warrants disposition of the issue without consideration by the jury.

In re Image Worldwide, Ltd.

Trustee (P) v. Creditor (D)

139 F.3d 574 (7th Cir. 1998).

NATURE OF CASE: Appeal from order granting trustee right to recover funds.

FACT SUMMARY: The Bankruptcy trustee (P) sought to avoid loan guarantees to a Corporate affiliate (D).

RULE OF LAW

Indirect benefits to a guarantor may be considered when determining whether a corporation receives reasonably equivalent value for a guarantee.

FACTS: Image Worldwide (IW) had guaranteed loans paid to an affiliate corporation, Image Marketing (IM) (D). When IW later filed for bankruptcy, the Trustee (P) alleged that the guarantees made IW insolvent and were fraudulent transfers because IW had not received reasonably equivalent value in exchange for its guarantees. When the court ruled in the Trustee's (P) favor, IM (D) appealed, claiming IW had received indirect benefits.

ISSUE: May indirect benefits to a guarantor be considered when determining whether a corporation receives reasonably equivalent value for a guarantee?

HOLDING AND DECISION: (Eschbach, J.) Yes. Indirect benefits to a guarantor may be considered when determining whether a corporation receives reasonably equivalent value for a guarantee. A bankruptcy trustee can avoid any transaction of the debtor that would be voidable by any actual unsecured creditor under state law. In this case, however, there were not two functioning corporations that benefited mutually from the loan. The bankruptcy court did not clearly err when it found that IW did not receive reasonably equivalent value for its guarantees. Affirmed.

ANALYSIS

Both corporations were owned by the same person. This case involved an involuntary Chapter 7 bankruptcy. The Trustee (P) had initially relied on the federal Uniform Fraudulent Transfer Act, but the one year statute of limitations had run, so the court applied the strong arm provision of the Bankruptcy Code.

Quicknotes

CORPORATION A distinct legal entity characterized by continuous existence; free alienability of interests held therein; centralized management; and limited liability on the part of the shareholders of the corporation.

FRAUDULENT TRANSFER The conveyance of title to property with the intent to defraud creditors or with the intent to deceive others.

INVOLUNTARY BANKRUPTCY Proceedings brought against a debtor by his creditors thereby forcing him into bankruptcy.

UNSECURED CREDITOR A creditor whose loan is not backed by specified collateral or a security agreement.

In re Video Depot, Ltd.

Bankruptcy trustee (P) v. Creditor (D)

127 F.3d 1195 (9th Cir. 1997).

NATURE OF CASE: Appeal from district court decision affirming bankruptcy court's judgment for trustee plaintiff.

FACT SUMMARY: The owner of Video Depot used corporate funds to pay off his personal gambling debts; the Bankruptcy trustee (P) later sought to recover the funds.

RULE OF LAW

A trustee may not recover from a subsequent transferee if the subsequent transferee accepted the transfer for value, in good faith, and without knowledge of the transfer's voidability.

FACTS: The owner of Video Depot purchased a check in the company's name and used it to pay his personal gambling debt at the Las Vegas Hilton (Hilton) (D). Video Depot later filed for bankruptcy and the Trustee (P) filed suit against Hilton (D) to recover the proceeds of the check. The parties stipulated that the payment to Hilton (D) was a fraudulent transfer. The bankruptcy court determined, and the district court agreed, that Hilton (D) was the initial transferee. Hilton (D) claimed that it was a subsequent transferee and appealed.

ISSUE: May a trustee recover from a subsequent transferee if the subsequent transferee accepted the transfer for value, in good faith, and without knowledge of the transfer's voidability?

HOLDING AND DECISION: (Nelson, J.) No. A trustee may not recover from a subsequent transferee if the subsequent transferee accepted the transfer for value, in good faith, and without knowledge of the transfer's voidability. The bankruptcy courts are split as to whether the principal of a debtor corporation necessarily is the initial transferee of corporate funds used to satisfy a personal obligation. The owner's control over the business operations of Video Depot does not, in itself, compel a finding that the owner had dominion and control over the funds transferred from Video Depot to Hilton (D). The owner was a courier, not a transferee. The bankruptcy court had enough grounds to find that Hilton (D) was an initial transferee. Affirmed.

ANALYSIS

Hilton (D) also unsuccessfully argued on appeal that the check was really a loan to the owner. The only issue in this case was whether the owner was the initial transferee. Since the check was made out to Hilton (D), the court found that the Video Depot owner had not had dominion over the funds.

Quicknotes

CORPORATION A distinct legal entity characterized by continuous existence; free alienability of interests held therein; centralized management; and limited liability on the part of the shareholders of the corporation.

FRAUDULENT CONVEYANCE Conveyances made within one year of filing the bankruptcy petition with intent to defraud creditors and which may be voidable.

VOIDABLE TRANSFER Conveyances made within one year of filing the bankruptcy petition with the intent to defraud creditors.

In re Bakersfield Westar, Inc.

Bankruptcy trustee (D) v. Debtors (P)

226 B.R. 227 (B.A.P. 9th Cir. 1998).

NATURE OF CASE: Review of denial of trustee's motion for partial summary judgment.

FACT SUMMARY: A Bankruptcy trustee (D) claimed that the Debtors' (P) pre-petition revocation of the Debtors' (P) subchapter S election was a fraudulent transfer under §§ 544 (b) and 548, and Cal. Civ. Code § 3439.

RULE OF LAW

A debtor's pre-petition right to revoke its election to be treated as a subchapter S corporation under I.R.C. § 1362, n.10 has value to a debtor's estate and is therefore properly characterized as property.

FACTS: The Saunders (P) operated an ambulance service and submitted to the Internal Revenue Service (IRS) an election to have their corporation treated as a subchapter S corporation for federal income tax purposes. The Saunders (P) later filed a statement of revocation, making their company a C corporation instead. When the Saunders (P) later filed for Chapter 7 bankruptcy, the Trustee (D) sought to have the revocation avoided as a fraudulent transfer. The Saunders (P) claimed they did not have the necessary actual fraudulent intent because the revocation was made on the advice of professionals. The bankruptcy court denied the Trustee's (D) motion for summary judgment because the Debtors' (P) revocation of its election to be treated as a subchapter S corporation did not constitute an interest of the debtor in property. The Trustee (D) appealed.

ISSUE: Does a debtor's pre-petition right to revoke its election to be treated as a subchapter S corporation under I.R.C. § 1362, n.10 have value to a debtor's estate and is it therefore properly characterized as property?

HOLDING AND DECISION: (Russell, J.) Yes. A debtor's pre-petition right to revoke its election to be treated as a subchapter S corporation under I.R.C. § 1362, n.10 has value to a debtor's estate and is therefore properly characterized as property. In this case, the Debtor's (P) estate will be required to pay the capital gains taxes on an administrative expense priority basis, and the tax payments will diminish the funds that would otherwise be available to pay other creditors. Reversed and remanded.

ANALYSIS

The court disagreed with the IRS who had argued on the side of the Debtors (P). The IRS argued that administrative havoc would result if trustees were allowed to avoid revocations of subchapter S elections. The court found that the concern was purely speculative.

Quicknotes

C-CORPORATION A corporation formed under Subchapter C of the Internal Revenue Code.

CHAPTER 7 BANKRUPTCY A legal proceeding whereby a debtor, who is unable to pay his debts as they become due, is relieved of his obligation to pay his creditors by liquidation and distribution of his remaining assets.

PRE-PETITION Before the bankruptcy petition has been filed.

REVOCATION The cancellation or withdrawal of some authority conferred or an instrument drafted, such as the withdrawal of a revocable contract offer prior to the offeree's acceptance.

SUBCHAPTER S CORPORATION A corporation that is formed with a limited number of shareholders pursuant to statute and is taxed to the shareholders at their usual income tax rates.

In re Carolee's Combine

Trustee (P) v. Capital investors (D)

3 B.R. 324 (Bankr. N.D. Ga. 1980).

NATURE OF CASE: Action by bankruptcy trustee to avoid certain payments.

FACT SUMMARY: Bankrupt Carolee's Combine made certain payments to de facto Investors (D) ahead of general creditors.

RULE OF LAW

Where one creditor improperly moves ahead of others, equitable subordination may be used to void the preference.

FACTS: Carolee's Combine was a venture organized to conduct an auction of certain building materials. Capital was partly obtained through "loans" that, by their terms, were in fact capital investments. Much of the material and labor obtained by Carolee's was on a deferred-payment basis. The auction was held, and Carolee's ended up over $200,000 in the red. Nonetheless, the Capital investors (D) were largely repaid at relatively high rates of return, up to 520 percent on an annual basis. Many of the laborers and materialmen ended up with nothing. After Carolee's declared bankruptcy, the Trustee (P) sought to avoid certain payments to the investors.

ISSUE: Where one creditor improperly moves ahead of others, may equitable subordination be used to void the preference?

HOLDING AND DECISION: (Robinson, J.) Yes. Where one creditor improperly moves ahead of others, equitable subordination may be used to void the preference. For the doctrine to apply, the subordinated creditor must have engaged in some type of unfair conduct, must have injured other creditors, and the subordination must not be inconsistent with the other Bankruptcy Code provisions. Here, although they were called "lenders" in the relevant instruments, the Individuals (P) were in fact investors, as evidenced by the rates of return. In a bankruptcy situation, creditors are to be paid before investors. Here, the situation was unfairly reversed. This was both unfair and contrary to bankruptcy law. The Investors (P) rightly should be subordinated to the general creditors. Petition granted.

ANALYSIS

Unlike most bankruptcy devices, equitable subordination was not, for a long time, statutory in nature. It was developed by courts in equity as a tool when other devices were found lacking. Its most salient characteristic is that a creditor upon whom it is used not only loses priority, but may be placed at the very end of the line. It, therefore, has a punitive element in it.

Quicknotes

SUBORDINATION The placement of a party's rights or claims in lower priority to the rights and claims of others.

VOIDABLE PREFERENCE A transfer made by the debtor to a creditor prior to filing a bankruptcy petition, giving a priority to one creditor over another, and which may be later set aside by the bankruptcy trustee.

In re SI Restructuring

Trustee (P) v. Insider creditors (D)

2008 U.S. App. Lexis 13140 (2008).

NATURE OF CASE: Appeal from affirmance of order in adversary proceeding equitably subordinating secured claims.

FACT SUMMARY: The Wooleys (D), former officers and directors, and the largest shareholders, of Schlotzsky's, Inc. (Schlotzsky's), contended that their secured claims should not be equitably subordinated and converted to unsecured claims because their conduct with respect to loans they made to Schlotzsky's was either not inequitable or did not injure Schlotzsky's or its general creditors.

RULE OF LAW

A secured claim belonging to a corporate debtor's insider creditors will not be equitably subordinated where there is no showing either that the creditors' conduct was inequitable, or that there was injury to the debtor or its other creditors.

FACTS: The Wooleys (D), officers and directors, and the largest shareholders, of Schlotzsky's, Inc. (Schlotzsky's), to relieve a critical cash crunch faced by Schlotzsky's, made two loans to the corporation: one in April for $1 million and another in November for $2.5 million. Both loans were secured with Schlotzsky's royalty streams from franchisees, intellectual property rights, and other intangible property. Schlotzsky's and the Wooleys (D) were represented by separate legal counsel for the April loan negotiations, the loan terms were approved by the audit committee and Schlotzsky's board of directors as a related-party transaction, and the transaction was disclosed in the company's filings with the SEC. Despite the April loan, the company still desperately needed capital, and efforts to obtain outside funding continued and were known to the board, and were addressed at an October board meeting. A bank finally agreed to permit the Wooleys (D) to personally borrow capital, which they in turn would be permitted to lend to Schlotzsky's. The bank formally approved the loan to the Wooleys (D) on November 10, and the board was notified on November 11 of a special meeting to be held on November 13 to approve the Wooleys' (D) loan to the company. Before the special meeting, the board members were provided with copies of the proposed promissory note and the security agreement along with e-mails from the company's counsel. When the loan was made, the Wooleys (D) had in place personal guarantees that guaranteed pre-existing Schlotzsky's debt. As part of the November loan package, the Wooleys (D) also secured this potential liability under the guarantees with the same collateral that secured the April and November loans. (The Wooleys' (D) potential obligation on the guaranty agreements was never triggered, however, because the company never defaulted on its principal obligation covered by the guarantees.) At the November 13 board meeting, conducted via telephone conference call, the board was told that without the infusion of additional funds, payroll could not be met and that the company would default on a payment to a secured creditor. All of the non-interested directors in attendance approved the loan without objection, an independent audit committee also approved the loan, and the transaction was publicly disclosed in SEC filings. The proceeds of the loan were used to pay the unsecured creditors and keep the company in operation. Several months later, the Wooleys (D) were terminated as officers and resigned as directors. Shortly afterward, the company filed for Chapter 11 bankruptcy protection, and the Wooleys (D) filed secured claims relating to the April and November loans. The committee of unsecured creditors brought an adversary proceeding against the Wooleys (D), seeking to have their secured claims equitably subordinated and treated as unsecured claims. The bankruptcy court found that the Wooleys (D) had breached their fiduciary duties with respect to the November loan for several reasons: first, because they had presented the loan to the board as the only option to the company collapsing; second, because the loans were putatively meant to be temporary, until permanent financing could be obtained, so there was no reason to secure the loans; third, because the collateral was the company's "crown jewels," so the Wooleys (D) took as much as they could for themselves; and fourth, because by securing their pre-existing contingent liability on their personal guarantees with the revenue stream of the franchise company, the Wooleys' (D) effectively released themselves as guarantors on the debt at the expense of the corporation and its unsecured creditors. Notwithstanding these conclusions, the bankruptcy court failed to make specific findings that the Wooleys' (D) regarding the loans or their pre-existing contingent liability on the guarantees resulted in harm to the corporation or to the unsecured creditors. It nevertheless ordered the Wooleys' (D) secured claims equitably subordinated and, thus, converted to unsecured status. The district court affirmed, and the court of appeals granted review.

ISSUE: Will a secured claim belonging to a corporate debtor's insider creditors be equitably subordinated where there is no showing either that the creditors' conduct was inequitable, or that there was injury to the debtor or its other creditors?

HOLDING AND DECISION: (Davis, J.) No. A secured claim belonging to a corporate debtor's insider creditors will not be equitably subordinated where there is no showing either that the creditors' conduct was inequitable, or

Continued on next page.

that there was injury to the debtor or its other creditors. The law regarding when equitable subordination should be applied is not found in the Code, but in case law, which provides that the claimant must have engaged in inequitable conduct; the misconduct must have resulted in injury to the creditors of the debtor or conferred an unfair advantage on the claimant; equitable subordination of the claim must not be inconsistent with the provisions of the Code; and a claim should be subordinated only to the extent necessary to offset the harm that the debtor or its creditors have suffered as a result of the inequitable conduct. Here, the bankruptcy court made no findings of inequitable conduct by the Wooleys (D) with respect to the April loan, and with regard to the November transactions, even assuming that there was inequitable conduct and unfair advantage, the bankruptcy court made no finding of harm, and the record does not support a finding that either the debtor or the unsecured creditors were harmed by the November transaction. Given that the proceeds of the loan were used to pay unsecured creditors, it cannot be said that unsecured creditors as a class were harmed by the November transaction, even if some unsecured creditors benefited at the expense of other unsecured creditors. Therefore, the argument by the Trustee (P) that when the company secured the Wooleys' (D) loan with franchise assets, the assets available to the unsecured creditors were reduced, thus injuring them, must fail. As to the Wooleys' (D) securing their existing personal guarantees with the same collateral used for the loans, there was never any harm to the company because the Wooleys' (D) potential obligation on the guaranty agreements was never triggered because the company never defaulted on its principal obligation covered by the guarantees. Thus, they also did not gain any unfair advantage as to this transaction. Finally, although the Trustee (P) denies it, it seems that he also is claiming damages under a "deepening insolvency theory," defined as prolonging an insolvent corporation's life through bad debt, causing the dissipation of corporate assets. The Trustee's (P) expert used this theory in determining that the company lost $3.5 million as a result of the loans. However, the bankruptcy court rejected this expert's testimony because it recognized that the Wooleys (D) were "highly committed" to keeping the company going. Moreover, the deepening insolvency theory has been rejected by many courts as a measure of damages, and, even if it were an accepted theory, it would not be supported by the record here, since there was no evidence that the company was undercapitalized or insolvent. For all these reasons, neither of the Wooleys' (D) claims should have been subordinated. Reversed.

ANALYSIS

Many courts, e.g., the Delaware Court of Chancery—the nation's preeminent court for corporate law matters—reject the doctrine of deepening insolvency as an independent cause of action or as a theory of damages. These courts reason that even when a company is insolvent, its directors may, in the appropriate exercise of their business judgment, take action that might, if it does not pan out, result in the company losing value or going into insolvency. The fact that the residual claimants of the company at that time are creditors does not mean that the directors cannot choose to continue the firm's operations in the hope that they can improve the company's financial health so that the company's creditors get a greater recovery. By doing so, however, the directors do not guaranty success—and do not breach their fiduciary duties.

Quicknotes

CHAPTER 11 REORGANIZATION A plan formulated pursuant to Chapter 11 of the Bankruptcy Code whereby a debtor, who is unable to pay his debts as they become due, is relieved of his obligation to pay his creditors through reorganization and payment from future income.

POST-PETITION After bankruptcy petition has been filed.

In re Malkus, Inc., Debtor

Debtor (P) v. Creditor (D)

2004 Bankr. LEXIS 2120 (Bankr. M.D. Fla. 2004).

NATURE OF CASE: Confirmation hearing for debtor's plan of reorganization under Chapter 11.

FACT SUMMARY: LaSalle National Bank (LaSalle) (D) challenged the Chapter 11 reorganization plan of Malkus, Inc. (P) as not feasible.

RULE OF LAW

A Chapter 11 plan of reorganization will not be confirmed where it is not feasible, as demonstrated by debtor's past performance.

FACTS: LaSalle National Bank (LaSalle) (D) held a mortgage note executed by Malkus, Inc. (P) that was secured by a first priority mortgage lien upon, and security interest in, all the real and personal property in a motel. Malkus, Inc. (P) filed a voluntary petition under Chapter 11 after LaSalle (D) started a foreclosure proceeding. Afterward, Malkus, Inc. (P) and LaSalle (D) entered into a stipulation, approved by the court, that required Malkus, Inc. (P) to pay LaSalle (D) at the end of every month the net cash generated from the operation of the motel, less the actual approved expenditures and the operating reserves; and to escrow $3,941 monthly in order to pay the post-petition real estate taxes. When Malkus, Inc. (P) failed to comply with the stipulation, the court lifted the automatic stay to permit LaSalle (D) to proceed with the foreclosure case through the entry of final judgment, with no sale to occur without further court order. Malkus, Inc. (P) made only one adequate protection payment to LaSalle (D) during the pendency of the case. Malkus, Inc. (P) sought to have its plan of reorganization confirmed, but LaSalle (D) challenged the plan as not feasible.

ISSUE: Will a Chapter 11 plan of reorganization be confirmed where it is not feasible, as demonstrated by debtor's past performance?

HOLDING AND DECISION: (Proctor, J.) No. A Chapter 11 plan of reorganization will not be confirmed where it is not feasible, as demonstrated by debtor's past performance. Pursuant to Code § 1129(a)(11), a plan of reorganization must be feasible. Although success does not have to be guaranteed, the plan must offer a reasonable prospect of success and be workable. A debtor's past performance is one of the most important measures of whether a debtor's plan will succeed. Here, LaSalle (D) argues that Malkus, Inc.'s (P) expenses, during the post-petition period of operations, exceeded its own budget in virtually every month (once adjusted for budgeted items—such as payments to LaSalle (D) (that were not made)—are figured in). In addition, LaSalle (D) asserts that Malkus, Inc. (P) even lost money in two of the months that were projected by the debtor to be successful, revenue-producing months. Although Malkus, Inc.'s (P) revenues have risen, its dismal track record spanning over the pendency of the case has clearly shown that the projections relied upon in the plan are unreasonable and unachievable. The motel's historical poor operating results cannot be overlooked merely because of a few months in which the debtor was either able to meet or surpass the motel's projected revenues. Therefore, the plan is not feasible, and Malkus, Inc. (P) has failed to carry its burden, as the proponent of the plan. Accordingly, the plan cannot be confirmed and the case must be dismissed.

ANALYSIS

The Code itself does not use the term "feasibility." Instead, the Code says that a plan will be confirmed only if "[c]onfirmation of the plan is not likely to be followed by the liquidation, or the need for further financial reorganization, of the debtor or any successor to the debtor under the plan, unless such liquidation or reorganization is proposed in the plan." Thus, feasibility goes to the ability of the debtor to survive long enough to make its scheduled payments. The test for feasibility is applied on a case-by-case basis and is left to the bankruptcy judge's discretion. The feasibility test must be satisfied regardless of whether all creditors have approved the plan.

Quicknotes

CHAPTER 11 REORGANIZATION A plan formulated pursuant to Chapter 11 of the Bankruptcy Code whereby a debtor, who is unable to pay his debts as they become due, is relieved of his obligation to pay his creditors through reorganization and payment from future income.

In re Made in Detroit, Inc., Debtor

Debtor (P) v. Creditor (D)

299 B.R. 170 (Bankr. E.D. Mich. 2003).

NATURE OF CASE: Confirmation proceeding for debtor's plan of reorganization under Chapter 11.

FACT SUMMARY: Made in Detroit, Inc. (Debtor) (P) filed a Chapter 11 petition and submitted a plan of reorganization for confirmation, but its creditors (D) objected, contending that the plan was not feasible because the proposed financing in the plan was conditional, so that Debtor (P) did not have exit financing to fund the plan.

RULE OF LAW

A Chapter 11 plan of reorganization will not be confirmed where it is not feasible, as demonstrated by conditional financing and a lack of exit financing.

FACTS: Made in Detroit, Inc. (Debtor) (P), which owned as its primary asset 410 acres of real estate, was delinquent on payments to secured creditors (D), who commenced foreclosure proceedings. As a result, Debtor (P) filed a Chapter 11 petition and submitted a plan of reorganization. The plan provided that it would be funded via a $9 million loan from Kennedy Funding, Inc. (Kennedy), and that the loan was contingent on certain conditions precedent, including a $270,000 commitment fee deposited in escrow and a $15 million "as is" quick sale valuation of the property. Debtor (P) intended to obtain these funds through loans or capital contributions from shareholders and/or loans from other persons. Kennedy was to bring investors into the transaction, but, if it was unable to do so, it had the right to cancel its loan obligations. The plan also provided that once the $9 million was obtained, the secured creditors and administrative claimants would be paid in full. The unsecured creditors (D) would receive an initial distribution of $750,000 (with the balance of claims to be paid from the proceeds of the sale of lots), and equity shareholders would retain their interest. The Official Committee of Unsecured Creditors (the "Committee") (D) filed objections to confirmation of the Debtor's (P) Plan. In addition, the Committee filed its own plan of reorganization.

ISSUE: Will a Chapter 11 plan of reorganization be confirmed where it is not feasible, as demonstrated by conditional financing and a lack of exit financing?

HOLDING AND DECISION: (McIvor, J.) No. A Chapter 11 plan of reorganization will not be confirmed where it is not feasible, as demonstrated by conditional financing and a lack of exit financing. Debtor's (P) plan fails to meet the requirement that a plan must be feasible. Feasibility is a mandatory requirement for confirmation. The Code prevents confirmation of visionary schemes that promise creditors more than the debtor can possibly attain after confirmation. A plan that is submitted on a conditional basis is not considered feasible, and thus confirmation of such a plan must be denied. The plan does not need to guarantee success, but it must present reasonable assurance of success. To provide such reasonable assurance, a plan must provide a realistic and workable framework for reorganization. The plan cannot be based on "visionary promises"; it must be doable; sincerity, honesty and willingness are not sufficient to make the plan feasible. Here, although Debtor (P) is acting in good faith, the plan is not realistic, and is based on wishful thinking. It is contingent on exit financing from Kennedy, and there is no assurance that the Kennedy loan will ever close or that the property will be appraised at a value high enough to provide the $9 million loan. Thus, it is not likely that the plan will be funded. The conditions precedent to Kennedy's funding of the loan were not satisfied as of the date of the confirmation hearing. Further, the evidence did not show that the satisfaction of such conditions was reasonably likely in the foreseeable future. The $270,000.00 loan commitment fee was never put into an escrow account or paid to Kennedy. Further, Debtor (P) did not meet its burden of showing that the funding was a loan that could be classified as an administrative expense because, under the totality of the circumstances, the funding appeared to constitute capital contributions, not a loan. In summary, Debtor (P) failed to show that it had exit financing to fund its plan. The proposed financing had so many contingencies that Debtor's (P) plan was conditional at best. Thus, the Debtor's (P) plan is not feasible under Code § 1129(a)(11), and the court must deny confirmation of the plan. Case dismissed.

ANALYSIS

Although the court found that Debtor's (P) plan was too shaky—based on too many conditions—it nevertheless confirmed the plan proposed by the Committee. That plan provided that it would be financed by an "as is" immediate cash sale of the property to the Trust for Public Land for $4,800,000. Under the terms of the Committee's plan, the secured creditors and administrative claimants were to be paid in full; the unsecured creditors (D) would receive a pro rata payment; and the equity shareholders would not receive any distribution nor would they retain any property interest. Obviously, the court found that Committee's plan was not conditional, given that the sale thereunder would occur "immediately" and reflected the value of the property.

Continued on next page.

Quicknotes

CHAPTER 11 REORGANIZATION A plan formulated pursuant to Chapter 11 of the Bankruptcy Code whereby a debtor, who is unable to pay his debts as they become due, is relieved of his obligation to pay his creditors through reorganization and payment from future income.

ESCROW A written contract held by a third party until the conditions therein are satisfied, at which time it is delivered to the obligee.

SK-Palladin Partners, L.P. v. Platinum Entertainment, Inc.

Unsecured creditor (P) v. Debtor (D)

2001 U.S. Dist. LEXIS 20710 (N.D. Ill. 2001).

NATURE OF CASE: Appeal from order confirming a joint plan of reorganization under Chapter 11.

FACT SUMMARY: SK-Palladin Partners, L.P. (Palladin) (P), an unsecured creditor of Platinum Entertainment Inc. (Platinum) (D), contended that Platinum's (D) joint reorganization plan under Chapter 11 was not in the best interests of creditors under Code § 1129(a)(7).

RULE OF LAW

A joint plan of reorganization under Chapter 11 will be confirmed where an objecting creditor cannot prove its claim that the plan is not in the creditors' best interests.

FACTS: Platinum Entertainment Inc. (Platinum) (D) filed a bankruptcy petition under Chapter 11, and prepared an offering memorandum for its assets, but no sale occurred. Consequently, it determined the liquidation value of its primary asset—a music catalogue—was $15 million. It also commenced settlement negotiations with The Harry Fox Agency, Inc. (Harry Fox) a lead plaintiff in pre-bankruptcy class action suits. Platinum (D) and the committee proposed the joint plan, which called for: (1) reorganization of Platinum's (D) legal and financial affairs; (2) resumption of Platinum's (D) business; (3) immediate deposit of $1 million for payment of unsecured claims; and (4) payment of $2 million to fund the Harry Fox settlement. SK-Palladin Partners, L.P. (Palladin) (P), a Class 3 holder of unsecured claims, objected to the joint plan. Palladin (P) argued the joint plan did not serve the best interest of creditors under Code § 1129 (a). Palladin (P) also claimed that the bankruptcy court erred by closing discovery and denying the admission of appraisals that purportedly demonstrated the value of the music catalogue was higher, and by failing to account for the catalogue's value after settlement of the class action suits. The bankruptcy court had determined that appraisals propounded by Palladin (P) were hearsay because it had failed to designate the appraiser as a witness. In addition, the bankruptcy court denied an extension of the discovery schedule because it found that Palladin (P) had not been diligent. The district court granted review.

ISSUE: Will a joint plan of reorganization under Chapter 11 be confirmed where an objecting creditor cannot prove its claim that the plan is not in the creditors' best interests?

HOLDING AND DECISION: (Conlon, J.) Yes. A joint plan of reorganization under Chapter 11 will be confirmed where an objecting creditor cannot prove its claim that the plan is not in the creditors' best interests. Pursuant to § 1129(a)(7), each of the creditors in a Chapter 11 reorganization must receive at least as much as they would under a Chapter 7 liquidation. Here, Palladin (P) asserts the Harry Fox class action suits diminished the value of Platinum's (D) music catalogue. According to Palladin (P), the bankruptcy court erred by closing discovery and denying the admission of appraisals that purportedly demonstrated the value of the music catalogue was higher; and not taking into account the music catalogue's value after settlement of the Harry Fox class action suits. Palladin's (P) assertions are meritless. First, the bankruptcy court's finding that Palladin (P) failed to perform discovery with due diligence is supported in the record. This lack of due diligence resulted in Palladin's (P) inability to offer its expert's valuation evidence at the hearing, nor did it offer its own testimony on the catalogue's value. Because the appraiser was unavailable as a witness, the bankruptcy court correctly barred the valuation evidence as hearsay. Thus, the bankruptcy court's ruling was not an abuse of discretion. Palladin (P) offered only unsupported assertions that the music catalogue's value was higher than $15 million because the class actions were settled. The bankruptcy court noted that a lender's $33 million secured claim and all administrative claims had to be paid before other creditors. Extensive efforts to sell Platinum's (D) assets proved fruitless. The bankruptcy court determined that was a "strong indication that the assets were not worth more than $33 million." Moreover, the bankruptcy court relied upon the only evidence of valuation presented at the hearing—Platinum's (D) submission that the music catalogue was worth $15 million. Because Platinum's (D) submissions were uncontroverted, the bankruptcy court reasonably relied on that evidence. Consequently, the bankruptcy court's factual finding was not clear error. Affirmed.

ANALYSIS

The burden in this situation was on Platinum (D) to show the liquidation value of the company, so as to show that creditors would get at least as much under the plan as they would in a Chapter 7 liquidation. Essentially, the court here is holding that Platinum (D) met that burden—or at least that Palladin (P) was insufficiently diligent to rebut Platinum's (D) evidence. The bankruptcy court did not take kindly to Palladin's (P) leisurely approach to discovery, saying "Your casual reference to the need for months to take discovery runs completely contrary to the manner in which bankruptcy cases are pursued."

Continued on next page.

Quicknotes

CLASS ACTION A suit commenced by a representative on behalf of an ascertainable group that is too large to appear in court, who shares a commonality of interests and who will benefit from a successful result.

HEARSAY An out-of-court statement made by a person other than the witness testifying at trial that is offered in order to prove the truth of the matter asserted.

In re U.S. Truck Co., Inc.

Debtor (P) v. Unsecured creditor (D)

800 F.2d 581 (6th Cir. 1986).

NATURE OF CASE: Appeal of order confirming Chapter 11 reorganization plan.

FACT SUMMARY: Creditor Teamsters Union (D) contended that a reorganization plan excluded it from a certain class of creditors for the sole purpose of plan approval.

RULE OF LAW

Excluding a creditor in a Chapter 11 reorganization from a class of similarly situated creditors for the sole purpose of plan approval may be invalid.

FACTS: U.S. Truck Co., Inc. (P) filed for bankruptcy under Chapter 11. One unsecured creditor was the Teamsters Union, (D) which had a collective bargaining agreement with the company. A reorganization plan was proposed that was not to the Union's (D) liking. However, the Union (D) was excluded from the class of general unsecured creditors, all of whom approved the plan, invoking the cramdown provisions of § 1129(b) of the Code. The plan was approved, and the Union (D) appealed, contending that the creditor classes had been gerrymandered solely for the sake of approval.

ISSUE: May the exclusion of a creditor in a Chapter 11 reorganization from a class of similarly situated creditors for the sole purpose of plan approval be invalid?

HOLDING AND DECISION: (Kennedy, J.) Yes. Excluding a creditor in a Chapter 11 reorganization from a class of similarly situated creditors for the sole purpose of plan approval may be invalid. Congress, in § 1129, specifically prohibited the inclusion of dissimilar creditors in the same class. There is no prohibition against not including similar creditors in the same class. Some courts have inferred this to mean that a similarly situated creditor may be excluded at will. This court disagrees. A trustee or debtor-in-possession is a fiduciary, and to exclude a creditor from a class to which it would otherwise belong solely for the purpose of obtaining plan approval constitutes a breach of that duty and will in many cases be invalid. [The court went on to hold that the Union (D) was, in fact, a uniquely situated creditor and was properly excluded from the class of unsecured creditors.] Affirmed.

ANALYSIS

As the opinion intimates, the rule announced here is not universally followed. Some courts have held that, because Congress did not prohibit the sort of class gerrymandering challenged here, it is acceptable. An example of this is *Barnes v. Whelan*, 689 F.2d 193 (D.C. Cir., 1982).

Quicknotes

COLLECTIVE BARGAINING Negotiations between an employer and employee that are mediated by a specified third party.

CRAMDOWN Refers to a court's confirmation of a reorganization plan in a bankruptcy proceeding despite the opposition of creditors.

DEBTOR-IN-POSSESSION In a Chapter 11 proceeding, refers to a debtor who retains control of assets or property pursuant to a plan of reorganization.

UNSECURED CREDITOR A creditor whose loan is not backed by specified collateral or a security agreement.

In re Bernhard Steiner Pianos USA, Inc.

Unsecured creditors (P) v. Debtor (D)

292 B.R. 109 (Bankr. N.D. Tex. 2002).

NATURE OF CASE: Objection to classification of creditors in Chapter 11 plan.

FACT SUMMARY: Unsecured floor plan creditors (P) objected to being classified separately from consignment creditors in Bernhard Steiner Pianos USA, Inc.'s (Debtor) (D) Chapter 11 reorganization plan.

RULE OF LAW

Under a Chapter 11 plan of reorganization, unsecured consignment creditors may be classified separately from general unsecured creditors where there are good business reasons to do so.

FACTS: Bernhard Steiner Pianos USA, Inc. (Debtor) (D) filed a Chapter 11 petition. The company sold new pianos, consigned used pianos, and repaired and refurbished pianos. Due to the Debtor's (D) cash crunch, funds were not turned over to the lenders providing the floor plan financing. The collateral for the floor plan lenders (P) was exceeded by the debt owed to those entities. Debtor (D) remained open for business during the pendency of the bankruptcy, and, early in the case, the floor plan creditors obtained relief from the automatic stay, and repossessed their remaining collateral. Debtor (D) entered into court-approved agreements with third parties whereby the third parties would provide pianos to Debtor (D) and would also pay for the cost of operations in return for a split of the profits. Debtor's (D) reorganization plan contemplated repayment of creditors on a 100 percent basis. There was testimony that in order for Debtor (D) to do so, Debtor (D) would have to maintain a successful operation, and that Debtor's (D) ability to continue successfully in business would require that the Debtor (D) attract good consignment pianos; the sale of new pianos alone would not suffice. In the piano industry, if a consignee gets the reputation that it is unwilling or unable to pay consignors, the consignee won't be able to attract good consignment pianos. Therefore, the quicker a debtor repays the consignment class, the quicker they get new consignment pianos. The plan was ultimately approved by all the impaired classes except for Class 6, of which the floor plan lenders were members. The plan separately classified creditors whose claims arose from consigned goods (Class 4) and general unsecured claims, including the claims of the floor plan lenders (P). The floor plan lenders (P) objected to this separate classification, given that both classes were unsecured creditors. Payments to Class 6 were scheduled to begin after full payment to Class 4, about a year after the effective date. The floor plan creditors (P) argued that both Class 4 and Class 6 should be placed in the same class.

ISSUE: Under a Chapter 11 plan of reorganization, may unsecured consignment creditors be classified separately from general unsecured creditors where there are good business reasons to do so?

HOLDING AND DECISION: (Hale, J.) Yes. Under a Chapter 11 plan of reorganization, unsecured consignment creditors may be classified separately from general unsecured creditors where there are good business reasons to do so. In this jurisdiction, separate classification is permitted for "good business reasons." Here, the Debtor (D) has met the good business reason test. Selling consigned pianos has historically been an important part of the Debtor's business and is contemplated to be an integral part of the Debtor's (D) future. Debtor presented evidence, which was not rebutted, that its consignment business had suffered significantly since word had leaked out that Debtor did not remit the proceeds from the sale of consigned pianos. The undisputed testimony is that the Class 4 consignment creditors were separately classified so as to accelerate repayment to them so Debtor (D) could begin expeditiously to repair its tarnished consignment name in a small market. Improving the consignment public's perception of Debtor (D) and restoring trust in the Debtor (D) among potential consignors as soon as possible is important to the success of the reorganization overall. Also, no evidence of gerrymandering was offered at the confirmation hearing. This is a good business reason for the separate classification and treatment of consignment creditors in Class 4 from the claims of the general unsecured creditors; therefore, the classification objection is overruled.

ANALYSIS

This case illustrates the principle followed in some jurisdictions that separate classification of legally similar claims is permissible, provided there is a good business justification for doing so. Other classification principles are that as a general premise, substantially similar claims, or those that share common priority and rights against the debtor's estate, should be placed in the same class. Also, small unsecured claims may be classified separately from their larger counterparts if the court so approves for administrative convenience. Finally, substantially similar claims are not permitted to be separately classified "in order to gerrymander an affirmative vote on a reorganization plan."

Continued on next page.

Quicknotes

CONSIGNMENT An agreement whereby one party is to deliver goods to another party who will pay the first party for those goods that the second party sells and will return any of the items that he does not sell.

GERRYMANDERING To create a civil division of an unusual shape for an improper purpose such as redistricting a state so that a maximum number of the elected representatives will be of a particular political party.

UNSECURED CREDITOR A creditor whose loan is not backed by specified collateral or a security agreement.

In re PPI Enterprises (U.S.), Inc.

Debtor (P) v. Landlord creditor (D)

324 F.3d 197 (3d Cir. 2003).

NATURE OF CASE: Appeal from affirmance of judgment in Chapter 11 bankruptcy case that, inter alia, a creditor was unimpaired.

FACT SUMMARY: Solow (D), a landlord creditor of PPI Enterprises, Inc. (PPIE) (P), contended that a broad reading of "claim" under Code § 1124(1) required a finding that he was an impaired creditor under PPIE's Chapter 11 reorganization plan because he was subject to the statutory cap of Code § 502 (b)(6), arguing that impairment occurred whether the source of impairment is the plan or a statute.

RULE OF LAW

A creditor is not impaired for purposes of voting on a reorganization plan where the creditor is subject to the statutory cap of Code § 502(b)(6).

FACTS: Solow (D) leased office space to PPI Enterprises, Inc. (PPIE) (P). PPIE's (P) indirect corporate parent guaranteed the lease obligations, and a bank issued a standby letter of credit on behalf of PPIE (P). After the parent became insolvent, PPIE (P) defaulted on the lease, and Solow (D) drew on the letter of credit, but there was still over $4.75 million in rent owing. PPIE (P) filed for Chapter 11 bankruptcy protection, seeking, inter alia, to limit the Solow's (D) lease termination damages under the statutory cap provisions in Code § 502(b)(6). After the bankruptcy court rejected Solow's (D) attempt to dismiss the Chapter 11 filing on grounds of bad faith, PPIE (P) filed its plan, under which Solow's (D) claim was classified as a "Class 2 non-insider general unsecured claim." PPIE (P) contended that plan approval by the classes of creditors was unnecessary since none were impaired. Nonetheless, PPIE (P) solicited votes from Classes 1, 2, and 3. Only two of seven ballots were returned from Class 2—Solow's (D) "no" vote and one "yes" vote. With no clear majority, Solow (D) contended Class 2 effectively rejected the plan. The bankruptcy court determined that Solow's (D) claim was subject to the statutory cap of Code § 502(b)(6) and reduced by application of the letter of credit; the bankruptcy was filed in good faith; and as an "unimpaired creditor," Solow (D) was deemed to have accepted the plan. The district court affirmed, and the court of appeals granted review.

ISSUE: Is a creditor impaired for purposes of voting on a reorganization plan where the creditor is subject to the statutory cap of Code § 502(b)(6)?

HOLDING AND DECISION: (Scirica, J.) No. A creditor is not impaired for purposes of voting on a reorganization plan where the creditor is subject to the statutory cap of Code § 502(b)(6). The bankruptcy court determined that the plan did not impair Solow's (D) legal, equitable, and contractual rights, since the limitation on Solow's (D) potential recovery was dictated by § 502(b)(6), which was independent of the plan. Solow (D) contends application of § 502(b)(6) alters his claim and entitles him to vote against the plan's confirmation. A "claim" refers broadly to a creditor's right to recovery. Solow (D) contends a broad definition of "claim" requires a finding of impairment whether the source of impairment is the plan or a statute. The bankruptcy court rejected Solow's (D) argument, finding he "confused two distinct concepts: (i) plan impairment, under which the debtor alters the 'legal, equitable, and contractual rights to which [the] claim entitles the holder of such claim,' and (ii) statutory impairment, under which the operation of a provision of the Code alters the amount that the creditor is entitled to under non-bankruptcy law." A closer look at the language of § 1124(1) reveals that "impairment by statute" is an oxymoron—impairment results only from what the plan does, not what the statute does. A plan that "leaves unaltered" the legal rights of a claimant is one that, by definition, does not impair the creditor. A plan that leaves a claimant subject to other applicable provisions of the Bankruptcy Code does no more to alter a claimant's legal rights than does a plan that leaves a claimant vulnerable to a given state's usury laws or to federal environmental laws. Thus, any alteration of legal rights is a consequence of the bankruptcy filing itself, not of the plan. Because the Bankruptcy Code, not the plan, is the only source of limitation on Solow's (D) pre-petition rights, Solow's (D) claim is not impaired under § 1124(1). Affirmed.

ANALYSIS

Solow (D) also alleged PPIE's (P) bankruptcy was a sham filing designed to create value for its indirect corporate parent and its creditors at his expense, and that the bankruptcy served no legitimate purpose. According to Solow (D), PPIE (P) did not intend its bankruptcy filing to effectuate a corporate reorganization because the company had no ongoing business, only one remaining employee, and "no assets other than stock certificates representing a 2 percent interest in Del Monte Foods Company." The bankruptcy court rejected Solow's (D) motion to dismiss on this ground. The court of appeals agreed with the bankruptcy court, holding that filing for Chapter 11 primarily to take advantage of the statutory cap is not per se a bad faith use of the bankruptcy law.

Continued on next page.

Quicknotes

BAD FAITH Conduct that is intentionally misleading or deceptive.

IMPAIRMENT The weakening or diminishing in power of a right.

In re Figter Ltd.

Debtor (P) v. Secured creditor (D)

118 F.3d 635 (9th Cir. 1997).

NATURE OF CASE: Appeal from decision that the holder of a first deed of trust bought twenty-one unsecured claims in good faith and that it could vote each one separately.

FACT SUMMARY: Figter Limited, a debtor in Chapter 11 bankruptcy, alleged that a secured creditor who bought out other unsecured claims acted in bad faith and should be limited to a single vote.

RULE OF LAW

On request of a party in interest, and after notice and a hearing, the court may designate (disqualify from voting) any entity whose acceptance or rejection of a plan was not in good faith.

FACTS: Figter Limited, a Chapter 11 debtor and owner of an apartment complex, proposed a reorganization plan that contemplated full payment of a promissory note, but at a disputed rate of interest. Under the plan, the secured creditor's claim was not impaired and unsecured claims were impaired at only 80 percent of their face value. The secured creditor then purchased twenty-one of the thirty-four unsecured claims and filed the proper notices of transfer of claims. As a result, Figter's plan was unconfirmable because it was unable to meet the requirement that there would not be an impaired, consenting class of claims. That would preclude a cramdown of the secured claim. Figter appealed in an attempt to avoid that result. Figter asserted that the secured creditor, Teachers Insurance and Annuity Association of America, should be precluded from voting its purchased claims because it did not buy them in good faith. Alternatively, Figter claimed that, even if they were purchased in good faith, Teachers could not vote them separately, but was limited to one total vote as a Class 3 creditor. The bankruptcy court decided that, in this case, Teachers was a creditor that acted in a good faith attempt to protect its interests and not with some ulterior motive, and that there was no reason to hold that the separate claims should suddenly become only one vote. The district court affirmed. Figter appealed.

ISSUE: On request of a party in interest, and after notice and a hearing, may the court designate (disqualify from voting) any entity whose acceptance or rejection of a plan was not in good faith?

HOLDING AND DECISION: (Fernandez, J.) Yes. On request of a party in interest, and after notice and a hearing, the court may designate (disqualify from voting) any entity whose acceptance or rejection of a plan was not in good faith. This provision of the Bankruptcy Code was intended to apply to those who were not attempting to protect their own proper interests, but who were, instead, attempting to obtain some benefit to which they were not entitled. Figter cites no authority for holding that in a single asset bankruptcy, claim purchasing activities like those of Teachers are in bad faith. It cannot be said that the bankruptcy court erred in deciding that Teachers acted in good faith and that it could vote each of its twenty-one claims separately. Affirmed.

ANALYSIS

Teachers ultimately was able to purchase enough of the unsecured claims in this case to block Figter's plan. Only impaired classes vote since the unimpaired classes are deemed to have accepted the plan. The definition of "impairment" is set forth in § 1124 of the Bankruptcy Code.

Quicknotes

CRAMDOWN Refers to a court's confirmation of a reorganization plan in a bankruptcy proceeding despite the opposition of creditors.

SECURED CREDITOR A creditor, the repayment of whose loan is secured by collateral sufficient to repay the debt owed.

In re Northwest Airlines Corp.

Debtor (P) v. Ad hoc committee (D)

363 B.R. 701 (Bankr. S.D.N.Y. 2007).

NATURE OF CASE: Motion to supplement a statement pursuant to Bankruptcy Rule 2019.

FACT SUMMARY: Northwest Airlines Corporation et al. (Debtors) (P) contended that a statement filed on behalf of an ad hoc committee (D) by its counsel pursuant to Rule 2019 was inadequate because it failed to list required information for each member of the committee.

RULE OF LAW

An ad hoc committee represented by counsel must disclose "the amounts of claims or interests owned by the members of the committee, the times when acquired, the amounts paid therefor, and any sales or other disposition thereof," as required by Bankruptcy Rule 2019.

FACTS: The law firm of Kasowitz, Benson, Torres & Friedman LLP (KBT&F) filed a statement pursuant to Rule 2019 on behalf of its client, an ad hoc committee (D) of equity security holders, in the Chapter 11 bankruptcy of Northwest Airlines Corporation et al. (Debtors) (P). KBT&F disclosed that there were 13 committee members with an aggregate of "19,065,644 shares of common stock of Northwest and claims against the debtors in the aggregate amount of $264,287,500." The Debtors (P) moved to supplement that statement, arguing that Rule 2019 required disclosure of "the amounts of claims or interests owned by the members of the committee, the times when acquired, the amounts paid therefor, and any sales or other disposition thereof." Rule 2019 requires that every committee, except an official committee, "representing more than one creditor or equity security holder" must disclose such information. The bankruptcy court heard the Debtors' (P) motion.

ISSUE: Must an ad hoc committee represented by counsel disclose "the amounts of claims or interests owned by the members of the committee, the times when acquired, the amounts paid therefor, and any sales or other disposition thereof," as required by Bankruptcy Rule 2019?

HOLDING AND DECISION: (Gropper, J.) Yes. An ad hoc committee represented by counsel must disclose "the amounts of claims or interests owned by the members of the committee, the times when acquired, the amounts paid therefor, and any sales or other disposition thereof," as required by Bankruptcy Rule 2019. Because the statement filed by KBT&F did not contain this information, it is facially deficient. Referring to Rule 2019's lead-in clause, the committee (D) argues that no member of the committee (D) represents any party other than itself, and that only KBT&F as counsel represents "more than one creditor or equity security holder." This argument fails, however, because the committee (D) is a unified entity. KBT&F was hired by the committee (D), not by its individual members, and it represents only the committee (D), not any of its constituent members. Although there may be cases where a law firm represents several individual clients and is the only entity required to file a Rule 2019 statement, on its own behalf, that is clearly not the case here. Rule 2019 is a longstanding rule, and there is no reason not to apply it as written. The statement must be amended to reflect the Rule's plain requirements. Motion granted.

ANALYSIS

Ad hoc or unofficial committees play an important role in Chapter 11 reorganization cases. By appearing as a "committee" of shareholders, the members purport to speak for a group and implicitly ask the court and other parties to give their positions a degree of credibility appropriate to a unified group with large holdings. Moreover, the Code specifically provides for the possibility of the grant of compensation to a non-official committee that makes a substantial contribution. A committee purporting to speak for a group has a better chance of meeting the "substantial contribution" test than an individual, given that a single creditor or shareholder is often met with the argument that it was merely acting in its own self-interest and was not making a "substantial contribution."

Quicknotes

AD HOC For a specific purpose.

EQUITY SECURITY An interest in property that may be sold upon a default in payment of the debt.

In re Malek

Creditors (P) v. Debtor (D)

35 B.R. 443 (Bankr. E.D. Mich. 1983).

NATURE OF CASE: Hearing on debtor's disclosure statement pursuant to reorganization.

FACT SUMMARY: Debtor Malek (D) submitted a disclosure statement to which certain creditors made objection.

RULE OF LAW

A debtor must provide a disclosure statement in conformity with the letter and spirit of the Code.

FACTS: Malek (D) filed for bankruptcy under Chapter 11. Pursuant to Code disclosure requirements, he submitted a disclosure statement to the court. Certain creditors (P) made objections thereto. A hearing was held on the validity of the statement.

ISSUE: Must a debtor provide a disclosure statement in conformity with the letter and spirit of the Code?

HOLDING AND DECISION: (Graves, J.) Yes. A debtor must provide a disclosure statement in conformity with the letter and spirit of the Code. Section 1125 mandates disclosure, and a debtor is therefore required to submit such a statement disclosing the information statutorily required. The statement should include, at the very least, the following: a description of the debtor's business, a history of the debtor, financial information, a description of the plan, how the plan is to be executed, a liquidation analysis, a description of debtor management and personnel, a projection of operations, all pending or contemplated litigation, all insider transactions, and tax consequences. The disclosure statement fell short of this. Objections sustained.

ANALYSIS

Disclosure problems can often complicate a Chapter 11 proceeding. A debtor may try to hide information bearing negatively on reorganization prospects. Disgruntled creditors often claim that the debtor hid material information. If objections to disclosure are made, a court must deal with the objections prior to approval.

Quicknotes

BANKRUPTCY A legal proceeding whereby a debtor, who is unable to pay his debts as they become due, is relieved of his obligation to pay his creditors either by liquidation and distribution of his remaining assets or through reorganization and payment from future income.

INSIDER Any person within a corporation who has access to information not available to the public.

LIQUIDATION The reduction to cash of all assets for distribution to creditors.

MANDATORY DISCLOSURE The required communication of certain facts by one party to another.

Bank of America National Trust & Savings Assn. v. 203 North LaSalle Street Partnership

Creditor (P) v. Debtor (D)

526 U.S. 434 (1999).

NATURE OF CASE: Review of approval of bankruptcy reorganization plan.

FACT SUMMARY: When the old equity holders in 203 North Lasalle (D) contributed new equity in exchange for ownership interests in the reorganized entity, Bank of America (P), the major senior creditor, objected.

RULE OF LAW

Plans providing junior interest holders with exclusive opportunities free from competition and without benefit of market valuation are prohibited under the Bankruptcy Code.

FACTS: 203 North LaSalle (D), an Illinois real estate limited partnership, was in Chapter 11 bankruptcy. Bank of America (P), the major senior creditor, objected to its reorganization plan because a group of old equity holders were to receive ownership interests in the reorganized entity and that opportunity had been given exclusively to the old equity holders without consideration of alternatives. Confirmation of the plan on a consensual basis was effectively blocked. 203 North LaSalle (D) proceeded to have the plan approved under the judicial cramdown process. To succeed under § 1129(b), the plan must be found to be fair and equitable, that is, the holder of any junior claim or interest should not receive or retain under the plan on account of such junior claim or interest any property. The plan was approved, and the appeals court affirmed. Bank of America (P) appealed, claiming that the plan was unfair, because the exclusive opportunity offered the old equity holders was property of some value that was obtained at no cost. The U.S. Supreme Court granted certiorari.

ISSUE: Are plans providing junior interest holders with exclusive opportunities free from competition and without benefit of market valuation prohibited under the Bankruptcy Code?

HOLDING AND DECISION: (Souter, J.) Yes. Plans providing junior interest holders with exclusive opportunities free from competition and without benefit of market valuation are prohibited under the Bankruptcy Code. The plan is unfair in that it vests equity in the reorganized business in 203 North LaSalle's (D) partners, without offering the opportunity to anyone else to compete for that equity. This opportunity should be treated as an item of property in its own right. Some form of market valuation should be applied to test the adequacy of the old equity holders' proposed contribution. Reversed and remanded.

CONCURRENCE: (Thomas, J.) I agree that the reorganization plan should not be confirmed. The analysis of the statute should begin with the text itself and not with external sources. The relevant Code provision does not expressly authorize pre-petition equity holders to receive or retain property in a reorganized entity in exchange for new capital. The court's unnecessary speculations only thickens the fog.

DISSENT: (Stevens, J.) The Court should now definitely resolve the issue whether § 1129(b)(2)(B)(ii) preserved or repealed the new value component of the absolute priority rule. If the debtor's plan would be entitled to approval if it had been submitted by a third party, it should not be disqualified simply because it did not include a unique provision that would not be required in an offer made by another party.

ANALYSIS

There is a split on the application of the absolute priority rule. The Seventh and Ninth Circuits have supported confirmation of such plans. The Second and Fourth Circuits have disapproved of similar plans. The Supreme Court did not resolve the issue in this case since it found that the statute would not be satisfied by either reading.

Quicknotes

CHAPTER 11 BANKRUPTCY A legal proceeding whereby a debtor, who is unable to pay his debts as they become due, is relieved of his obligation to pay his creditors through reorganization and payment from future income.

CHAPTER 11 REORGANIZATION A plan formulated pursuant to Chapter 11 of the Bankruptcy Code whereby a debtor, who is unable to pay his debts as they become due, is relieved of his obligation to pay his creditors through reorganization and payment from future income.

CRAMDOWN Refers to a court's confirmation of a reorganization plan in a bankruptcy proceeding despite the opposition of creditors.

EQUITY Fairness; justice; the determination of a matter consistent with principles of fairness and not in strict compliance with rules of law.

SECURED CREDITOR A creditor, the repayment of whose loan is secured by collateral sufficient to repay the debt owed.

In re MJ Metal Products, Inc.

Debtor (P) v. Creditors (D)

292 B.R. 702 (Bankr. D. Wyo. 2003).

NATURE OF CASE: Confirmation proceeding for Chapter 11 reorganization plan.

FACT SUMMARY: MJ Metal Products, Inc. (the debtor) (P) contended that its Chapter 11 plan of reorganization should be confirmed, even though it was not accepted by an impaired class of creditors (D), and even though it violated the absolute priority rule, because, the debtor (P) asserted, the vote of one of the creditors should not have been counted, because the creditors did not raise the absolute priority rule as an issue, and because the new value exception to the rule was satisfied, in any event.

RULE OF LAW

A Chapter 11 plan of reorganization is not confirmable where an impaired class does not accept the plan and the plan violates the absolute priority rule, even if no creditor raises the rule as an issue.

FACTS: MJ Metal Products, Inc. (the debtor) (P) was a close corporation owned by two shareholders. Under its Chapter 11 reorganization plan, the debtor (P) would pay general unsecured creditors (Class 8), but not the full amount owed. Thus, this class was impaired. One of these creditors (D) was the National Labor Relations Board (NLRB), which had obtained a judgment against the debtor (P) for back wages owed to three employees. The plan also provided that all of the debtor's (P) common stock would be cancelled and that new stock in the reorganized debtor would be sold to the highest bidder. However, only the two current shareholders would be eligible to bid for the stock. Only 52 percent of the voting Class 8 creditors accepted the plan; the NLRB did not accept it. The bankruptcy court had to decide whether the plan was confirmable.

ISSUE: Is a Chapter 11 plan of reorganization confirmable where an impaired class does not accept the plan and the plan violates the absolute priority rule, even if no creditor raises the rule as an issue?

HOLDING AND DECISION: (McNiff, J.) No. A Chapter 11 plan of reorganization is not confirmable where an impaired class does not accept the plan and the plan violates the absolute priority rule, even if no creditor raises the rule as an issue. Under Code § 1129(a)(8), each class of claims must either accept the plan, or the treatment of that class must be unimpaired. Here, Class 8 was an impaired class of claims because it was not receiving payment in full, and "two-thirds in amount" of the voting creditors did not accept the plan. Nonetheless, a plan proponent may obtain confirmation of a plan that does not satisfy § 1129(a)(8) if that class of unsecured claims is paid in full (which in this case it was not), or if the plan complies with the absolute priority rule, i.e., no holder of an interest junior to the claims in the class will receive an interest in any property under the plan. Here, the plan proposed that one or the other shareholder would receive stock in the reorganized debtor. This was in direct violation of the absolute priority rule. The debtor (P) argues that because there is no creditor in Class 8 raising the issue of the absolute priority rule, the court should confirm the plan regardless of whether or not the rule is satisfied. The debtor is wrong, as the court has an independent duty to determine whether a plan complies with § 1129. Also rejected is the debtor's (P) argument that the NLRB should be precluded from voting the claims of the employees because it has not filed as a representative of the employees as creditors. However, here, it is the NLRB that obtained the judgment against the debtor (P), and, therefore, the NLRB is a party in interest, not a representative. Moreover, even if the NLRB were removed, along with one of the employee creditors, still only 63 percent of the voting creditors of Class 8 (D) could be deemed to have approved the plan. Finally, the debtor (P) contends that the absolute priority rule is satisfied because the provision providing for a sale of the reorganized debtor's stock to the existing shareholders satisfies the new value exception to the rule. Here, by providing an exclusive right to the existing shareholders to bid for shares in the reorganized debtor, the plan would contravene the intention of the exception, which, if it exists, must provide for exposure to the market to obtain that new value. For these reasons, the plan is not confirmable.

ANALYSIS

The debtor (P) here had other options that could have resulted in a confirmable plan. As the court pointed out, the debtor could have exposed the sale of the reorganized shares to the market, or could have attempted to obtain additional accepting votes in Class 8, or could have paid the unsecured creditors in full. Moreover, the plan did not preclude other parties from proposing their own plan. Accordingly, the court's order made provision for an amended or new plan.

Quicknotes

CHAPTER 11 BANKRUPTCY A legal proceeding whereby a debtor, who is unable to pay his debts as they become due, is relieved of his obligation to pay his creditors through reorganization and payment from future income.

CHAPTER 11 REORGANIZATION A plan formulated pursuant to Chapter 11 of the Bankruptcy Code whereby a debtor, who is unable to pay his debts as they become due, is relieved of his obligation to pay his creditors through reorganization and payment from future income.

PRE-PETITION Before bankruptcy petition has been filed.

UNSECURED CREDITOR A creditor whose loan is not backed by specified collateral or a security agreement.

In re Channel Master Holdings, Inc.

Debtors (P) v. Creditors (D)

309 B.R. 855 (Bankr. D. Del. 2004).

NATURE OF CASE: Objection to Chapter 11 professional fees applications.

FACT SUMMARY: Lenders (D) in a Chapter 11 bankruptcy objected to professional fees submitted by the Official Unsecured Creditors' Committee's (the Committee) (D) professionals on the ground that those fees exceeded a $75,000 cap approved in the DIP Finance Motion budget, and that the fees were excessive.

RULE OF LAW

(1) A cap on professional fees in an approved financing order does not preclude a court from approving any fees that are in excess of the cap.

(2) A court may reduce requested professional fees that are based on unnecessary services or necessary services that are overvalued.

FACTS: Channel Master Holdings, Inc. and its affiliates (collectively "the debtors") (P) filed for protection under Chapter 11. At the final hearing on the DIP Financing Motion, the debtors (P) presented a budget that capped the fees of the Official Unsecured Creditors' Committee's (the Committee's) (D) professionals at $75,000. The budget also capped fees for the debtors' (P) professionals ($990,000) and the pre-petition and post-petition lenders' (Lenders') (D) advisors ($350,000). There was also a miscellaneous category for Chapter 11 expenses of $225,000. Over the Committee's objections, the court approved the budget, but reserved authority to allocate the budgeted fees among the professionals on a pro-rata basis. All the debtors' (P) assets were eventually sold for far less than was owed to the Lenders (D). The case was ultimately converted to a Chapter 7 case, and the professional for the debtors (P) and the Committee (D) filed final fee applications for all services rendered prior to conversion. The fees requested by the Committee's (D) professionals exceeded the $75,000 carve-out in the financing order budget, and the Lenders (D) objected to fees in excess of that amount. The Lenders (D) asserted that the financing order precluded the court from approving any fees in excess of the $75,000 cap. They also asserted that the fees requested were excessive because the professional performed many unnecessary services and the value of the necessary services was substantially less than requested.

ISSUE:

(1) Does a cap on professional fees in an approved financing order preclude a court from approving any fees that are in excess of the cap?

(2) May a court reduce requested professional fees that are based on unnecessary services, or necessary services that are overvalued?

HOLDING AND DECISION: (Walrath, C.J.)

(1) No. A cap on professional fees in an approved financing order does not preclude a court from approving any fees that are in excess of the cap. The existence of a cap on fees for the Committee's (D) professionals in the DIP Financing Order does not limit allowance or payment of fees to those professionals. A court has the inherent power to direct disgorgement of fees by any professional and to redistribute those disgorged fees among all professionals in order to assure that none receives more than its pro rata share. Here, the court stated its intent to consider disgorgement of fees, despite the carve-out caps in the budget, as appropriate. In the instant case, the estate is administratively insolvent and reallocation of fees may be warranted. To enforce the carve-out caps and allow all requested fees, the debtors' (P) professionals would get 100 percent of their fees, whereas the Committee's (D) professionals would get only 27 percent. Because there are sufficient funds available from the $225,000 cap for miscellaneous expenses to cover the fees of the Committee's professionals even without invading the balance of the debtors' (P) cap it is unnecessary to require the debtors' (P) professionals to disgorge any fees.

(2) Yes. A court may reduce requested professional fees that are based on unnecessary services or necessary services that are overvalued. Even if there were no objections, the court has an independent duty to review all professional fee requests to assure the services rendered were necessary and appropriate, and that the fees are reasonable. Here, the Lenders objected, arguing that because the unsecured creditors appeared to be entitled to nothing from the inception of the case, the Committee's (D) professionals should not have performed services that were neither designed nor likely to result in a recovery for the unsecured creditors (D). Although success is not a prerequisite to allowance of fees in Chapter 11, Chapter 11 is not a license to perform services and generate fees in a vacuum without considering the possibilities of recovery. Here, a reasonable professional representing the Committee would have performed many of the services performed by the professionals in this case, but not to the extent that the professionals did in this case. Specifically, it was reasonable for the professionals to review a Key Employee Retention Plan (KERP). However, the professionals reviewed it too extensively (to the amount of $34,000). A reasonable professional under the circumstances would have incurred only a $5,000 fee. The requested fees for these services will be reduced

Continued on next page.

accordingly. Conversely, work by the professionals in connection with the sale process was not excessive, although it amounted to fees of $103,000. This is because auctions in bankruptcy can result in substantially increased bids. These fees will be allowed. Similarly, the fees incurred for analyzing the perfection of the Lenders' (D) liens are allowed because if the liens had been avoided, it would have resulted in a recovery for the unsecured creditors.

ANALYSIS

A point to keep in mind with regard to professional fees is that a security interest in most of a debtor's assets will mean that there may be no source of payment for the debtor's professionals or those hired by the creditor's committee absent the secured party's consent. Here, the court obviously considered protection of the unsecured creditors to be an essential part of the bankruptcy process, even if it did mean that the lenders were paying for such protection out of their collateral.

Quicknotes

COLLATERAL Property that secures the payment of a debt.

POST-PETITION After bankruptcy petition has been filed.

PRE-PETITION Before bankruptcy petition has been filed.

UNSECURED CREDITOR A creditor whose loan is not backed by specified collateral or a security agreement.

In re Dana Corp.

Debtors (P) v. Creditors, workers, trustee (D)

351 B.R. 96 (Bankr. S.D.N.Y. 2006).

NATURE OF CASE: Motion to approve a proposed compensation plan.

FACT SUMMARY: The Debtors (P) proposed a compensation plan for top executives that included payment of base salary, annual incentive plan (AIP) bonuses, a "Target Completion Bonuses," a Senior Executive Retirement Program, and a noncompete component. Various groups, including creditors, noteholders, unions, and the Trustee (collectively, "Objecting Parties") (D), objected to the compensation plan primarily on the grounds that it violated the limitations set forth in 11 U.S.C. § 503(c) relating to Key Employee Retention Plans (KERPs).

RULE OF LAW

Where an insider compensation plan mostly has compensation elements that effectively serve to retain insiders regardless of performance and that provide severance pay, the plan must comply with the provisions of 11 U.S.C. § 503(c) before the plan will be approved.

FACTS: The corporate Debtors (P), Dana Corp. and related entities, who were voluntarily in Chapter 11 bankruptcy protection, proposed a compensation plan in a Compensation Motion for top executives that included payment of base salary, annual incentive plan (AIP) bonuses, a "Target Completion Bonuses," a Senior Executive Retirement Program, and a noncompete component. The most favorable compensation under the plan was for the company's CEO, Mr. Burns. Under the AIP, reward of an annual bonus would be conditioned upon Dana's short-term financial performance and the size of the award would depend on whether the company met threshold, target, or superior performance goals established by Dana's Compensation Committee. The executives would also receive a Completion Bonus, part of which would be awarded without regard to performance or creditor recovery, payable in cash on the effective date of a plan of reorganization if the employee was still with the company, the other part of which would be paid as an uncapped, variable component based on the Total Enterprise Value of the Debtors (TEV) six months after a reorganization's effective date. A severance pay/noncompete component for Mr. Burns would pay him certain amounts upon involuntary dismissal or resignation, contingent on his executing a noncompete agreement, and he would also receive some or all of his Completion Bonus, depending on whether the reorganization plan's effective date had been reached. Mr. Burns' Senior Executive Retirement Program (SERP) would be assumed by the company upon his termination or the company's emergence from Chapter 11. Various groups, including creditors, noteholders, unions, and the Trustee (collectively, "Objecting Parties") (D), objected to the compensation plan. The Objecting Parties (D) contended that the proposed plan's provisions violated the limitations set forth in 11 U.S.C. § 503(c) relating to Key Employee Retention Plans (KERPs) and did not constitute a "Produce Value for Pay" plan to be scrutinized under a business judgment standard as set forth in § 363.

ISSUE: Where an insider compensation plan mostly has compensation elements that effectively serve to retain insiders regardless of performance and that provide severance pay, must the plan comply with the provisions of 11 U.S.C. § 503(c) before the plan will be approved?

HOLDING AND DECISION: (Lifland, J.) Yes. Where an insider compensation plan mostly has compensation elements that effectively serve to retain insiders regardless of performance and that provide severance pay, the plan must comply with the provisions of 11 U.S.C. § 503 (c) before the plan will be approved. Section 503(c) establishes specific evidentiary standards that must be met before a bankruptcy court may authorize payments made to an insider for the purpose of inducing such person to remain with a debtor's business, or payments made on account of severance. If an element of a proposed compensation plan comes within the scope of § 503(c), the business judgment standard of review is inapplicable. Here, the first part of the Completion Bonus, awarded to an executive for merely staying with the company until it emerges from bankruptcy, is in substance a retention bonus, and thus governed by § 503(c). Even the variable part of this bonus is more akin to a retention bonus because artificially low thresholds for the payment of this part of the Completion Bonus more or less guarantees that it will be paid. Similarly, the payments upon involuntary termination or resignation that are conditioned on the executive's signing a noncompete agreement, are in substance severance payments, which occur upon termination of employment. Here, the Debtors (P) have not met their burden of demonstrating that those payments are not severance payments. Under § 503(c)(2), a severance payment to an insider may not be approved unless it is established that the payment is part of a program generally applicable to all full-time employees and the amount of the payment is not more than 10 times the amount of mean severance given to non-management employees in that calendar year. Here, the Debtors (P) have not shown that the severance payments comply with this requirement. For these reasons, the proposed compensation plan does not satisfy § 503(c). Debtors' (P) motion is denied.

Continued on next page.

ANALYSIS

Senator Edward Kennedy proposed the amendment to § 503 of the Bankruptcy Code as a last-minute addition to the Bankruptcy Abuse Prevention and Consumer Protection Act (BAPCPA), expressing his concern over the "glaring abuses of the bankruptcy system by the executives of giant companies like Enron Corp. and WorldCom Inc., and Polaroid Corporation, who lined their own pockets, but left thousands of employees and retirees out in the cold." See Statement of Senator Edward Kennedy on the Bankruptcy Bill (March 1, 2005). Other members of Congress were concerned that Senator Kennedy's amendment would prevent responsible companies that needed to retain key employees to reorganize successfully and suggested that § 503 should only prevent payments to insiders in the event of fraud, mismanagement, and conduct contributing to the debtor's insolvency. Those concerns, however, were never included in the final bill.

Quicknotes

NONCOMPETE CLAUSE A provision, typically contained in an employment contract or a contract for the sale of a business, pursuant to which the promisor agrees not to compete with the promisee for a specified time period and/or within a particular geographic area.

In re Dana Corp.

Debtors (P) v. Workers, retirees, trustee (D)

358 B.R. 567 (Bankr. S.D.N.Y. 2006).

NATURE OF CASE: Motion to approve a revised compensation plan.

FACT SUMMARY: After their initial compensation plan was rejected as violating 11 U.S.C. § 503(c), the Debtors (P) negotiated with creditor and equity committees and proposed a revised plan that was intended to be a true incentivizing plan that included base salary, an annual incentive plan (AIP), assumption of pension benefits, severance, and a long-term performance based incentive plan (LTIP). Various union groups, retirees, and the trustee (the "Objecting Parties") (D) objected, claiming that the plan was retentive in nature and violated § 503(c).

RULE OF LAW

Where an insider compensation plan mostly has compensation elements that incentivize insiders to increase the debtor's value, with only incidental retentive features, and that provide severance pay in accordance with limits set forth in 11 U.S.C. § 503(c), the plan will be approved if it otherwise is within the debtor's business judgment.

FACTS: The corporate Debtors (P), Dana Corp. and related entities, were voluntarily in Chapter 11 bankruptcy protection. An initial compensation plan proposed by the Debtors (P) was found to be a Key Employee Retention Plan (KERP) that violated 11 U.S.C. § 503(c). Consequently, the Debtors (P) negotiated with the official committee of unsecured creditors (the "Creditors' Committee") and official committee of equity security holders (the "Equity Committee") in an effort to reach a consensus on an acceptable compensation package. The Debtors (P) moved in an Executive Compensation Motion for approval of the plan, which the committees and the Debtors (P) claimed was a true incentivizing package for senior management, rather than a KERP. The plan included base salary, an annual incentive plan (AIP), assumption of pension benefits, severance, and a long-term performance based incentive plan (LTIP). The plan would assume executives' pension plans. Assumption would take place upon emergence from bankruptcy or the senior executives' involuntary termination without cause, and with respect to the CEO, voluntary termination for good reason. The pension benefits would only be assumed on the condition that the salaried and bargaining unit defined benefit pension plans of Dana employees were not terminated. The pension benefits did not vest until the executive had been at Dana for five years, and various interim accruing factors determined the actual amount of the benefits. Although the executives had already earned certain of the pension benefits, with more to be earned in the future, the assumption of such benefits would not increase the amount of pension benefits to which they were currently entitled. Moreover, such assumption was not contingent upon any executive continuing to be employed by Dana for any particular period of time after assumption. The plan would also pay severance in amounts complying with § 503 (c)(2). In consideration for the assumption of their employment agreements and receipt of payments under the LTIP, the executives would execute new noncompete, nonsolicitation, nondisclosure and nondisparagement agreements (collectively, the "NDA Agreements"). Under the LTIP, the executives would be eligible for a graded long-term incentive bonus if the company reached certain benchmarks tied to Earnings Before Interest, Taxes, Depreciation, Amortization and Restructuring Costs (EBITDAR). The AIP, a short-term incentive plan, would be similar to the company's AIP of 50 years. Various union groups, a committee of retirees, and the trustee (the "Objecting Parties") (D) opposed the plan, claiming that it was primarily retentive and violated § 503 (c) both as to this aspect and as to severance limits.

ISSUE: Where an insider compensation plan mostly has compensation elements that incentivize insiders to increase the debtor's value, with only incidental retentive features, and that provide severance pay in accordance with limits set forth in 11 U.S.C. § 503(c), will the plan be approved if it otherwise is within the debtor's business judgment?

HOLDING AND DECISION: (Lifland, J.) Yes. Where an insider compensation plan mostly has compensation elements that incentivize insiders to increase the debtor's value, with only incidental retentive features, and that provide severance pay in accordance with limits set forth in 11 U.S.C. § 503(c), the plan will be approved if it otherwise is within the debtor's business judgment. As to the assumption of the executives' pension benefits, the Objecting Parties (D) contend that it is retentive and in the nature of severance pay. However, given that the pension plans are true pension plans insofar as they has a five-year vesting schedule and the assumption of the pension benefits does not increase the amount of benefits to which the executives are entitled, to the extent these conditions have any retentive impact, it is merely incidental to the terms of the pension plans and are ordinary and customary in such plans. Moreover, the evidence supports the Debtors' (P) contention that they exercised fair and reasonable business judgment in determining to assume the executives' employment agreements. As to the AIP, which is similar to the Debtors' (P) pre-petition practice of 50 years, it is within the ordinary course of Debtors' (P) business. Although the Code does not provide guidance as to whether a particular transaction has been

Continued on next page.

conducted "in the ordinary course of business." courts have applied a two-step "horizontal and vertical test" that considers the reasonableness of the transaction from an industry-wide (horizontal) perspective and from the viewpoint of a creditor (vertical). The horizontal test asks if the transaction is of the sort commonly undertaken by companies in that industry. The vertical test asks whether the transaction subjects a creditor to economic risk of a nature different from those he accepted when he decided to extend credit. The AIP passes both these test. However, the payments to be made under the AIP must be considered in the context of determining whether the overall compensation proposal is a proper exercise of the Debtors' (P) business judgment. As to the LTIP, the Objecting Parties (D) argue that EBITDAR benchmark levels virtually guaranty that the executives will be paid their minimum LTIP, but the uncontroverted evidence shows, to the contrary, that achievement of the EBITDAR benchmarks is uncertain, at best. Looking at the proposed compensation packages as a whole, it is not clear whether the cost or expense is reasonable and in the best interests of the Debtors' (P) estate. Having both an LTIP and an AIP may render the plan unreasonable, disproportionate, and too generous, and, therefore, not supportive of the goal of "sharing the pain." Therefore, the LTIP should be approved, but with the limitation that an appropriate yearly ceiling is placed on each of the executives' total compensation earned during the reorganization period. Overall, the proposed compensation package is an incentivizing package, so that § 503(c)(1) is inapplicable. Also, because the severance payments are designed to meet § 503(c)(2), that section is also satisfied. The assumption of the pension agreements, and the adoption of the LTIP, are reasonable and well within the Debtors' (P) business judgment. Therefore, the Debtor's (P) motion is granted, with the condition that an appropriate ceiling or cap be placed on the total yearly compensation of the executives during the course of the bankruptcy proceedings.

ANALYSIS

The Bankruptcy Code is designed to allow a debtor-in-possession the flexibility to engage in ordinary transactions without unneeded oversight by creditors or the court, while at the same time giving creditors an opportunity to contest those transactions that are not ordinary. This balance between allowing businesses to continue their daily operations on the one hand, and protecting creditors from squandering the estate's assets on the other, is reflected in § 363(c)(1), which provides that:

> If the business of the debtor is authorized to be operated under . . . this title and unless the court orders otherwise, the trustee may enter into transactions . . . in the ordinary course of business, without notice or a hearing, and may use property of the estate in the ordinary course of business without notice or a hearing.

As the court indicates, a two-part, "horizontal" and "vertical" test is used to determine whether the subject transaction was entered into in the "ordinary course of business."

Quicknotes

DEBTOR-IN-POSSESSION In a Chapter 11 proceeding, refers to a debtor who retains control of assets or property pursuant to a plan of reorganization.

NONCOMPETE CLAUSE A provision, typically contained in an employment contract or a contract for the sale of a business, pursuant to which the promisor agrees not to compete with the promisee for a specified time period and/or within a particular geographic area.

In re Loral Space & Communications, Ltd.

Shareholders of public company (P) v. Debtors and creditors (D)

2004 WL 2979785 (S.D.N.Y. 2004).

NATURE OF CASE: Appeal from denial of motion for the appointment of an examiner.

FACT SUMMARY: The Loral Stockholders Protective Committee (the LSPC) (P), representing the shareholders of Loral Space & Communications, Ltd. and its affiliates (collectively Loral) (debtors) (D), contended that because the $5,000,000 debt threshold was met under Code § 1104(c)(2), the bankruptcy court did not have discretion to deny the appointment of an examiner to value Loral (D), which LSPC (P) had requested.

RULE OF LAW

A bankruptcy court does not have discretion to deny appointment of an examiner where the $5,000,000 debt threshold is met under Code § 1104(c)(2) and shareholders of a public company have moved for the appointment of an examiner.

FACTS: The Loral Stockholders Protective Committee (the LSPC) (P), representing the shareholders of Loral Space & Communications, Ltd. and its affiliates (collectively Loral) (debtors) (D), had submitted a motion that requested that the bankruptcy court appoint an examiner who would independently value Loral's (D) assets and liabilities. The LSPC (P) had contended that the debtors (D) and creditors (D) had colluded to undervalue Loral's (D) assets by several hundreds of millions of dollars. The bankruptcy court denied the LSPC's (P) motion, contending that because the $5,000,000 debt threshold was met under Code § 1104(c)(2), the bankruptcy court did not have discretion to deny the appointment of an examiner to value Loral (D), which LSPC (P) had requested. The district court reversed and remanded the bankruptcy court's decision to deny the LSPC's motion for the appointment of an examiner and ordered the bankruptcy court to appoint an examiner within ten days. Notwithstanding that on remand the bankruptcy judge recognized the debtors' (D) fixed, liquidated, unsecured debts, other than debts for goods, services, or taxes, or owing to an insider, exceeded $5,000,000, and also acknowledged that Loral (D) was a public company and that the legislative history of Code § 1104(c)(2) indicates that the purpose of establishing the threshold figure of $5,000,000 was to protect equity holders of public companies, the judge departed from the majority view and again denied the appointment of an examiner to determine Loral's (D) going concern value. The court of appeals granted review, again.

ISSUE: Does a bankruptcy court have discretion to deny appointment of an examiner where the $5,000,000 debt threshold is met under Code § 1104(c)(2) and shareholders of a public company have moved for the appointment of an examiner?

HOLDING AND DECISION: (Patterson, J.) No. A bankruptcy court does not have discretion to deny appointment of an examiner where the $5,000,000 debt threshold is met under Code § 1104(c)(2) and shareholders of a public company have moved for the appointment of an examiner. On its face, § 1104(c)(2) mandates the appointment of an examiner where a party in interest moves for an examiner and the debtor has $5,000,000 of qualifying debt. Furthermore, as the bankruptcy judge noted prior to denying the LSPC's (P) motion, "the legislative history of Section 1104(c)(2) reflects Congress's desire to provide extra protection to stockholders of public companies through the mechanism of an independent functionary." Although this Circuit has not ruled on this issue, the majority view is that appointment of an examiner under § 1104(c)(2) is mandatory where the threshold amount of qualifying debt is met. As those courts have concluded, unless paragraph (c)(2) requires appointment of an examiner in cases exceeding the debt threshold, "it becomes indistinguishable from paragraph (c)(1)." In light of the straightforward language and legislative history of Code § 1104(c)(2), the bankruptcy court did not have discretion to deny LSPC's (P) request for appointment of an examiner. Reversed and remanded.

ANALYSIS

A decision by the Bankruptcy Court for the Northern District of Illinois made it clear that under the Code, when the debt threshold is met, appointment of an examiner is mandatory, as otherwise there would be no need to set a debt threshold. The court observed: "If paragraph (c)(2) were not mandatory, then § 1104(c) would have the following meaning: 'If specified debt is less than $5 million, it is in the court's discretion to appoint an examiner; and if specified debt is more than $5 million, it is in the court's discretion to appoint an examiner.'" *In re UAL Corp.*, 307 B.R. 80, at 85 n.2 (Bankr. N.D. Ill. 2004).

Quicknotes

ASSET An item of real or personal property that is owned and has tangible value.

LIABILITY Any obligation or responsibility.

Signature Combs, Inc. v. United States

Owner of polluted land (P) v. Federal government (D)

253 F. Supp. 2d 1028 (W.D. Tenn. 2003).

NATURE OF CASE: Motion for judgment on the pleadings in action to recover environmental response costs under the Comprehensive Environmental Response, Compensation and Liability Act, 42 U.S.C.S. § 9601 et seq.

FACT SUMMARY: Signature Combs, Inc. (Plaintiffs) (P) sought to recover environmental response costs under the Comprehensive Environmental Response, Compensation and Liability Act, 42 U.S.C.S. § 9601 et seq. from Mason and Dixon Lines, Inc. (MDL) (D). MDL asserted that Plaintiffs' (P) claims against it were discharged pursuant to MDL's (D) Chapter 11 bankruptcy reorganization.

RULE OF LAW

Post-reorganization environmental claims brought against a debtor under the Comprehensive Environmental Response, Compensation and Liability Act have not been previously discharged in Chapter 11 where the Environmental Protection Agency could not have fairly contemplated the debtor's potential liability prior to its reorganization.

FACTS: Two Superfund sites contaminated with hazardous waste were cleaned up by the Environmental Protection Agency (EPA) and its state counterpart. Under the Comprehensive Environmental Response, Compensation and Liability Act (CERCLA), 42 U.S.C.S. § 9601 et seq., the government obtained reimbursement for the cleanup costs, known as response costs, from Signature Combs, Inc. (Plaintiffs) (P). The Plaintiffs (P) then sought reimbursement of some of these costs from Mason and Dixon Lines, Inc. (MDL) (D), which defended by asserting that Plaintiffs' (P) claims against it were discharged pursuant to MDL's (D) Chapter 11 bankruptcy reorganization, which became final 12 years before Plaintiffs (P) instituted their action. MDL (D) contended that its liability to Plaintiffs (P) depended on whether it was potentially liable to the United States (D), and that such liability had been discharged. MDL (D) moved for judgment on the pleadings.

ISSUE: Have post-reorganization environmental claims brought against a debtor under the Comprehensive Environmental Response, Compensation and Liability Act (CERCLA) been previously discharged in Chapter 11 where the Environmental Protection Agency (EPA) could not have fairly contemplated the debtor's potential liability prior to its reorganization?

HOLDING AND DECISION: (Donald, J.) No. Post-reorganization environmental claims brought against a debtor under the Comprehensive Environmental Response, Compensation and Liability Act (CERCLA) have not been previously discharged in Chapter 11 where the Environmental Protection Agency (EPA) could not have fairly contemplated the debtor's potential liability prior to its reorganization. The issue here—when a party's contingent CERCLA liability may be discharged through bankruptcy—is an issue of first impression for this court, but other courts that have considered this issue are split on the standards to apply in determining the issue. Some courts take a "right to payment" approach, which discharge a claim only when all four elements of a CERCLA claim existed prior to bankruptcy. This approach has been criticized for failing to address bankruptcy law and policy and for undermining the fresh start policy because the debtor cannot receive a fresh start from its CERCLA liabilities stemming from pre-bankruptcy conduct if any of the four elements (some of which are not in the debtor's control) have not been met. Another criticism is that under bankruptcy law, a claim is defined more broadly than under CERCLA, so that non-bankruptcy law should not control what constitutes a claim. Further, this approach might encourage some creditors to delay cleanup until after the close of bankruptcy proceedings, thereby increasing the response costs. Another approach, known as the "underlying act approach," discharge is possible provided the underlying polluting act occurred prior to the debtor's bankruptcy. This means that even if the EPA does not yet know of a potential CERCLA claim against the debtor, the debtor's liability is discharged so long as the debtor's conduct relating to the contamination concluded prior to its bankruptcy petition. This approach favors bankruptcy law (unlike the "right to payment" approach), but has been criticized as unfair to creditors because it would allow a polluting party to undergo bankruptcy proceedings and receive a discharge from any liabilities before the EPA or any other creditor ever has a reason to know about the debtor's polluting acts. This approach would enable the circumvention of CERCLA's goal of making polluters accountable for their actions. Moreover, this approach could cause the EPA to divert its energies from cleaning up sites to determining a debtor's potential status as a responsible party and might risk violating the EPA's or other creditors' right to reasonable notice prior to the discharge of a claim. A third approach, known as the "debtor-creditor relationship" approach provides that CERCLA liability is discharged if the creditor and debtor began a relationship before the debtor filed for bankruptcy, so long as the underlying act occurred before the bankruptcy petition was filed. Because some of the courts that have used this approach have defined "relationship" very broadly, this approach has been criticized as becoming the equivalent of the "underlying acts" approach. Still, a fourth approach, known as the "fair

Continued on next page.

contemplation" or "foreseeability" approach, posits that that a contingent CERCLA claim arises pre-petition only if it is "based upon pre-petition conduct that can fairly be contemplated by the parties at the time of the debtors' bankruptcy." Under such an approach, a claim accrues when the potential CERCLA claimant, at the time of bankruptcy, "could have ascertained through the exercise of reasonable diligence that it had a claim" against the debtor. This standard allows a claim to accrue earlier than the right to payment standard because the potential claimant need not incur response costs (the fourth CERCLA element) for a contingent claim to arise under this standard. At the same time, the standard requires more awareness of a potential CERCLA claim by a potential creditor than do the underlying act or debtor-creditor relationship standards, both of which allow claims to accrue even if the potential creditor had no idea that it might have a CERCLA claim against the debtor. Thus, the "fair contemplation" approach attempts to reconcile the goals of both the bankruptcy courts and CERCLA—which the Supreme Court has directed to be reconciled whenever possible. It attempts to accommodate both the fresh start goal of bankruptcy and the speedy cleanup and polluter accountability CERCLA goals, and, unlike the other approaches, it does not violate notice requirements because creditors must be aware of potential claims against debtors before such claims can be discharged. Finally, it might also encourage bankruptcy goals in addition to the fresh start objective. One such goal is to provide creditors with the maximum recovery on their claims. The fair contemplation approach may support this goal because "including uncertain future CERCLA claims in the bankruptcy plan may entail added transaction costs that place an additional drain on the debtor company and actually diminish the creditors' recovery." By using the fair contemplation standard, these added costs can be diminished or eliminated. Since the fresh start goal may not be appropriate for a corporation seeking reorganization, the fair contemplation standard further supports bankruptcy goals in the context of CERCLA claims. For all these reasons, the fair contemplation approach is the appropriate approach for determining whether MDL's (D) liability had been discharged. Nothing in the record indicates that at the time of reorganization order the EPA fairly contemplated or had reason to foresee MDL's (D) potential liability to it for the contaminated sites. Therefore, based on the evidence presented in the pleadings, it cannot be said that the EPA had a contingent claim against MDL (D) at the time MDL (D) discharged its "claims" in its bankruptcy reorganization. Motion dismissed.

ANALYSIS

One criticism of the fair contemplation approach is that in situations where the debtor itself does not know of its potential CERCLA liability until well after the close of its bankruptcy proceedings, because its liability stems from the wrongful conduct of a third party, applying a fair contemplation standard requiring contemplation by the EPA of the debtor's potential liability makes it highly unlikely that the debtor will ever be able to discharge its contingent CERCLA liabilities through bankruptcy.

Quicknotes

CERCLA Enacted to fill gaps in environmental clean-up efforts left by Resource Conservation and Recovery Act of 1976. Permits both the government and private plaintiffs to recover clean-up costs.

CHAPTER 11 REORGANIZATION A plan formulated pursuant to Chapter 11 of the Bankruptcy Code whereby a debtor, who is unable to pay his debts as they become due, is relieved of his obligation to pay his creditors through reorganization and payment from future income.

Kane v. Johns-Manville Corp.

Claimants (P) v. Debtor (D)

843 F.2d 636 (2d Cir. 1988).

NATURE OF CASE: Appeal challenging the legality of a Chapter 11 reorganization plan.

FACT SUMMARY: Kane (P), representing a group of asbestos claimants (collectively referred to as Kane (P), challenged the Chapter 11 reorganization plan submitted by Johns-Manville Corp. (D) and confirmed by the bankruptcy court on several grounds, including that the plan submitted and approved failed to comply with the requirements of 11 U.S.C. § 1129(a) and (b).

RULE OF LAW

Corporations faced with "mass tort" litigation may attempt to resolve liability through a Chapter 11 reorganization plan so long as the plan is submitted in good faith in an attempt to accomplish a successful reorganization of the corporation and creditors are at least assured of receiving what they would have received had the corporation undergone a liquidation pursuant to Chapter 7 of the Bankruptcy Code.

FACTS: Johns-Manville (D), a major manufacturer of products containing asbestos, was faced with an estimated $2 billion liability associated with present and anticipated asbestos-related disease claims. To attempt to address such claims, it filed a voluntary petition in bankruptcy under Chapter 11. A legal representative was appointed to represent the interests of those who were termed "future asbestos health claimants." A plan was ultimately submitted whereby a trust was created out of which all present and future claimants would be paid. The trust was funded by insurance proceeds, cash, notes, receivables, long-term notes, and 20 percent of Johns-Manville's (D) profits, until all claims were paid. Through a multimedia notice campaign, potential asbestos claimants were notified of the plan and given the opportunity to vote on the plan by submitting a combined "proof of loss and voting" form. For voting purposes, each claim was valued at one dollar. Roughly 96 percent of those submitting forms approved the plan. The plan included an injunction against bringing suit directly against Johns-Manville (D) or its insurers, provided for a procedure whereby a claimant could proceed against the Trust, and by its terms applied to all claimants, present and future. Kane (P), representing a group of present asbestos claimants, challenged the plan, contending it discharged the rights of future claimants who did not technically have a dischargeable claim under Chapter 11. Kane (P) further argued that notice of the plan was inadequate, that the voting procedures utilized violated the Bankruptcy Code, and that the plan failed to conform with the requirements of 11 U.S.C. § 1129 (a) and (b). The plan was confirmed despite these objections, and the district court affirmed. Kane (P) appealed.

ISSUE: Can a corporation faced with "mass tort" litigation attempt to resolve its liability through a Chapter 11 reorganization plan if the plan is submitted in good faith in an attempt to accomplish a successful reorganization of the corporation and assures creditors of receiving at least as much as they would have received under a Chapter 7 liquidation of the corporation?

HOLDING AND DECISION: (Newman, J.) Yes. Corporations faced with "mass tort" litigation may attempt to resolve liability through a Chapter 11 reorganization plan so long as the plan is submitted in good faith in an attempt to accomplish a successful reorganization of the plan, and creditors are at least assured under the plan of receiving what they would have received had the corporation undergone a Chapter 7 liquidation. This is what is required under 11 U.S.C. § 1129(a) and (b). The court first found that Kane (P) lacked standing to assess claims on behalf of any future third-party claimants because as a present claimant his interests were potentially opposed to those claimants because those claimants were already represented by the legal representative in these hearings and because the legal representative had expressly stated on appeal that he did not wish Kane (P) to assert the future claimants' rights. The court also rejected any challenge by Kane (P) as to the voting procedures employed, determining that any error in voting procedures constituted harmless error, and that any of the procedures claimed to be required by Kane (P) under the Bankruptcy Code would have resulted in no changes in the ultimate vote. The court was within its discretion in determining that the plan as submitted by Johns-Manville (D) was a good-faith attempt to accomplish a successful reorganization while keeping the best interests of all the creditors in mind. The court accepted the figures submitted by Johns-Manville (D) that the claimants would receive 100 percent payment on their claims, considerably higher than if there was Chapter 7 liquidation, and its acceptance of those findings was not clearly erroneous. The long-arm funding techniques employed by the Trust assure the continued payment of claims, while the injunction allows Johns-Manville (D) its best attempt to successfully reorganize, without the yoke of the continuing asbestos-disease litigation. The court's finding that the reorganization plan offers reasonable assurance of success is not clearly erroneous. Affirmed.

Continued on next page.

ANALYSIS

Even though there are a great many problems associated with employing a bankruptcy solution to mass tort litigation, it continues to be a primary response to such litigation. Such an approach has been utilized in the pharmaceutical context. In *In re A.H. Robbins,* 880 F.2d 769 (4th Cir. 1989), A. H. Robbins utilized the bankruptcy courts in order to resolve its liability arising out of the manufacture of the Dalkon Shield intrauterine device. It is interesting to note that one of Kane's (P) claims in the present litigation proved to be true: Shortly after the plan's inception, the Trust began to run out of money.

Quicknotes

CHAPTER 11 REORGANIZATION A plan formulated pursuant to Chapter 11 of the Bankruptcy Code whereby a debtor, who is unable to pay his debts as they become due, is relieved of his obligation to pay his creditors through reorganization and payment from future income.

INJUNCTION A court order requiring a person to do, or prohibiting that person from doing, a specific act.

TORT A legal wrong resulting in a breach of duty by the wrongdoer, causing damages as a result of the breach.

TRUST The holding of property by one party for the benefit of another.

In re Fairchild Aircraft Corp.

Debtor (P) v. Crash victims' families (D)

184 B.R. 910 (Bankr. W.D. Tex. 1995).

NATURE OF CASE: Adversary proceeding for declaratory and injunctive relief.

FACT SUMMARY: When an airplane manufactured by Fairchild Aircraft Corporation (FAC) crashed and several people were killed, the successor to the estate of FAC after bankruptcy filed suit to avoid any liability.

RULE OF LAW

Where a debtor has not made any provision for the interests of tort claimants in its financial restructuring plan, those interests cannot be said to have been discharged in the bankruptcy.

FACTS: Fairchild Aircraft Corporation (FAC) manufactured and sold commuter aircraft until 1990 when it filed for Chapter 11 bankruptcy. The trustee sold the company's assets as a going concern to Fairchild Acquisition, Inc. (FAI) (P). The asset purchase agreement stated that the purchaser would not assume any liabilities or obligations, and enjoined all creditors, claimants, and persons claiming or having any interest whatsoever from commencing suits against FAI (P). When one of the planes manufactured by FAC crashed and four people were killed, their families claimed that the aircraft had been defectively manufactured and sued FAI (P) on a successor liability theory. FAI (P) filed an adversary proceeding as a preemptive strike, seeking declaratory and injunctive relief, based on provisions of the Chapter 11 bankruptcy plan, the asset purchase agreement, and the court's order confirming the plan. The families alleged that their interests had not been adequately provided for in the bankruptcy plan.

ISSUE: Where a debtor has not made any provision for the interests of tort claimants in its financial restructuring plan, can those interests be said to have been discharged in the bankruptcy?

HOLDING AND DECISION: (Clark, J.) No. Where a debtor has not made any provision for the interests of tort claimants in its financial restructuring plan, those interests cannot be said to have been discharged in the bankruptcy. FAC could have estimated the number of its aircraft that were likely to crash and the number of persons to be injured and appoint a legal representative to protect those interests. Because this was not done, though it could have been done, these alleged claims cannot be treated as bankruptcy claims. The order of sale did not insulate FAI (P) from liability and the court lacked jurisdiction to enjoin these claimants. Summary judgment for defendants granted.

ANALYSIS

The court was concerned with ensuring fundamental fairness for future claimants. The debtor was required to show that it had anticipated that type of claim. The debtor would also have to show that such potential claims were adequately provided for in the plan.

Quicknotes

CHAPTER 11 BANKRUPTCY A legal proceeding whereby a debtor, who is unable to pay his debts as they become due, is relieved of his obligation to pay his creditors through reorganization and payment from future income.

PRODUCT LIABILITY The legal liability of manufacturers and sellers for damages and injuries suffered by buyers, users, and even bystanders because of defects in goods purchased.

TRUSTEE A person who is entrusted to keep or administer something.

FCC v. NextWave Personal Communications, Inc.

Federal agency (D) v. Debtor licensee (P)

537 U.S. 293 (2003).

NATURE OF CASE: Appeal from judgment that FCC's cancellation of licenses for nonpayment of license fees by a Chapter 11 debtor violated the Bankruptcy Code.

FACT SUMMARY: The Federal Communications Commission (FCC) (D) contended that Code § 525 did not prohibit it from revoking spectrum licenses it had granted to NextWave Personal Communications, Inc. (NextWave) (P) merely because NextWave (P) was a debtor in bankruptcy that had failed to make timely payments owed to the FCC (D) for purchase of the licenses because, the FCC (D) argued, NextWave's (P) license obligations were "regulatory conditions" not dischargeable in bankruptcy.

RULE OF LAW

Bankruptcy Code § 525 prohibits the Federal Communications Commission (FCC) from revoking licenses held by a debtor in bankruptcy upon the debtor's failure to make timely payments owed to the FCC for purchase of the license.

FACTS: Pursuant to provisions of the Communications Act of 1934 authorizing the Federal Communications Commission (FCC) (D) to award spectrum licenses to small businesses through competitive bidding, and to allow them to pay for the licenses in installments, the FCC (D) auctioned off certain broadband personal communications services licenses to NextWave Personal Communications, Inc. (NextWave) (P). NextWave (P) made a down payment on the purchase price, signed promissory notes for the balance, and executed agreements giving the FCC (D) a first lien on, and security interest in, NextWave's (P) rights and interest in the licenses, which recited that they were conditioned upon the full and timely payment of all monies due the FCC (D), and that failure to comply with this condition would result in their automatic cancellation. NextWave (P) eventually filed for Chapter 11 bankruptcy protection and suspended payments to all creditors, including the FCC (D), pending confirmation of its reorganization plan. The FCC (D) objected to the plan, asserting that NextWave's (P) licenses had been canceled automatically when the company missed its first payment-deadline, and announced that NextWave's (P) licenses were available for auction. The bankruptcy court invalidated the cancellation of the licenses, but the Second Circuit Court of Appeals reversed, holding that exclusive jurisdiction to review the FCC's (D) regulatory action lay with the District of Columbia Circuit Court of Appeals. After the FCC (D) denied NextWave's (P) petition for reconsideration of the license cancellation, the District of Columbia Circuit held that the cancellation violated 11 U.S.C. § 525(a), which prohibits governmental units from revoking a license to a debtor solely because such debtor has not paid a debt that is dischargeable in bankruptcy. The Supreme Court granted certiorari.

ISSUE: Does Bankruptcy Code § 525 prohibit the Federal Communications Commission (FCC) from revoking licenses held by a debtor in bankruptcy upon the debtor's failure to make timely payments owed to the FCC for purchase of the license?

HOLDING AND DECISION: (Scalia, J.) Yes. Bankruptcy Code § 525 prohibits the Federal Communications Commission (FCC) from revoking licenses held by a debtor in bankruptcy upon the debtor's failure to make timely payments owed to the FCC for purchase of the license. Even though the FCC (D) concedes that it canceled NextWave's (P) licenses because of nonpayment, the FCC (D) nonetheless contends that § 525 does not apply because the FCC (D) had a "valid regulatory motive" for canceling the licenses. The fact that the FCC (D) had a valid regulatory motive for its action is irrelevant. Section 525 means nothing more or less than that the failure to pay a dischargeable debt must alone be the proximate cause of the cancellation ("solely because"), whatever the agency's ultimate motive may be. That section cannot reasonably be understood to include, among the other causes whose presence can preclude application of the prohibition, the governmental unit's motive in effecting the cancellation; an exception for regulatory motive would consume the rule.

Also rejected is the FCC's (D) contention that regulatory conditions like full and timely payment are not properly classified as debts under § 525(a). This is just another way of claiming that regulatory conditions are exempt from § 525. However, no matter how the FCC (D) casts it, this argument loses.

Finally, this interpretation of § 525 does not, as the FCC (P) contends, create a conflict with the Communications Act by obstructing the functioning of that Act's auction provisions. Nothing in those provisions demands that cancellation be the sanction for failure to make agreed-upon periodic payments or even requires the Commission to permit payment to be made over time. What the FCC (D) describes as a conflict boils down to nothing more than a policy preference on the FCC's (D) part for (1) selling licenses on credit and (2) canceling licenses rather than asserting security interests when there is a default. Such administrative preferences cannot be the basis for denying NextWave (P) rights provided by a law's plain terms. Affirmed.

Continued on next page.

ANALYSIS

Justice Breyer, dissenting, argued that Code § 525(a) was not intended to apply to cases in which the licensor was also a creditor, but rather was intended to protect the debtor from discriminatory license terminations. He concluded that the majority's literal interpretation of the statute threatened to create a serious anomaly, under which, seemingly, a government cannot ever enforce a lien on property that it has sold on the installment plan as long as (1) the property is a license, (2) the buyer has gone bankrupt, and (3) the government wants the license back solely because the buyer did not pay for it. "After all, in such circumstances, it is virtually always the case that the buyer will not have paid a debt that is in fact 'dischargeable,' and that 'event' alone will have 'triggered' the government's 'decision' to revoke the license." He saw no reason why the government should not be able to enforce a sales contract through repossession, unless the government's action is discriminatory and undercuts the "fresh start" purpose of bankruptcy.

Quicknotes

CERTIORARI A discretionary writ issued by a superior court to an inferior court in order to review the lower court's decisions; the Supreme Court's writ ordering such review.

DISCHARGEABLE DEBTS Debts subject to discharge in a bankruptcy proceeding.

LIEN A claim against the property of another in order to secure the payment of a debt.

PROMISSORY NOTE A written promise to tender a stated amount of money at a designated time and to a designated person.

In re U.S.H. Corp.

Claimant (P) v. Post-confirmation debtor (D)

223 B.R. 654 (Bankr. S.D.N.Y. 1998).

NATURE OF CASE: Motion to dismiss suit on grounds that pre-petition claims were barred by confirmation of defendant debtor's reorganization plan.

FACT SUMMARY: Homeowners (P) who brought suit against U.S. Home Corporation (US Home) (debtor) (D), a construction company, contended that their pre-petition claims were not barred by the confirmation of US Home's (D) plan because they were not given formal notice of the bankruptcy proceeding. US Home (D) countered that the homeowners (D) failed to state a claim and that they were unknown creditors who had received constructive notice by publication.

RULE OF LAW

Pre-petition claims are barred where the claimants are unknown creditors and the bankruptcy proceedings were published in accordance with law.

FACTS: U.S. Home Corporation (US Home) (debtor) (D), a construction company, developed and built homes from 1989-1991 in a certain subdivision in Texas. US Home (D) filed a Chapter 11 bankruptcy petition in 1991, and, in 1993, its reorganization plan was confirmed. US Home (D) published notices of the bar date in numerous national and regional newspapers and publications. In 1995, when the homeowners (P) of the subdivision developed by US Home (D) applied for insurance, they discovered that their homes had not been built in compliance with the building code requirements of the Texas Catastrophe Property Insurance Association (CAT-POOL). Those standards, however, were voluntary. In 1996, the homeowners (P) brought suit against US Home (D) for deceptive trade practices. US Home (D) responded that the confirmation order permanently enjoined litigation against US Home (D) based on pre-petition claims. The homeowners (P) then commenced an action seeking an order determining that they were not bound by the confirmation order because they were not given formal notice of the bankruptcy proceeding. US Home (D) countered, first, that the CAT-POOL guidelines were voluntary and, therefore, the homeowners (P) failed to state a claim upon which relief could be granted. Second, US Home (D) argued, as unknown creditors who received constructive notice by publication of the bankruptcy proceeding, the homeowners' (D) claims were barred by the discharge provisions contained in the confirmation order, plan and Code § 1141(d).

ISSUE: Are pre-petition claims barred where the claimants are unknown creditors and the bankruptcy proceedings were published in accordance with law?

HOLDING AND DECISION: (Lifland, J.) Yes. Pre-petition claims are barred where the claimants are unknown creditors and the bankruptcy proceedings were published in accordance with law. Ordinarily, an order confirming a reorganization plan operates to discharge all unsecured debts and liabilities, even those of tort victims who were unaware of the debtor's bankruptcy. Once confirmed, the plan binds the debtor and all creditors, whether or not a creditor has accepted the plan. Discharge under the Bankruptcy Code, however, presumes that all creditors bound by the plan have been given notice sufficient to satisfy due process. When a creditor is unknown to the debtor, publication notice of the claims bar date may satisfy the requirements of due process. However, if a creditor is known to the debtor, notice by publication is not constitutionally reasonable, and actual notice of the relevant bar dates must be afforded to the creditor. Thus, here, the principal issue was whether the homeowners (P) were "known" or "unknown" claimants at the time of the bar order. As US Home (D) published notices of the bar date in numerous national and regional publications and newspapers, its publication notices were more than sufficient to satisfy due process if the homeowners (P) were "unknown" creditors. A "known" creditor is one whose identity is either known or "reasonably ascertainable by the debtor." An "unknown" creditor is one whose "interests are either conjectural or future or, although they could be discovered upon investigation, do not in due course of business come to knowledge [of the debtor]." A creditor's identity is "reasonably ascertainable" if that creditor can be identified through "reasonably diligent efforts." However, reasonable diligence does not require impracticable or extended searches. Under the facts and circumstances of this case, the homeowners (P) were unknown creditors, given there was no mandatory building code or standard that required US Home (D) to build in accordance with CAT-POOL standards. Without the linchpin of a duty of US Home (D) to build in accordance with CAT-POOL standards, US Home (D) could not have been expected to discover any potential claim of the homeowners (P) prior to confirmation, particularly one so remote. It was not the duty of US Home (D) to search out "each conceivable or possible creditor." If the homeowners (P) were to be considered known creditors at the time of the confirmation, the universe of creditors entitled to actual notice would defeat the purpose of Title 11's expedited and cost-effective claims resolution process. Motion to dismiss is granted.

Continued on next page.

ANALYSIS

This case illustrates the fact that often in a situation where a pre-petition claim is brought after the reorganization plan is confirmed, whether the claimant received adequate notice is often determined by the merits of the claims, as the merits will often determine whether the claimant was a "known" or "unknown" creditor, and, therefore, what the debtor's obligations were vis-à-vis the claimant.

Quicknotes

ENJOIN The ordering of a party to cease the conduct of a specific activity.

PRE-PETITION Before bankruptcy petition has been filed.

In re Howe

Debtors (P) v. Creditors (D)

913 F.2d 1138 (5th Cir. 1990).

NATURE OF CASE: Appeal from affirmance of dismissal, on res judicata grounds, of state-law lender liability claims.

FACT SUMMARY: The Howes (P) (debtors) contended that their state-law lender liability claims against Premier Bank (Premier) (D) and Vaughan (D) should not have been dismissed on res judicata grounds because their claim did not involve the same cause of action that was disposed of their earlier bankruptcy proceeding and plan confirmation.

RULE OF LAW

Claims that could have been brought in reorganization plan confirmation proceedings are barred by res judicata where these subsequent claims are based on the same nucleus of operative facts and were discoverable during the bankruptcy proceedings.

FACTS: The Howes (P) (debtors) filed for Chapter 11 bankruptcy and negotiated a plan of reorganization. Several years after the plan's confirmation, the Howes (P) sued Premier Bank (Premier) (D) and Vaughan (D) in state court for lender liability claims, asserting that Premier (D), Vaughan (D), and others had induced the Howes (P) to incur substantial indebtedness without regard to their ability to repay the borrowed sum. The aim, according to the Howes (P), had been to drive the Howes (P) into financial ruin so they would have to give up their land for development. However, during bankruptcy proceedings that had occurred five years earlier, in a fourth amended plan of reorganization, the Howes' (P) lender liability claims were not scheduled as an asset of the estate, nor were they disclosed or treated in the plan, which was confirmed. The plan specifically treated the Howes' (P) indebtedness to Premier (D) as an allowed claim. The case was removed to the federal court and subsequently referred to the bankruptcy court, where Premier Bank (Premier) (D) and Vaughan (D) moved to dismiss. The Howes (P) moved to abstain and remand, alleging that their claims were better left for the state court. The bankruptcy court dismissed their action on res judicata grounds, and the district court affirmed. The court of appeals granted review.

ISSUE: Are claims that could have been brought in reorganization plan confirmation proceedings barred by res judicata where these subsequent claims are based on the same nucleus of operative facts and were discoverable during the bankruptcy proceedings?

HOLDING AND DECISION: (King, J.) Yes. Claims that could have been brought in reorganization plan confirmation proceedings are barred by res judicata where these subsequent claims are based on the same nucleus of operative facts and were discoverable during the bankruptcy proceedings. A plan is binding on all parties once it is confirmed, and all questions that could have been raised pertaining to the plan are res judicata. The test for res judicata is that: (1) the parties be identical in both suits; (2) a court of competent jurisdiction rendered the prior judgment; (3) there was a final judgment on the merits in the previous decision; and (4) the plaintiff raises the same cause of action or claim in both suits. Here, the Howes (P) concede that the first three elements of the test are met. They contend, however, that their claim does not involve the same cause of action as the earlier bankruptcy proceeding because "there was not an order in the bankruptcy proceeding . . . specifically addressing the relationship that existed by and among" the parties. The critical issue, thus, is whether the two suits are based on the same nucleus of operative facts. The rule is that res judicata bars all claims that were or could have been advanced in support of the cause of action on the occasion of its former adjudication, not merely those that were adjudicated. The loan transaction at the heart of the present litigation was also the source of Premier's (D) claim against the estate. The Howes (P) vigorously contested the validity of Premier's (D) lien in adversary proceedings in the bankruptcy court and contended that Premier's loan was usurious. Premier's (D) loan was the only major claim against the estate and was the subject of extensive negotiations prior to confirmation of the plan of reorganization. Therefore, the Howes' (P) present allegations merely assert new theories based on the same nucleus of operative facts that informed their earlier bankruptcy proceedings. The two actions, therefore, constitute the same claim or cause of action for res judicata purposes. The Howes' (P) argument that although they were aware of the basic facts underlying their claims, they were not aware of the significance of those facts is rejected; their ignorance is an inadequate excuse for their failure to raise their claims in the earlier proceedings. They do not suggest that the facts forming the basis of those claims were undiscoverable until after those proceedings. Nor do they suggest that the adversary proceedings lacked the procedural mechanisms that would have allowed them to bring their claims. Affirmed.

ANALYSIS

The court in this case adopted the transactional approach of the Restatement (Second) of Judgments for determining whether two suits involve the same claim for res judicata purposes. Under this approach, the critical issue is not the

Continued on next page.

relief requested or the theory asserted, but whether the plaintiff bases the two actions on the same nucleus of operative facts. Under the transactional test, the same action for res judicata purposes includes all the remedial rights of the plaintiff against the defendant growing out of the relevant transaction (or series of connected transactions). A party may not avoid the preclusive affect of res judicata by asserting a new theory or a different remedy.

Quicknotes

RES JUDICATA The rule of law that a final judgment by a court precludes subsequent litigation between the parties regarding the same cause of action.

In re Metromedia Fiber Network, Inc.

Creditors (P) v. Debtor (D)

416 F.3d 136 (2d Cir. 2005).

NATURE OF CASE: Appeal from affirmance of order confirming a plan of reorganization.

FACT SUMMARY: Creditors (P) of Metromedia Fiber Network, Inc. and its subsidiaries (collectively, "Metromedia") (D), challenged the release in Metromedia's (D) reorganization plan of nondebtors, including the Kluge Trust, contending that the releases were unauthorized by the Code, at least on the bankruptcy court's findings.

RULE OF LAW

A nondebtor's release in a plan of reorganization will not be approved where there is no finding of unique circumstances that would make the release important to the success of the plan.

FACTS: The bankruptcy court confirmed the reorganization plan of Metromedia Fiber Network, Inc. and its subsidiaries (collectively, "Metromedia") (D). As part of the reorganization, the Kluge Trust and other nondebtors received a comprehensive release from creditor claims Kluge Trust received the release, along with certain interests in the reorganized Metromedia, in exchange for forgiving unsecured claims against Metromedia (D); converting senior secured claims to equity in reorganized Metromedia; investing capital in the reorganized Metromedia; and purchasing unsold common stock in the reorganized Metromedia's planned stock offering. In confirming the release, the bankruptcy court found that Kluge Trust made a "material contribution" to the bankruptcy estate. Metromedia's (D) creditors (P) challenged the releases on the grounds that they were not authorized by the Bankruptcy Code. (At that point, however, the reorganization plan had been largely implemented.) The district court affirmed the bankruptcy court's confirmation, and the court of appeals granted review.

ISSUE: Will a nondebtor's release in a plan of reorganization be approved where there is no finding of unique circumstances that would make the release important to the success of the plan?

HOLDING AND DECISION: (Jacobs, J.) No. A nondebtor's release in a plan of reorganization will not be approved where there is no finding of unique circumstances that would make the release important to the success of the plan. Case law provides that a court may enjoin a creditor from suing a nondebtor third party, provided the injunction plays an important part in the debtor's reorganization plan. Such an injunction is rarely granted. It is expressly authorized by the Code only in asbestos cases—and some Circuits have held that nondebtor releases may be granted only in that type of case. In addition, such releases lend themselves to abuse because, in effect, they may operate as a bankruptcy discharge arranged without a filing and without the safeguards of the Code. The potential for abuse is heightened when releases afford blanket immunity, as in the instant case. Nondebtor releases may be tolerated if the affected creditors consent, or if there are unique circumstances that render the release terms important to the reorganization plan's success. Here, there were no findings of either. Although the bankruptcy court found that Kluge Trust made a "material contribution" to the estate, it made no finding that the release was itself important to the plan, nor was there any finding as to whether the breadth of the release—which covered numerous third parties in addition to the Kluge Trust, and which covered any and all claims relating to Metromedia (D)—was necessary to the plan. Without such findings, the release should not have been approved. However, given that the plan has already been implemented, and because the creditors (P) did not seek a stay of the plan pending appeal, the plan will be confirmed due to equitable mootness. Affirmed.

ANALYSIS

Unique circumstances that have warranted a comprehensive release have included situations where: the estate received substantial consideration; the enjoined claims were "channeled" to a settlement fund rather than extinguished; the enjoined claims would indirectly impact the debtor's reorganization by way of indemnity or contribution; and the plan otherwise provided for the full payment of the enjoined claims.

Quicknotes

ENJOIN The ordering of a party to cease the conduct of a specific activity.

IMMUNITY Exemption from a legal obligation.

RELEASE The relinquishment of a claim against another party.

In re Bernhard Steiner Pianos USA, Inc.

Objecting creditors (P) v. Debtor (D)

292 B.R. 109 (Bankr. N.D. Tex. 2002).

NATURE OF CASE: Objection to provision in confirmed Chapter 11 plan permitting a temporary stay against claims brought against third-party guarantors.

FACT SUMMARY: Creditors (P) objected to provisions in a modified Chapter 11 plan of reorganization permitting a temporary stay against claims brought against third-party guarantors to the extent those provisions acted as a release of their claims against Kahn, the Debtor's (D) principal.

RULE OF LAW

A Chapter 11 plan of reorganization may be confirmed where it provides a temporary injunction against enforcement of claims against a third-party guarantor where the third party enjoys an identity of interest with the debtor such that the claims against the third party are essentially claims against the debtor, and where the third-party claims would have an adverse effect on the debtor's ability to accomplish reorganization.

FACTS: Creditors (P) objected to modified paragraph 10.03 of the Debtor's (D) plan of reorganization. That paragraph provided that while no guarantors of the Debtor's (D) debt were released by the plan, the exclusive remedy for payment of any debt so long as the plan was not in default was the plan itself. It provided that "to the extent necessary, any applicable statute of limitations against collection from any third party (e.g., guarantor) is specifically tolled from the period of time from the bankruptcy petition date until the date upon which the debtor fails to cure any written notice of default as set forth in the plan." The creditors (P) objected to these provisions to the extent they acted as a release of their claims against Kahn, the Debtor's (D) principal. The confirmation order provided a ten-day cure period and relief from modified paragraph 10.03 upon "changed circumstances."

ISSUE: May a Chapter 11 plan of reorganization be confirmed where it provides a temporary injunction against enforcement of claims against a third-party guarantor where the third party enjoys an identity of interest with the debtor such that the claims against the third party are essentially claims against the debtor, and where the third-party claims would have an adverse effect on the debtor's ability to accomplish reorganization?

HOLDING AND DECISION: (Hale, J.) Yes. A Chapter 11 plan of reorganization may be confirmed where it provides a temporary injunction against enforcement of claims against a third-party guarantor where the third party enjoys an identity of interest with the debtor such that the claims against the third party are essentially claims against the debtor, and where the third-party claims would have an adverse effect on the debtor's ability to accomplish reorganization. Generally, a plan of reorganization cannot be confirmed if the plan purports to release guarantors of the debtor's debts and a creditor objects to the release. Here, paragraph 10.3 specifically states that guarantors are not discharged or released from any liability under the plan. Therefore, on its face, the plan does not purport to grant a release for third parties, such as Kahn. Further, nothing in paragraph 10.3 affects Kahn's ultimate liability under any guaranty agreement. Instead, it merely controls the timing of when a claim, if any, against Kahn, can be brought. And, under the plan the temporary stay could lift upon uncured default under the plan, or upon a change in circumstances for Kahn. If the objecting creditors (P) are not paid under the plan, they may pursue their guarantor, Kahn. If his circumstances improve, or if the situation warrants, the objecting creditors (P) can seek relief from the stay imposed by the plan. Post-confirmation permanent injunctions that effectively release a non-debtor from liability are prohibited. However, temporary injunctions may be proper under unusual circumstances. These circumstances include (1) when the non-debtor and debtor enjoy such an identity of interest that the suit against the non-debtor is essentially a suit against the debtor, and (2) when the third-party action will have an adverse impact on the debtor's ability to accomplish reorganization. Here, those circumstances have been met, because Debtor's (D) success or failure depends primarily on Kahn, who, for practical purposes, can be deemed to be the Debtor (D). The Debtor (D) will survive and creditors will be paid only if Kahn is allowed to conduct the Debtor's (D) business without distraction. Thus, suit against Kahn is tantamount to suit against the Debtor (D), and pursuit of such suit would have an adverse impact on Debtor's (D) successful reorganization. Here, too, paragraph 10.03 has the effect of a temporary injunction, and the Debtor (D) must meet the burden of obtaining an injunction. Here, the Debtor (D) has met that burden. It has shown that it can likely reorganize successfully, but that it will suffer irreparable harm, i.e., will not successfully reorganize, if the objecting creditors are permitted to pursue their individual guaranty claims against Kahn. This would harm not only the Debtor (D) but also its other creditors. On the other hand, the objecting creditors would merely not be repaid as quickly as they would like. They are free to pursue Kahn on his guaranties in the event Debtor (D) defaults on its plan payments and the default is not cured within 10 days. At that time, they need only to obtain an order lifting the "stay" and allowing them to proceed against Kahn directly. Thus,

Continued on next page.

the harm to Debtor (D) far outweighs the harm to the objecting creditors (P). Finally, granting a temporary injunction in this case would not be against public policy. The plan, as modified, is approved.

ANALYSIS

By essentially giving the Debtor (D) and Kahn time to effect the reorganization plan, the court's decision in this case is in line with the ultimate purpose of Chapter 11: to give business in financial difficulties an opportunity to reorganize their business affairs, provide repayment to their creditors, and emerge from their bankruptcy case in a financially sound manner.

Quicknotes

CHAPTER 11 REORGANIZATION A plan formulated pursuant to Chapter 11 of the Bankruptcy Code whereby a debtor, who is unable to pay his debts as they become due, is relieved of his obligation to pay his creditors through reorganization and payment from future income.

GUARANTOR A party who agrees to be liable for the debt or default of another.

INJUNCTION A court order requiring a person to do, or prohibiting that person from doing, a specific act.

In re Lee

Law firm applicant (P) v. Bankruptcy court (D)

94 B.R. 172 (Bankr. C.D. Cal. 1989).

NATURE OF CASE: Parallel employment applications for appointment as counsel for two Chapter 11 debtors.

FACT SUMMARY: The law firm Lee, Scott & Young sought appointment as counsel for both Seoul Corporation and Lee (P), who was one of Seoul's shareholders, but the law firm's application failed to disclose its retainer with Lee (P).

RULE OF LAW

A single attorney or law firm will be disqualified from representing two or more Chapter 11 debtors when the lawyer has failed to disclose a retainer or the existence of parallel employment applications or when the joint representation gives rise to an actual conflict of interest.

FACTS: Seoul Corporation, a seller of general merchandise and wholesale costume jewelry, filed for Chapter 11 bankruptcy. One week later, its sole shareholders, including Lee (P), also filed for Chapter 11 protection. The schedules of both debtors revealed that there was a substantial overlap of creditors for the individuals and for the corporation. Both Seoul Corporation and Lee (P) filed employment applications for the appointment of the law firm Lee, Scott & Young as counsel for the debtors. However, the applications failed to disclose that the firm had received a $2,500 retainer from Lee (P) (but not from Seoul Corporation) and that there were parallel applications. The firm's declaration to the court represented that it did not represent any adverse interests to the bankruptcy estates. When the court discovered the parallel applications, it issued an order to show cause why the law firm should not be disqualified in both cases for failure to disclose them.

ISSUE: Will an attorney or law firm be disqualified from representing two or more Chapter 11 debtors when it has failed to disclose a retainer or the existence of parallel employment applications or when the joint representation gives rise to an actual conflict of interest?

HOLDING AND DECISION: (Bufford, J.) Yes. An attorney or law firm will be disqualified from representing two Chapter 11 debtors when it has failed to disclose a retainer or the existence of parallel employment applications or when the joint representation gives rise to an actual conflict of interest. There is a presumption that for two or more related bankruptcy cases it is improper to appoint a single trustee, creditor's committee, or the same counsel for trustees, creditor's committee, or debtors in possession when: (1) creditors of the debtors have dealt with such debtors as an economic unit; (2) there is a substantial overlap of creditors; (3) the affairs of the debtors are substantially entangled; (4) assets have been transferred from one debtor to another in non-arm's length transactions; or (5) the corporate veil of one of the debtors should be pierced. Here Lee, Scott & Young did not disclose its retainer with Lee (P) or its parallel employment applications, both in violation of Bankruptcy Rule 2014(a). Further, Seoul Corporation and Lee (P) have joint liability on many of the debts owing by the respective estates, and thus the interests of Seoul Corporation and Lee (P) were in actual conflict. Bankruptcy Code § 327(a) prohibits an attorney from representing a debtor if he is not disinterested or holds an interest adverse to the bankruptcy estate. Therefore, on any of these three grounds, the law firm may be disqualified from representing either Seoul Corporation or Lee (P) or both. Because such nondisclosures and conflicts are common in the district, the court will only disqualify the firm from representing Lee (P) and will grant the employment application with regard to Seoul Corporation; the standards set forth in the opinion will be applied prospectively.

ANALYSIS

This case demonstrates one influential bankruptcy judge's attempt to enunciate ethical standards governing the appointment of counsel who attempt to represent Chapter 11 debtors with relating estates. Because bankruptcy counsel can serve only with court approval under Bankruptcy Code § 327(a), and the counsel's fees must be approved by the court under §§ 328(a) and 329(b), the court exercises final supervision over the debtor's choice of counsel.

Quicknotes

CONFLICT OF INTEREST Refers to ethical problems that arise, or may be anticipated to arise, between an attorney and his client if the interests of the attorney, another client or a third-party conflict with those of the present client.

RETAINER Fee paid upon employing an attorney in advance of services rendered; sometimes paid to prevent employment by adversary.

TRUSTEE A person who is entrusted to keep or administer property for the benefit of another.

In re SONICblue Inc.

Trustee and creditors (P) v. Debtor's counsel (D)

2007 WL 926871 (Bankr. N.D. Cal. 2007).

NATURE OF CASE: Motions for disqualification of debtors' counsel and disgorgement of attorneys' fees; appointment of a Chapter 11 trustee; and conversion of the debtors' case to Chapter 7.

FACT SUMMARY: Counsel for SONICblue Inc. and its subsidiaries (the "debtors") in their Chapter 11 bankruptcy was Pillsbury Winthrop Shaw Pittman LLC (PWSP) (D). PWSP (D) had issued a pre-petition opinion letter, several years before the bankruptcy, assuring payment to certain of the debtors' senior bondholders who effectively controlled the creditors' committee in the debtors' bankruptcy. After the opinion letter came to light when the senior bondholders demanded indemnification from PWSP (D), and only after PWSP (D) failed to disclose the conflict in its initial disclosures, the U.S. Trustee moved to disqualify PWSP (D) and to appoint a Chapter 11 trustee. Because of PWSP's (D) conflict of interest, which had not been timely disclosed, a claims trader that acquired claims against the estate moved to convert the case to Chapter 7.

RULE OF LAW

(1) Where debtor's counsel has failed to disclose a material conflict of interest, it is in the creditors' best interest to disqualify counsel and to have counsel replaced by a Chapter 11 trustee.

(2) Conversion of a Chapter 11 case to a Chapter 7 case is not preferable to appointing a Chapter 11 trustee and in the creditors' best interest where the committee of unsecured creditors and its counsel may not be fulfilling their duties to the creditor class.

FACTS: In 2001, SONICBlue Inc. formed S3 Graphics Co., Ltd., a joint venture with VIA Technologies, Inc. (VIA), and contributed certain intellectual property assets to the joint venture. In April 2002, SONICblue raised financing in a private placement issuance of $75 million in 7 3/4 percent senior secured subordinated convertible debentures. Three institutional bondholders acquired the senior debentures at a discount for $62.5 million. The indenture provided for the subordination of the senior debentures to certain obligations to VIA. In its capacity as counsel to SONICblue, Pillsbury Winthrop Shaw Pittman LLC (PWSP) (D) issued to the senior bondholders a written opinion as to the enforceability of the debentures. The opinion indicated that the debentures were enforceable against SONICblue, but, most likely as the result of a scrivener's error, the opinion failed to indicate that enforceability would be limited by bankruptcy or similar circumstances. In October 2002, SONICblue retained PWSP (D) as bankruptcy counsel in the Chapter 11 bankruptcy that SONICblue and its subsidiaries (the "debtors") had filed, and in April 2003, PWSP (D) filed an employment application accompanied by a verified statement pursuant to Bankruptcy Rule 2014, which failed to disclose PWSP's (D) potential conflict of interest resulting from the issuance of the opinion letter to the senior bondholders one year earlier. PWSP (D) was appointed debtors' counsel. Smith, the company's CFO, was appointed responsible individual. PWSP (D) diligently filed supplemental disclosures between May 2003 and June 2006, none of which mentioned the opinion letter. In addition, the Office of the United States Trustee appointed an Official Committee of Unsecured Creditors in March 2003, and the court authorized the employment of Bender of the law firm Levene, Neale, Bender, Rankin & Brill LLP (LNBRB) as the committee's counsel. The committee was dominated by the three senior bondholders. The debtors anticipated exhausting their cash reserves, and the cases became Chapter 11 liquidating cases. The debtors held nearly $80 million in funds for distribution and anticipated receiving an additional $6 million from preference settlements. Secured claims were paid in full from the proceeds of sale, and a distribution of 33 percent to unsecured creditors was anticipated. After most of the assets were liquidated, PWSP (D), along with LNBRB, engaged in prosecuting avoidance actions and objections to claims. In doing so, PWSP (D) discovered that the bondholders may have received post-petition interest on their unsecured claim, contravening the prohibition in 11 U.S.C. § 502(b)(2)—which meant that SONICblue could challenge the bondholders' claim. In response, the bondholders asserted that they had relied on the opinion letter, which they interpreted as assuring that their claims were allowable in a subsequent bankruptcy case, and in September 2006 sought indemnification from PWSP (D) for any losses resulting from SONICblue's challenge to their claim—which could amount to $43 million. PWSP (P) turned the handling of the objection to the claim over to Bender, and informed him of the indemnification demand, but still did not disclose to the court the senior bondholders' claim or the opinion letter on which it was based. It was not until March 2007, after the United States Trustee (P) had filed motions both to appoint a trustee and to disqualify PWSP (D), as well as for disgorgement of attorneys' fees, that PWSP (D) finally provided a disclosure and detailed explanation of PWSP's (D) conflict of interest with the senior bondholders. In addition to the Trustee's (P) motions, a claims trader, SB Claims, moved to convert the case to a Chapter 7 case.

ISSUE:

(1) Where debtor's counsel has failed to disclose a material conflict of interest, is it in the creditors' best interest to

Continued on next page.

disqualify counsel and to have counsel replaced by a Chapter 11 trustee?

(2) Is conversion of a Chapter 11 case to a Chapter 7 case preferable to appointing a Chapter 11 trustee and in the creditors' best interest where the committee of unsecured creditors and its counsel may not be fulfilling their duties to the creditor class?

HOLDING AND DECISION: (Morgan, J.)

(1) Yes. Where debtor's counsel has failed to disclose a material conflict of interest, it is in the creditors' best interest to disqualify counsel and to have counsel replaced by a Chapter 11 trustee. Under § 327(a), a debtor in possession may employ attorneys that do not hold an interest adverse to the estate and that are disinterested persons, and, therefore, to serve as debtor's counsel, counsel must be free of all conflicting interests that might impair the impartiality and neutral judgment that they are expected to exercise. To disqualify PWSP (D) and to have a Chapter 11 trustee appointed, the Trustee (P) need only prevail either under § 1104(a)(1) and show cause, or under § 1104(a)(2), and show that the requested action is in the creditors' best interest; the Trustee (P) does not have to prevail under both. A review of the facts clearly demonstrates that PWPS (D) knew it had a continuing duty to update its Rule 2014 disclosures upon learning of any undisclosed connections or conflicts, that as of August 2006 it knew it had a disabling conflict of interest because it immediately sought the aid of LNBRB in an attempt to resolve the conflict, and that in the face of its duties it nonetheless failed to apprise the court of these facts. Its attempt to characterize its failings as mere oversight is highly unpersuasive, especially since it made ongoing supplemental disclosures. These facts also demonstrate the need for a strong, independent, neutral trustee to restore creditor confidence. Since the creditors also have their doubts about Smith as responsible individual—since he does not report to a board, his duties are only part-time, and he had been named as a defendant in a breach of fiduciary duty action in regard to the issuance of the senior debentures—the appointment of a trustee will allay these concerns as well. For these reasons, appointment of a trustee is warranted. Motion as to this issue granted.

(2) No. Conversion of a Chapter 11 case to a Chapter 7 case is not preferable to appointing a Chapter 11 trustee and in the creditors' best interest where the committee of unsecured creditors and its counsel may not be fulfilling their duties to the creditor class. The main reason to convert to Chapter 7 would be to remove the influence of the creditors' committee from the case, since there seems to be at least the appearance of impropriety by the committee and LNBRB. The bondholders appear to have used their position on the committee to insert themselves into the settlement negotiations without revealing a hidden agenda, so that they may have breached their fiduciary duties to the unsecured creditor body. It also appears that LNBRB may have failed to fulfill its role as a watchdog on behalf of the unsecured creditors. When the conflict arose between PWSP (D) and the senior bondholders, LNBRB accepted responsibility for prosecuting the objections to the bondholders' claims without considering its own connections to the bondholders and the fact, or at least appearance, that it might also be conflicted. Professionals retained by an official committee of unsecured creditors owe fiduciary duties to the committee and the entire creditor class. Therefore, SB Claims's concerns about the committee and its counsel are substantial. Because of these troubling improprieties, having an active trustee who will formulate an independent strategy and direct its own counsel is critical. Additionally, by having the case remain in Chapter 11, the United States Trustee's (P) application for an order approving either the appointment or the election of a trustee would have to include a disclosure of all the proposed trustee's connections to the debtor, creditors and other parties in interest; there is no similar disclosure requirement in Chapter 7. For these reasons the case will not be converted to a Chapter 7 case. Motion as to this issue denied.

ANALYSIS

At some point in its opinion, the court noted that there were serious allegations that the case was being run by and for the benefit of counsel. PWSP's (D) actions, as well as those of LNBRB, which seemed to be self-interested acts aimed at protecting referral sources and revenue, are the kind of conduct that the Bankruptcy Reform Act of 1978 intended to put an end to. The legislative history of that Act decried the "opprobrious" bankruptcy ring and cronyism that the "protective atmosphere surrounding the close-knit referral circle" of attorneys in this case seems to manifest.

Quicknotes

CHAPTER 7 BANKRUPTCY A legal proceeding whereby a debtor, who is unable to pay his debts as they become due, is relieved of his obligation to pay his creditors by liquidation and distribution of his remaining assets.

CHAPTER 11 BANKRUPTCY A legal proceeding whereby a debtor, who is unable to pay his debts as they become due, is relieved of his obligation to pay his creditors through reorganization and payment from future income.

CONFLICT OF INTEREST Refers to ethical problems that arise, or may be anticipated to arise, between an attorney and his client if the interests of the attorney, another client or a third-party conflict with those of the present client.

In re Martin

Debtors (P) v. Bankruptcy court (D)

817 F.2d 175 (1st Cir. 1987).

NATURE OF CASE: Appeal from order invalidating a mortgage.

FACT SUMMARY: The Martins (P) did not have more than $500 to put up as a cash retainer to hire a law firm to file its Chapter 11 petition, so they made out a $100,000 demand note payable to the firm, secured by a second mortgage on improved real estate they owned.

RULE OF LAW

Whether a mortgage given to an attorney to secure the payment of his fees by a Chapter 11 debtor-client gives rise to an actual, perceived, or potential conflict of interest necessitating its invalidation is to be determined on a case-by-case basis.

FACTS: The Martins (P), who ran a failing restaurant business, consulted a law firm and decided to file a Chapter 11 petition. They could not afford to put up a $5,000 cash retainer, but instead agreed to a $500 cash retainer and a $100,000 demand note payable to the firm and secured by a second mortgage on improved real estate that did not serve as their residence or their place of business. In the firm's employment application to the bankruptcy court, the terms of the fee arrangement, including the note and mortgage, were fully disclosed. The bankruptcy court found that the mortgage constituted an interest adverse to the bankrupts' estate, contrary to 11 U.S.C. § 327(a), and therefore invalidated it. The Martins (P) appealed.

ISSUE: Should the bankruptcy court determine on a case-by-case basis whether a mortgage given to an attorney to secure the payment of his fees by a Chapter 11 debtor-client gives rise to an actual, perceived, or potential conflict of interest?

HOLDING AND DECISION: (Selya, J.) Yes. Whether a mortgage given to an attorney to secure the payment of his fees by a Chapter 11 debtor-creditor gives rise to an actual, perceived, or potential conflict of interest necessitating its invalidation is to be determined on a case-by-case basis. In determining whether the mortgage makes an attorney a creditor with an interest adverse to his Chapter 11 client, the court should consider: the reasonableness of the fee arrangement and whether it was negotiated in good faith; whether the security demanded was commensurate with the predictable magnitude and value of the foreseeable services; whether it was a needed means of ensuring the engagement of competent counsel; and whether or not there are telltale signs of overreaching. Doubts are to be resolved in favor of invalidation. Here, however, the grant of a mortgage by the Martins (P) as security for the payment of fees was not impermissible per se. Order is vacated; matter remanded for further proceedings.

ANALYSIS

Here, the conflict-of-interest question arose merely because the attorney representing the Chapter 11 debtor was attempting to assure payment of fees for services rendered. The First Circuit was reluctant to invalidate, posthaste, the mortgage, partly out of a desire to balance the debtor's need for bankruptcy counsel with the risk of overreaching by fee-hungry attorneys.

Quicknotes

CONFLICT OF INTEREST Refers to ethical problems that arise, or may be anticipated to arise, between an attorney and his client if the interests of the attorney, another client or a third-party conflict with those of the present client.

MORTGAGE An interest in land created by a written instrument providing security for the payment of a debt or the performance of a duty.

Commodity Futures Trading Commission v. Weintraub

Federal agency (P) v. Attorney (D)

471 U.S. 343 (1985).

NATURE OF CASE: Appeal of reversal of court-ordered waiver of privilege.

FACT SUMMARY: A bankruptcy trustee waived the attorney-client privilege for prefiling communications.

RULE OF LAW

A bankruptcy trustee may waive the attorney-client privilege for prefiling corporate communications.

FACTS: Chicago Discount Commodity Brokers, Inc. was put into receivership. Notz was appointed trustee. Pursuant to an investigation of alleged illegalities, Weintraub (D), a former attorney for CDCB, was called to testify. Weintraub (D) refused to answer several questions, asserting attorney-client privilege. Notz then waived the privilege. Weintraub (D) balked, contending that Notz did not have standing to do so respecting prefiling communications. The district court ordered Weintraub (D) to answer the questions, but the court of appeals reversed. The Commodity Futures Trading Commission (P) appealed.

ISSUE: May a bankruptcy trustee waive the attorney-client privilege for prefiling corporate communications?

HOLDING AND DECISION: (Marshall, J.) Yes. A bankruptcy trustee may waive the attorney-client privilege for prefiling corporate communications. It is settled law that management of corporations may waive the attorney-client privilege. It is also settled that when new management takes over, either through succession or corporate ouster, the new management may waive the privilege for communications made prior to its taking over. When a corporation files for bankruptcy, the trustee takes on the managerial duties of the corporation; he or she is analogous to new management. It therefore follows that the trustee may waive the privilege to the extent new management could. That is precisely what Notz did here. As the court finds no congressional intent otherwise and no policy reason not to extend to the trustee the waiving powers of new management, the court of appeals is reversed.

ANALYSIS

Weintraub (D) advanced a couple of policy reasons not to adopt the rule the Court did. One was that the trustee represented creditors, not shareholders. The Court said this was simply part of the nature of bankruptcy. Weintraub (D) also argued that the rule would apply to individual bankrupts. The Court disagreed.

Quicknotes

ATTORNEY-CLIENT PRIVILEGE A doctrine precluding the admission into evidence of confidential communications between an attorney and his client made in the course of obtaining professional assistance.

OUSTER The unlawful dispossession of a party lawfully entitled to possession of real property.

WAIVER The intentional or voluntary forfeiture of a recognized right.

CHAPTER 9

Domestic Jurisdiction

Quick Reference Rules of Law

PAGE

1. **The 1984 Amendments.** The Seventh Amendment assures the right to a jury trial of a claim by a Chapter 11 trustee to recover a fraudulent conveyance. (Granfinanciera, S.A. v. Nordberg) *144*

2. **The 1984 Amendments.** Bankruptcy jurisdiction exists so long as it is possible that a proceeding may impact on the debtor's rights, liabilities, options, or freedom of action. (In re Dow Corning Corp. [I]) *145*

3. **The 1984 Amendments.** A district court cannot employ 28 U.S.C. § 1334(c)(1) to abstain globally without examination of a single individual claim. (In re Dow Corning Corp. [II]) *146*

4. **The 1984 Amendments.** Where a bankruptcy claim directly affects a core bankruptcy function, it is a core proceeding. (In re United States Lines, Inc.) *147*

5. **The 1984 Amendments.** A court must consider judicial economy, timeliness, fairness, the efficient administration of the estate, and the interest of justice when considering a transfer of venue. (In re Enron Corp.) *148*

Granfinanciera, S.A. v. Nordberg

Recipient of conveyance (P) v. Trustee (D)

492 U.S. 33 (1989).

NATURE OF CASE: Appeal from denial of right to jury trial in bankruptcy trustee's action to recover fraudulent conveyance.

FACT SUMMARY: When Nordberg (P), the trustee in bankruptcy for Chapter 11 debtor Chase & Sanborn, filed suit against Granfinanciera (D) for a fraudulent conveyance made within one year after the Chapter 11 filing, Granfinanciera (D) sought and was denied a jury trial on the claim.

> **RULE OF LAW**
> The Seventh Amendment assures the right to a jury trial of a claim by a Chapter 11 trustee to recover a fraudulent conveyance.

FACTS: Chase & Sanborn filed for Chapter 11 protection. Nordberg (P), the Chapter 11 trustee, filed an action against Granfinanciera (D) seeking to recover an alleged fraudulent conveyance of $1.7 million received from Chase & Sanborn's predecessor within one year of the Chapter 11 petition without receipt of consideration or reasonably equivalent value in return. Granfinanciera (D) sought a jury trial of Nordberg's (P) claim, but was denied one by the Eleventh Circuit on the grounds that both fraudulent conveyance claims and claims in bankruptcy were equitable, not legal, in nature.

ISSUE: Does the Seventh Amendment assure the right to a jury trial of a claim by a Chapter 11 trustee to recover a fraudulent conveyance?

HOLDING AND DECISION: (Brennan, J.) Yes. The Seventh Amendment assures the right to a jury trial of a claim by a Chapter 11 trustee to recover a fraudulent conveyance. Although the Chapter 11 trustee's right to sue for constructive fraud is statutory and set forth in the Bankruptcy Code, 11 U.S.C. § 548(1)(2), the Seventh Amendment still governs actions brought to enforce statutory rights that are analogous to common law causes of action heard by late-eighteenth-century English courts at law rather than at equity. Actions to recover preferential or fraudulent transfers were typically brought at law in common law England. Further, although suits to recover preferences are related to bankruptcy proceedings and have been designated as "core proceedings" under the 1984 amendments that may be adjudicated by bankruptcy judges subject to referral by a district court, they still are separate, plenary suits to which the Seventh Amendment applies. The trustee's right to recover a fraudulent conveyance is a private, not public (arising out of a federal regulatory scheme), right which resembles state common law contract claims brought by bankrupt corporations to augment the bankrupt estate—not a creditor's claim to a pro rata share of the bankruptcy estate itself. Because Granfinanciera (D) did not file a claim against the estate itself, Granfinanciera's (D) Seventh Amendment right to a trial by jury cannot be deprived. Reversed.

DISSENT: (White, J.) An action to recover a fraudulent conveyance is "integrally related" to the essence of bankruptcy proceedings, and creditor-debtor disputes involve "public" rights. The Court should defer to Congress, which has defined fraudulent conveyance actions as being at the "core" of bankruptcy proceedings and triable in bankruptcy courts before bankruptcy judges, without a jury.

DISSENT: (Blackmun, J.) The action to recover a fraudulent conveyance here arises under a federal statute and is related to the bankruptcy process as a common device to undermine the fair distribution of assets among creditors. Although Congress may not abridge Seventh Amendment rights, it has not crossed an impermissible "line" by characterizing a fraudulent conveyance action on the eve of bankruptcy as a "core proceeding."

ANALYSIS

The principal critical issue left undecided by the majority here is whether the Seventh Amendment or Article III allows jury trials in fraudulent conveyance actions to be held before non-Article III bankruptcy judges subject to the oversight provided by the district court. The only claims subsequent to the 1984 amendments that appear to be excluded from adjudication by bankruptcy judges as non-"core proceedings" or not "related to" the bankruptcy are personal injury and wrongful death claims against an estate under 11 U.S.C. § 157(b) and (c); and § 1334(c)(1). The district court itself may try the case or exercise its discretion to remove the matter to the state court.

Quicknotes

CHAPTER 11 BANKRUPTCY A legal proceeding whereby a debtor, who is unable to pay his debts as they become due, is relieved of his obligation to pay his creditors through reorganization and payment from future income.

CREDITOR A person or party to whom a debt or obligation is owed.

FRAUDULENT CONVEYANCE Conveyances made with intent to defraud creditors; may be voidable.

SEVENTH AMENDMENT Provides that no fact tried by a jury shall be otherwise re-examined in any court of the United States, other than according to the rules of the common law.

In re Dow Corning Corp. (I)

Claimants (P) v. Debtor (D)

86 F.3d 482 (6th Cir. 1996).

NATURE OF CASE: Appeal from denial of transfer motions.

FACT SUMMARY: The district court claimed it lacked subject matter jurisdiction over claims that were not related to Dow Corning's bankruptcy proceedings.

RULE OF LAW

Bankruptcy jurisdiction exists so long as it is possible that a proceeding may impact on the debtor's rights, liabilities, options, or freedom of action.

FACTS: Dow Corning was the predominant producer of silicone gel breast implants and supplied silicone raw materials to other manufacturers. Dow Corning and other manufacturers and suppliers of silicone gel-filled implants were codefendants in a large number of personal injury lawsuits. Dow Corning filed for Chapter 11 bankruptcy. When claimants moved to transfer claims for compensatory and punitive damages to the federal district court, sitting as a bankruptcy court, the court ruled it did not have subject matter jurisdiction. An appeal followed.

ISSUE: Does bankruptcy jurisdiction exist so long as it is possible that a proceeding may impact on the debtor's rights, liabilities, options, or freedom of action?

HOLDING AND DECISION: (Martin, J.) Yes. Bankruptcy jurisdiction exists so long as it is possible that a proceeding may impact on the debtor's rights, liabilities, options, or freedom of action. The usual test to determine whether a civil proceeding is related to bankruptcy is whether the outcome of that proceeding could conceivably have any effect on the estate being administered in bankruptcy. In addition to the claims asserted by personal injury claimants, Dow Chemical and Corning Incorporated have asserted cross-claims on each other, and that will also have an effect on the bankruptcy estate. Claims for indemnification and contribution obviously would affect the size of the estate, as well. Section 1334 (b) jurisdiction exists over breast implant claims pending against Dow Corning and one or both of its parents. The district court is in a better position to make abstention determinations. Reversed and remanded.

ANALYSIS

The district court later abstained. The case was returned to same court in 1997. The court then issued a writ of mandamus.

Quicknotes

COMPENSATORY DAMAGES Measure of damages necessary to compensate victim for actual injuries suffered.

CONTRIBUTION The right of a person or party who has compensated a victim for his injury to seek reimbursement from others who are equally responsible for the injury in proportional amounts.

INDEMNIFICATION Reimbursement for losses sustained or security against anticipated loss or damages.

PERSONAL INJURY Harm to an individual's person or body.

PUNITIVE DAMAGES Damages exceeding the actual injury suffered for the purposes of punishment, deterrence and comfort to plaintiff.

SUBJECT MATTER JURISDICTION A court's ability to adjudicate a specific category of cases based on the subject matter of the dispute.

In re Dow Corning Corp. (II)

Claimants (P) v. Debtor (D)

113 F.3d 565 (6th Cir. 1997).

NATURE OF CASE: Appeal and petition for writ of mandamus.

FACT SUMMARY: When the district court refused to transfer claims from claimants who had not joined the global settlement pool, Dow Corning appealed.

RULE OF LAW

A district court cannot employ 28 U.S.C. § 1334 (c)(1) to abstain globally without examination of a single individual claim.

FACTS: In an earlier case, the court ruled that various claims from many jurisdictions should all be transferred to the same bankruptcy court handling Dow Corning's bankruptcy. When the case was remanded to the district court, the court exercised discretionary and mandatory abstention and declined to transfer the cases. Dow Corning and its shareholders appealed, petitioning the court for a writ of mandamus.

ISSUE: May a district court employ 28 U.S.C. § 1334 (c)(1) to abstain globally without examination of a single individual claim?

HOLDING AND DECISION: (Martin, C.J.) No. A district court cannot employ 28 U.S.C. § 1334(c)(1) to abstain globally without examination of a single individual claim. The requirements for mandatory abstention dictate that each case must be examined individually. In many of the cases there does not even appear to have been a motion for abstention filed by the plaintiff in the proceeding. The court's exercise of discretionary abstention was also troubling. A writ of mandamus is issued ordering the district court to transfer the claims against shareholders and to evaluate each case individually. Petition granted.

ANALYSIS

The court's use of mandamus was necessary due to the unusual nature of the case. The huge number of claims filed in the multi-forum breast-implant litigation necessitated such action. No hearing was conducted, and no evidence was presented to the district court.

Quicknotes

BANKRUPTCY A legal proceeding whereby a debtor, who is unable to pay his debts as they become due, is relieved of his obligation to pay his creditors either by liquidation and distribution of his remaining assets or through reorganization and payment from future income.

MANDAMUS A court order issued commanding a public or private entity, or an official thereof, to perform a duty required by law.

In re United States Lines, Inc.

Debtor (P) v. Insurers (D)

197 F.3d 631 (2d Cir. 1999).

NATURE OF CASE: Interlocutory appeal.

FACT SUMMARY: When former employees filed claims for asbestos-related injuries sustained while they worked on United States Lines (USL) ships, USL (P) filed for bankruptcy and sought to recover insurance proceeds.

RULE OF LAW

Where a bankruptcy claim directly affects a core bankruptcy function, it is a core proceeding.

FACTS: The United States Lines (P) and United States Lines (S.A.) Inc. Reorganization Trust sued in bankruptcy court seeking a declaratory judgment to establish their rights under several insurance contracts. USL (P) also sought punitive damages for creation of an insurance maze. The bankruptcy court held that the action was within its core jurisdiction and denied the insurance companies' (D) motion to compel arbitration. The district court reversed, ruling that the insurance contract disputes were not core proceedings. The district court ordered arbitration to proceed and certified its order for interlocutory appeal.

ISSUE: Where a bankruptcy claim directly affects a core bankruptcy function, is it a core proceeding?

HOLDING AND DECISION: (Walker, J.) Yes. Where a bankruptcy claim directly affects a core bankruptcy function, it is a core proceeding. The impact that these contracts have on other core bankruptcy functions render them core, notwithstanding the fact that claims are on pre-petition contracts. The bankruptcy court has core jurisdiction over claims arising from a contract formed post-petition. There are circumstances in which a bankruptcy court may stay arbitration, and in this case the bankruptcy court was correct that it had discretion to do so. Reversed and remanded.

CONCURRENCE: (Newman, J.) I concur in the result. The efficient functioning of the bankruptcy system would be better served by a bright-line rule that treats as core proceeding all suits alleging post-petition breaches of pre-petition contracts.

CONCURRENCE: (Calabresi, J.) I would be inclined to follow a case-by-case approach.

ANALYSIS

The claims by employees were complicated by a pay-first provision in the insurance contracts. The insurer's liability was not triggered until the insured paid the claim of the personal injury victim. All of the insurance contracts had been issued prior to bankruptcy.

Quicknotes

ARBITRATION An agreement to have a dispute heard and decided by a neutral third party, rather than through legal proceedings.

CHAPTER 11 REORGANIZATION A plan formulated pursuant to Chapter 11 of the Bankruptcy Code whereby a debtor who is unable to pay his debts as they become due is relieved of his obligation to pay his creditors through reorganization and payment from future income.

DECLARATORY JUDGMENT An adjudication by the courts that grants not relief but is binding over the legal status of the parties involved in the dispute.

INTERLOCUTORY APPEAL The appeal of an issue that does not resolve the disposition of the case, but is essential to a determination of the parties' legal rights.

In re Enron Corp.

Consideration of appropriate venue.

274 B.R. 327 (Bankr. S.D.N.Y. 2002).

NATURE OF CASE: Motion for transfer of venue.

FACT SUMMARY: Enron Corporation (Enron), a large multinational corporation headquartered in Houston, Texas, filed multiple bankruptcy petitions in a New York bankruptcy court. Several parties moved for a transfer of venue from New York to a Texas bankruptcy court.

RULE OF LAW

A court must consider judicial economy, timeliness, fairness, the efficient administration of the estate, and the interest of justice when considering a transfer of venue.

FACTS: Enron, consisting here of 18 affiliated debtor companies, filed bankruptcy petitions in a New York bankruptcy court. One subsidiary properly filed in New York and then the others were allowed to file as "affiliates" under 28 U.S.C. § 1408(2). Several parties involved in the bankruptcy case moved to transfer venue from New York to Texas. Several facts weigh in favor of each New York and Texas. No debtor company affiliated with Enron is organized under the laws of New York and Enron is headquartered in Houston, Texas. The corporate books and records are substantially located in Texas. Enron has litigation matters in both New York and Texas courts. Most of Enron's management, officers, and directors are located in Texas. The largest unsecured creditor of Enron, JP Morgan Chase, is headquartered in New York and is represented in the bankruptcy proceedings by New York counsel. Six of fifteen members of the Official Committee of Unsecured Creditors (the "Committee") are located in New York, with three in Texas, and the six others each located in separate states or countries. Of the seventeen largest Enron creditors, none is located in Texas. New York, however, has multiple creditor listings. The vast majority of Enron employees are located in Houston, Texas. Their interest in the Enron litigation primarily involves the Enron 401(k) plan, although other issues involve bonus and severance payments to employees largely located in Texas. Enron has hired multiple law firms with main offices in New York and subsidiary offices in Texas. Enron itself had 145 attorneys in its employ and an entire floor dedicated to Arthur Andersen employees, with both departments operating out of the Houston office. Most of the immediate interest of Enron employees involves the Texas venue. New York, though, is one of the world's most accessible cities and a major financial marketplace. A roundtrip flight from Houston to New York takes approximately seven hours and costs approximately $1,800 for a coach seat. No flights from Houston arrive in New York prior to 10:00 a.m. EST.

ISSUE: Must a court consider judicial economy, timeliness, fairness, the efficient administration of the estate, and the interest of justice when considering a transfer of venue?

HOLDING AND DECISION: (Gonzalez, J.) Yes. A court must consider judicial economy, timeliness, fairness, the efficient administration of the estate, and the interest of justice when considering a transfer of venue. A prospective debtor may elect the venue for Chapter 11 reorganization under § 1408(1). If a transfer of venue is desired, the burden is on the movant to demonstrate that a transfer is warranted; transfer is highly burdensome to a bankruptcy proceeding, and a debtor's proper choice of forum is given great weight. A transfer is appropriate if it is in the interest of justice or for the convenience of the parties. A number of factors play into a determination of convenience, but the most weight is given to the "promotion of the economic and efficient administration of the estate." In this case, the number and location of creditors is quite expansive. This may be the largest bankruptcy ever filed and creditors exist worldwide. Texas may be more inconvenient for more of the creditors, as New York is so accessible globally. Texas is certainly not a better venue for the convenience of the creditors. The Committee, as a fiduciary to and representative of Enron's unsecured creditors, has strongly opposed transfer and its opposition is certainly relevant. A creditor offering $1 billion in post-petition financing opposes transfer. The movants argue that the majority of necessary creditor parties are located in or convenient to Texas, but they take into account the large number of inter-company Debtors. If that argument is accepted, 88 percent of the trade and vendor debt amount is held by Texas entities, but then 90 percent of the overall debt holders oppose transfer, so that argument falls. The employees may certainly find it burdensome to travel to New York to attend hearings, but their concerns are primarily related to the 401(k) issues, which are not necessarily before this court. Given that fact, the existence of a majority of employees in Texas is not a factor in favor of transfer. Few employees, if any, would be required to appear in this court and teleconferences may be arranged if necessary. Finally, the most important factor is for the economic and efficient administration of the case. New York is a global financial giant and offers innumerable resources for restructuring Enron's debt. Most of those companies responsible for restructuring the debt are located in New York and administration of the restructuring will be more convenient and efficient in New York. The

Continued on next page.

interest of justice, however, must still be considered, which could result in transfer. While the efficient administration of the estate will best be served in New York, this court must also consider the "learning curve" associated with transferring this case to a new venue. This court has had to gain familiarity with a broad array of issues and emergency matters. Movants argue that a "learning curve" should not be considered given that they timely filed a motion to transfer, but many of the already-heard motions were considered on short notice or an emergency basis and much has transpired in this case. Delays would be inevitable on a transfer of venue. Retaining jurisdiction in New York will best serve the interests of this case. Motion denied.

ANALYSIS

The larger creditors won out over the smaller creditors and the employees in this case. Perhaps it was a strategic move to have the larger creditors making the initial decisions such as choice of forum. In the wake of this case, a U.S. Senator from Texas moved to restrict choice of venue to the location of the principal place of business. The criticism is that large companies such as Enron moved to "far off" venue locations to avoid heavy smaller creditor and employee involvement. The "far off" court may not be as sensitive to "local" issues.

Quicknotes

CHAPTER 11 BANKRUPTCY A legal proceeding whereby a debtor, who is unable to pay his debts as they become due, is relieved of his obligation to pay his creditors through reorganization and payment from future income.

CHAPTER 11 REORGANIZATION A plan formulated pursuant to Chapter 11 of the Bankruptcy Code whereby a debtor, who is unable to pay his debts as they become due, is relieved of his obligation to pay his creditors through reorganization and payment from future income.

SECURED CREDITOR A creditor, the repayment of whose loan is secured by collateral sufficient to repay the debt owed.

UNSECURED CREDITOR A creditor whose loan is not backed by specified collateral or a security agreement.

VENUE The specific geographic location over which a court has jurisdiction to hear a suit.

CHAPTER 10

Transnational Bankruptcies

Quick Reference Rules of Law

1. **Choice of Forum: United States.** A foreign corporation with a subsidiary having a U.S. office may be subject to U.S. jurisdiction for purposes of a Chapter 11 proceeding. (In re McLean Industries, Inc. [I]) *152*

2. **Choice of Forum: United States.** A creditor cannot escape a contempt order by assigning its claim against a bankrupt. (In re McLean Industries [II]) *153*

3. **Choice of Forum: Elsewhere.** The bankrupt estate includes property located outside of the country. (X. v. Schenkius [Receiver for Y]) *154*

4. **Cooperating with the Home Country Court: United States.** Where foreign bankruptcy proceedings are not pending in a country where a debtor has its center of its main interests (COMI) or where it has an "establishment," the foreign proceedings are not eligible for relief as main or nonmain proceedings under Chapter 15. (In re Bear Stearns High-Grade Structured Credit Strategies Master Fund, Ltd.) *155*

5. **Cooperating with the Home Country Court: United States.** Recognition of an ancillary foreign insolvency proceeding will be granted under former § 304 of the Bankruptcy Code where the foreign proceeding comports with due process, ensures just treatment of creditors, and does not violate public policy. (In re Board of Directors Telecom Argentina, S.A.) *157*

6. **Cooperating with the Home Country Court: Elsewhere.** English courts have the authority to remit assets of an entity of a relevant country to liquidators in that country to be distributed in accordance with the insolvency laws of that country even where doing so will favor some creditors at the expense of others. (McGrath v. Riddell) *159*

7. **Choice of Law.** Bankruptcy courts may best be able to effectuate the purposes of the bankruptcy law by cooperating with foreign courts on a case-by-case basis. (In re Maxwell Communication Corp. PLC) *161*

In re McLean Industries, Inc. (I)

Shipping company debtor (P) v. Creditor (D)

68 B.R. 690 (Bankr. S.D.N.Y. 1986).

NATURE OF CASE: Petition for preliminary injunction and contempt citation in Chapter 11 bankruptcy.

FACT SUMMARY: A foreign corporation with a subsidiary having a U.S. office contended it was not subject to U.S. jurisdiction for purposes of a Chapter 11 proceeding.

RULE OF LAW

A foreign corporation with a subsidiary having a U.S. office may be subject to U.S. jurisdiction for purposes of a Chapter 11 proceeding.

FACTS: United States Lines, Inc. (P), a shipping company, filed for bankruptcy under Chapter 11. One creditor was GAC Marine Fuels, Ltd. (D), a British corporation with offices around the world. A wholly-owned subsidiary of GAC (D) had an office in New Jersey, at which it solicited business for GAC (D). After U.S. Lines (P) filed for bankruptcy, GAC (D) obtained an order in Hong Kong attaching a ship owned by U.S. Lines (P), which brought a petition in bankruptcy court seeking a contempt citation and an injunction. GAC (D) contended it was not subject to U.S. jurisdiction.

ISSUE: May a foreign corporation with a subsidiary having a U.S. office be subject to U.S. jurisdiction for purposes of a Chapter 11 proceeding?

HOLDING AND DECISION: (Buschman, J.) Yes. A foreign corporation with a subsidiary having a U.S. office may be subject to U.S. jurisdiction for purposes of a Chapter 11 proceeding. The law as it relates to personal jurisdiction in bankruptcy is governed by standard due process considerations. A foreign entity will be subject to U.S. jurisdiction if it transacts business in the United States and if either the cause of action arose out of U.S. business or the entity's contacts are so continuous as to provide general personal jurisdiction. If an entity's contracts are through a subsidiary, jurisdiction will be afforded if the subsidiary's acts are for the benefit of the parent. Here, it appears that the subsidiary's New Jersey office made seven to fifteen transactions per month on account of GAC (D), and this is sufficient to confer general personal jurisdiction. Petition granted.

ANALYSIS

The jurisdictional analysis here was identical to the analysis underlying state "long arm" jurisdictional statutes. Arguments have been made that the U.S. government has such a strong interest in its bankruptcy proceedings that its jurisdiction should have a broader reach than such state laws. The court here declined to rule on this issue, finding it unnecessary.

Quicknotes

JURISDICTION The authority of a court to hear and declare judgment in respect to a particular matter.

LONG-ARM STATUTE A state statute conferring personal jurisdiction to state courts over a defendant not residing in the state, when the cause of action arises as a result of activities conducted within the state or affecting state residents.

SUBSIDIARY A company, a majority of whose shares are owned by another corporation and which is subject to that corporation's control.

In re McLean Industries, Inc. (II)

Shipping company debtor (P) v. Creditor (D)

76 B.R. 291 (Bankr. S.D.N.Y. 1987).

NATURE OF CASE: Petition for interlocutory judgment of continuing contempt in a bankruptcy.

FACT SUMMARY: Creditor GAC Marine Fuels (D), under a contempt order, assigned its claims against the bankrupt.

RULE OF LAW

A creditor cannot escape a contempt order by assigning its claim against a bankrupt.

FACTS: In a Chapter 11 proceeding, debtor United States Lines (P) had obtained a contempt citation against creditor GAC Marine Fuels, Ltd. (D) for the latter having obtained attachment orders against ships belonging to U.S. Lines (P), which were harbored in Hong Kong and Singapore. The contempt order mandated that GAC (D) take steps to discontinue the attachments. Instead, GAC (D) assigned its claims to another corporation, which continued the attachments. U.S. Lines (P) argued that since it no longer owned the claims against U.S. Lines (P), it could not comply with the order.

ISSUE: Can a creditor escape a contempt order by assigning its claim against a bankrupt?

HOLDING AND DECISION: (Buschman, J.) No. A creditor cannot escape a contempt order by assigning its claim against a bankrupt. When a court issues a contempt citation against a creditor for violating the automatic stay, a creditor is under a duty to take whatever steps it must to end the violation. To transfer its claim to another entity hardly constitutes a fulfillment of this obligation and justifies an order of continuing contempt. Petition granted.

ANALYSIS

GAC (D) had originally made an in personam jurisdictional objection, which it had lost. In this action, it raised an in rem objection. This proved equally unsuccessful. The Code, at § 541, includes within its ambit all property of a debtor, "wherever situated."

Quicknotes

AUTOMATIC STAY Upon the filing of a voluntary bankruptcy petition, creditors are prohibited from attempting to recover payment from the debtor or his property.

IN REM An action against property.

INTERLOCUTORY Intervening; temporary; refers to an issue that is determined during the course of a proceeding and which does not constitute a final judgment on the merits.

X. v. Schenkius (Receiver for Y)

Divorced spouse (P) v. Receiver (D)

Court of Appeal of 'S-Hertogenbosch, 6 July 1993, KG 1993, 406; NIPR 1993 No. 469; NJ 1994, 250.

NATURE OF CASE: Appeal from order in bankruptcy hearing.

FACT SUMMARY: X was ordered by the court to aid in the sale of former community property assets located in Spain for the purpose of liquidation of her ex-husband's estate.

RULE OF LAW

The bankrupt estate includes property located outside of the country.

FACTS: X (P) and Y filed for a divorce in the district court in the Netherlands, and the divorce was unofficially granted on June 6, 1988. Y filed for bankruptcy in the same court, and the bankruptcy order was granted on July 18, 1988. Schenkius (D) was appointed receiver. Their divorce decree became final on December 6, 1988. Part of their community assets was a piece of land in Spain on which there were two houses. The receiver demanded that X (P) execute a power of attorney to facilitate the sale of the Spanish land. X (P) contested the order, claiming that the territorial effect of Dutch bankruptcy law could not reach property in Spain. The district court found for Schenkius (D). X (P) appealed.

ISSUE: Does the bankrupt estate include property located outside of the country?

HOLDING AND DECISION: [Judge not stated in casebook excerpt.] Yes. The bankrupt estate includes property located outside of the country. The bankruptcy necessarily covers the entire estate. Because the bankruptcy in this case was filed in the Netherlands, the entire estate is subject to Dutch bankruptcy law. Simply because Dutch law may not have an extraterritorial effect does not mean that X (P), who resides in the Netherlands, must not comply with all court orders attempting to include the property in the bankruptcy. The district court is affirmed.

ANALYSIS

Bankruptcy was traditionally treated as completed territorially. Japan adheres to the strictly territorial approach, not touching any property outside of Japan itself. The court in this case is trying to break away from the strict interpretation, but without claiming extraterritorial effect; the Netherlands has a say in what should happen to the property, but the extent it can enforce its opinion is admittedly limited.

Quicknotes

COMMUNITY PROPERTY In community property jurisdictions, refers to all money or property acquired during the term of the marriage in which each spouse has an undivided one-half interest.

RECEIVER An individual who is appointed by the court to maintain the holdings of a corporation, individual or other entity involved in a legal proceeding.

In re Bear Stearns High-Grade Structured Credit Strategies Master Fund, Ltd.

Foreign joint provisional liquidators (P) v. Creditors (D)

374 B.R. 122 (Bankr. S.D.N.Y. 2007).

NATURE OF CASE: Petition for recognition of foreign liquidation proceedings as either foreign main or foreign nonmain proceedings under Chapter 15.

FACT SUMMARY: Joint provisional liquidators (JPLs) (P) of two investment funds (the "Funds") petitioned the bankruptcy court for recognition of liquidation proceedings of the Funds in the Cayman Island courts as either foreign main or foreign nonmain proceedings under Chapter 15.

RULE OF LAW

Where foreign bankruptcy proceedings are not pending in a country where a debtor has its center of its main interests (COMI) or where it has an "establishment," the foreign proceedings are not eligible for relief as main or nonmain proceedings under Chapter 15.

FACTS: Joint provisional liquidators (JPLs) (P) of two open-ended investment funds (the "Funds") petitioned the bankruptcy court for recognition of liquidation proceedings (Foreign Proceeding) of the Funds in the Cayman Island courts as either foreign main or foreign nonmain proceedings under Chapter 15. The JPLs (P) sought foreign main recognition pursuant to section 1517 of the Bankruptcy Code, the granting of related relief pursuant to Code § 1520, and additional relief pursuant to § 1521(a). In the alternative, if foreign main recognition was denied, they sought foreign nonmain recognition pursuant to § 1502(5) and concomitant relief under § 1521. Only related entities from Merrill Lynch (D) objected to the petitions. The Funds were both Cayman Islands exempted LLCs with registered offices in the Cayman Islands, but there were no employees or managers in the Cayman Islands. The investment manager for the Funds was located in New York, the administrator that ran the back-office operations of the Funds was in Massachusetts, the Funds' books and records were in Delaware, and prior to the commencement of the Foreign Proceeding, all of the Funds' liquid assets were located in the United States. The investor registries were maintained and located in Ireland, accounts receivables were located throughout Europe and the United States, counterparties to master repurchase and swap agreements were based both inside and outside the United States but none were claimed to be in the Cayman Islands. Moreover, there apparently existed the possibility that prepetition transactions conducted in the United States could be avoidable under U.S. law.

ISSUE: Where foreign bankruptcy proceedings are not pending in a country where a debtor has its center of its main interests (COMI) or where it has an "establishment," are the foreign proceedings eligible for relief as main or nonmain proceedings under Chapter 15?

HOLDING AND DECISION: (Lifland, J.) No. Where foreign bankruptcy proceedings are not pending in a country where a debtor has its center of its main interests (COMI) or where it has an "establishment," the foreign proceedings are not eligible for relief as main or nonmain proceedings under Chapter 15, the goal of which is to provide effective mechanisms for dealing with cases of cross-border insolvency. The court must make an independent determination as to whether the foreign proceedings meet the definitional requirements of foreign main or nonmain proceedings. The determination is a single-step, formulaic determination as to whether the definitions in §§ 1502 and 101(23) and (24) have been met. If the foreign proceeding is to obtain recognition, it must meet those definitions and the recognition must be characterized as either main or nonmain. A foreign main proceeding is defined under § 1502(4) as a "foreign proceeding pending in the country where the debtor has the center of its main interests" (COMI). Under § 1502(5), foreign nonmain proceeding means any other proceeding "pending in a country where the debtor has an establishment." Section 1502(2) defines "establishment" as "any place of operations where the debtor carries out a nontransitory economic activity." Section 1516(c) provides that "[i]n the absence of evidence to the contrary, the debtor's registered office, . . . is presumed to be the center of the debtor's main interests." However, this presumption is not a preferred alternative where there is a separation between a corporation's jurisdiction of incorporation and its real seat. The foreign petitioner carries the burden of proof on this issue. Thus, if there is evidence that the COMI might not be in the country of the registered office, the petitioner must prove that the COMI is in fact in the same country as the registered office. Indicia of COMI can include the following: the location of the debtor's headquarters; the location of those who actually manage the debtor (which, conceivably could be the headquarters of a holding company); the location of the debtor's primary assets; the location of the majority of the debtor's creditors or of a majority of the creditors who would be affected by the case; and/or the jurisdiction whose law would apply to most disputes. Here, the factors that inform the determination come from the JPL's (P) own evidentiary submissions, guided by the

Continued on next page.

application of similar statutes by foreign jurisdictions. Such foreign guidance, e.g., the European Union Convention on Insolvency Proceedings, provides that COMI is "the place where the debtor conducts the administration of his interests on a regular basis and is therefore ascertainable by third parties." Applying these guidelines, it is clear from the evidence that the Funds' only connection to the Cayman Islands is that they are registered there. There are no employees there, and the investment manager, administrator, books and records, registries, accounts receivable, and counterparties are located elsewhere. Finally, pre-petition transactions conducted in the United States might be avoidable under U.S. law. For these reasons, the Funds do not have their COMI in the Cayman Islands and the foreign proceedings cannot be characterized as foreign main proceedings; the presumption that the COMI is the place of the Funds' registered offices has been rebutted. As to whether the foreign proceedings may be characterized as nonmain proceedings, there is no evidence that the Funds have a place of business in the Cayman Islands, which is tantamount to saying they do not have an "establishment" there. Moreover, the JPLs' (P) reliance on former § 304 is misplaced, since Chapter 15 imposes a rigid procedural structure for recognition of foreign proceedings as either main or nonmain, whereas § 304 did not. Therefore, the Foreign Proceedings cannot be characterized as nonmain. In sum, they are not eligible for relief as main or nonmain proceedings under Chapter 15. Petition denied.

ANALYSIS

Nonrecognition of the foreign proceedings in this case, however, did not leave the JPLs (P) without the ability to obtain relief from U.S. courts; they could still obtain relief under 11 U.S.C. §§ 303(b)(4) and 1509(f). Section 303(b)(4) of the Bankruptcy Code specifically provides that an involuntary case may be commenced under Chapter 7 or 11 by a foreign representative of the estate in a foreign proceeding so that a foreign representative is not left remediless upon nonrecognition, and that section does not require that the foreign proceeding be recognized. This flexibility leaves open the potential coordination of a case filed in the United States under Title 11 with the foreign proceeding. In addition, § 1509(f) provides that the failure of a foreign representative to obtain recognition does not affect any right the foreign representative may have to sue in a court in the United States to collect or recover a claim that is the property of the debtor.

Quicknotes

LIQUIDATION The reduction to cash of all assets for distribution to creditors.

PRE-PETITION Before bankruptcy petition has been filed.

In re Board of Directors Telecom Argentina, S.A.

Foreign debtor (P) v. Creditor (D)

528 F.3d 162 (2d Cir. 2008).

NATURE OF CASE: Appeal from affirmance of grant of petition for recognition of an ancillary foreign insolvency proceeding.

FACT SUMMARY: Argo (D), one of Telecom Argentina, S.A.'s (Telecom's) (P) creditors, contended that Telecom's (P) debt restructuring under Argentine law should not be recognized as an ancillary foreign insolvency proceeding under former § 304 of the Bankruptcy Code because the foreign proceeding did not provide for just treatment of creditors and violated public policy.

RULE OF LAW

Recognition of an ancillary foreign insolvency proceeding will be granted under former § 304 of the Bankruptcy Code where the foreign proceeding comports with due process, ensures just treatment of creditors, and does not violate public policy.

FACTS: Telecom Argentina, S.A. (Telecom) (P), a major Argentine telecommunications company, suffered a severe liquidity crisis during a deep recession. Telecom (P), which held approximately US $3.3 billion in outstanding unsecured debt (Old Debt), had suspended principal payments on all of its Old Debt, and then sought to restructure the debt under Argentina's Insolvency Law through an acuerdo preventivo extrajudicial (APE). An APE permits a debtor that suspends its payments or has financial difficulties to seek court approval of a privately negotiated, majority-approved restructuring plan and thereby make the plan binding on all creditors. After receiving the requisite approval, Telecom (P) submitted it to an Argentine commercial court for review, and the court approved the APE. The court found that the proposed restructuring was not abusive, fraudulent or discriminatory. Argo (D), one of Telecom's (P) non-consenting creditors, instructed the indenture trustee not to exchange its notes, and, consequently, around US$ 80 million in Old Debt held by non-consenting creditors was not cancelled and was placed in a trust. Telecom (P) then initiated by petition a case ancillary to a foreign proceeding pursuant to 11 U.S.C. § 304, seeking a judgment declaring that the Argentine approval order and the APE should be given full force and effect in the United States, should be binding on all creditors and their agents, and should result in the cancellation of the Old Debt. The bankruptcy court granted the petition, and the district court affirmed. Argo (D) appealed, and the court of appeals granted review.

ISSUE: Will recognition of an ancillary foreign insolvency proceeding be granted under former § 304 of the Bankruptcy Code where the foreign proceeding comports with due process, ensures just treatment of creditors, and does not violate public policy?

HOLDING AND DECISION: (Sotomayor, J.) Yes. Recognition of an ancillary foreign insolvency proceeding will be granted under former § 304 of the Bankruptcy Code where the foreign proceeding comports with due process, ensures just treatment of creditors, and does not violate public policy. To determine whether to recognize the foreign proceeding, the court looks at six factors enumerated in § 304(c). As to one of these factors, Argo (D) argues that the APE process does not provide for just treatment of creditors because it allows for "only limited objections and limited recourse against a majority-approved APE." However, contrary to Argo's (D) assertions, the APE plan provided for an orderly, centralized administration of Telecom's (P) debt restructuring. Argo (D) had notice of the APE proceedings throughout the process. Argo (D) also had the opportunity to present objections to the Argentine court. Moreover, Argentine law prohibits courts from approving a restructuring plan that is abusive, and the court in this case determined that the plan was not abusive, fraudulent, or discriminatory. The court even directed that non-consenting creditors should get an additional opportunity to select among their options after the APE was approved. For these reasons, the bankruptcy court did not abuse its discretion by finding that the APE proceeding comported with due process and ensured just treatment of creditors. As to another § 304(c) factor, Argo (D) also contends that the APE violated public policy because it was inconsistent with three Bankruptcy Code requirements: (1) protection of bondholders' rights under § 316(b) of the Trust Indenture Act (TIA); (2) the best interests of the creditor requirement under § 1129(a)(7); and (3) the good-faith requirement under § 1129(a)(3). Because of these inconsistencies, Argo (D) argues that the APE should not be granted comity, which is defined as "the recognition which one nation allows within its territory to the legislative, executive or judicial acts of another nation, having due regard both to international duty and convenience, and to the rights of its own citizens, or of other persons who are under the protection of its laws." The TIA protects the holder of a bond issued under a qualified indenture from majority-imposed impairment of its rights, but since TIA protected bonds are subject to restructuring under U.S. bankruptcy law, a bankruptcy court may grant enforcement of foreign insolvency proceedings that restructure TIA protected bonds so long as recognition of those proceedings is otherwise valid. Argo (D) claims that even if that is the case, a nonconsensual reorganization under U.S. bankruptcy law is permissible notwithstanding TIA because of the protections offered by the good faith and best-interest-

Continued on next page.

of-the-creditors requirements. Thus, Argo (D) reasons that because Argentine law does not provide these protections, the APE is not entitled to comity. Comity, however, does not require that foreign protections be identical to U.S. protections. In essence, Argo's (D) argument is that comity should not be granted because creditors could receive a smaller distribution on their unsecured claim under foreign law than they would receive under U.S. law. However, provided the other § 304(c) factors are satisfied, the statute does not require that the amount of a distribution in a foreign insolvency proceeding be identical to the hypothetical amount the creditor would have received in a proceeding under U.S. law. Although Telecom (P) was not required to prepare a liquidation analysis as required by U.S. law, the APE provided creditors with options to receive from 80 to 100% of the outstanding principal face amount of their claim—which seems like excellent consideration. In addition, there is no support in the record for Argo's (D) claim that the APE was not undertaken in good faith. Argo (D) did not adduce evidence to support its allegation that Telecom (P) could have paid all of its debts in full, but was using the APE law to enrich its shareholders. Telecom (P) experienced very real financial hardship, and obtained overwhelming creditor approval for the APE. Also, Argo (D) failed to object to any of the APE proceedings in Argentina; it is now barred from doing so in the U.S., which recognizes that foreign courts have an interest in conducting insolvency proceedings concerning their own domestic business entities. For these reasons, the bankruptcy court did not abuse its discretion in granting comity to the APE. Affirmed.

ANALYSIS

The six factors that the court considers under § 304(c) are: (1) just treatment of all claimholders; (2) protection for U.S. claimholders against prejudice and inconvenience in claims processing; (3) prevention of preferential or fraudulent dispositions of property; (4) distribution of proceeds substantially in the order prescribed by U.S. bankruptcy law; (5) comity; and (6) if appropriate, an opportunity for a "fresh start" if the foreign proceeding concerns an individual. Courts must "conduct a case-by-case balancing of the [se] statutory factors." In this case, Argo (D) challenged the court's analysis of only two of the § 304(c) factors—just treatment of all creditors and comity.

Quicknotes

COMITY A rule pursuant to which courts in one state give deference to the statutes and judicial decisions of the court of another state.

DUE PROCESS The constitutional mandate requiring the courts to protect and enforce individuals' rights and liberties consistent with prevailing principles of fairness and justice and prohibiting the federal and state governments from such activities that deprive its citizens of life, liberty, or property interest.

LIQUIDATION The reduction to cash of all assets for distribution to creditors.

McGrath v. Riddell

[Parties not identified.]

House of Lords [2008] UKHL 21.

NATURE OF CASE: Appeal from English lower court judgments denying a request to remit assets of Australian companies to Australian liquidators for distribution.

FACT SUMMARY: An Australian court requested that the English assets of four Australian companies in liquidation be remitted to Australian liquidators for distribution in accordance with Australian insolvency law.

RULE OF LAW

English courts have the authority to remit assets of an entity of a relevant country to liquidators in that country to be distributed in accordance with the insolvency laws of that country even where doing so will favor some creditors at the expense of others.

FACTS: Four Australian insurance companies were in liquidation in Australia. Some of their assets—mostly reinsurance claims on policies taken out in London—were situated in England. Provisional liquidators were appointed in England to protect these assets. In Australia, liquidators were also appointed. As part of the liquidation process, an Australian court made a request to the appropriate English court requesting that the English provisional liquidators be directed, after payment of their expenses, to remit the assets to the Australian liquidators for distribution. The Australian court made its request pursuant to section 426 (4) of England's Insolvency Act 1986, which provides that: "The courts having jurisdiction in relation to insolvency law in any part of the United Kingdom shall assist the courts having the corresponding jurisdiction in . . . any relevant country." The English Secretary of State has the power to designate a country as "relevant" and has so designated Australia. Section 426(5) provides that the court to which a request is made under § 426(4) has the authority "to apply, in relation to any matters specified in the request, the insolvency law which is applicable by either court in relation to comparable matters falling within its jurisdiction." The alternative to granting the Australian court's request was a separate liquidation and distribution of the English assets in accordance with the Insolvency Act. The outcome under each scenario would be different for different classes of creditors. The lower court denied the request, on the grounds that the distribution in Australia would not be pari passu, but would give preference to some creditors (the policy holders) at the expense of other creditors (the rest of the creditors). The Court of Appeal affirmed, and the House of Lords granted review.

ISSUE: Do English courts have the authority to remit assets of an entity of a relevant country to liquidators in that country to be distributed in accordance with the insolvency laws of that country even where doing so will favor some creditors at the expense of others?

HOLDING: Yes. English courts have the authority to remit assets of an entity of a relevant country to liquidators in that country to be distributed in accordance with the insolvency laws of that country even where doing so will favor some creditors at the expense of others.

OPINION: (Lord Hoffmann) The courts' authority derives from case law principles, and is reinforced by Insolvency Law § 462. Prior to that statute's enactment, case law provided for international cooperation in corporate insolvency based on principles of private international law and comity, and that bankruptcy should be unitary and universal. This principle holds that the unitary bankruptcy proceeding in the court of the bankrupt's country receives international recognition and applies to all the bankrupt's assets. In the United States, this aspirational principle is known as "modified universalism." Full universalism is achieved only be treaty. The judicial practice that developed around this principle in ancillary cases was to limit the powers and duties of liquidators to collecting the English assets and settling a list of the creditors who sent in proofs. The English liquidators were given the authority to remit the English assets to the liquidators in the relevant country. Some courts denied such authority where distribution would not be made in accordance with English law, reasoning that they did not have jurisdiction to do otherwise because creditors in an English liquidation (principal or ancillary) cannot be deprived of their statutory rights under English law. However, once it is accepted that the court has the authority to direct an English ancillary liquidator to remit the assets for distribution by the principal liquidator, it logically follows that those assets do not have to be distributed according to English law to endow the court with jurisdiction to order the remittal in the first place. As a practical matter, most countries have their own lists of preferential creditors that differ from those of England. Thus, the court has jurisdiction at common law to direct the remittal. The court is not, under § 462, applying Australian law to the distribution, but ordering the remittal under English law for distribution in Australia, in accord with that country's laws. The decision the English court is making is that there is a foreign jurisdiction more appropriate than England for dealing with the liquidation. The court is not deciding a choice of law question. Here, applying these principles of universalism, it would not offend any principles of justice for the assets to be remitted to

Continued on next page.

Australia. The Australian court's request should have been granted. Appeal allowed (Reversed).

OPINION: (Lord Scott of Foscote) Although the courts do have the authority to order remittal of the assets in this case, the authority derives not, as Lord Hoffmann argues, from common law, but only from § 462 as part of England's insolvency law. To hold, as the lower courts did, that remittal cannot occur because the result would be different than under English insolvency law, would be to thwart § 462's intended potential to promote a universal scheme for insolvency distribution. However, where § 462 is not implicated in an ancillary proceeding, where a "relevant country" is not involved, the courts do not have inherent common law jurisdiction to deprive creditors of their English liquidation rights. In such cases, there is a conflict between the goal of universality and the obligation of English courts to accord creditors their English insolvency rights. This conflict has been resolved by § 462, but only with regard to "relevant countries." Appeal allowed (Reversed).

OPINION: (Lord Phillips of Worth Matravers) The assets should be remitted based on § 462, which gives the court jurisdiction to accede to the Australian court's request, and because the particular facts of the case warrant remittal. Doing so is in accord with principles of international comity and universalism, and the question of whether jurisdiction is available under the common law does not have to be reached. Appeal allowed (Reversed).

OPINION: (Lord Walker of Gestingthorpe) Lord Hoffmann's approach to § 462 is the correct approach. The Australian court's request should have been granted. Appeal allowed (Reversed).

OPINION: (Lord Neuberger of Abbotsbury) The courts have common law authority to remit assets, but where the distribution will not be in accordance with the English insolvency regime, the power to do so derives from § 426. Here, the remittal should have been ordered. Appeal allowed (Reversed).

ANALYSIS

The United States has not been designated a "relevant country" by England's Secretary of State for purposes of § 462. Thus, if a U.S. bankruptcy trustee or court made a request similar to the one made by the Australian court in this case, Lord Scott would not have permitted remittal—but it seems that a majority of the other Lords would have.

Quicknotes

COMITY A rule pursuant to which courts in one state give deference to the statutes and judicial decisions of the court of another state.

COMMON LAW A body of law developed through the judicial decisions of the courts as opposed to the legislative process.

In re Maxwell Communication Corp. PLC

Debtor (P) v. Banks (D)

93 F.3d 1036 (2d Cir. 1996).

NATURE OF CASE: Appeal from dismissal of debtor's Chapter 11 complaints to recover funds from pre-petition transfers.

FACT SUMMARY: Maxwell Communication (P), an international corporation and a debtor estate in Chapter 11 bankruptcy, sought to recover under American law millions of dollars transferred to foreign banks (D) shortly before filing for bankruptcy.

RULE OF LAW

Bankruptcy courts may best be able to effectuate the purposes of the bankruptcy law by cooperating with foreign courts on a case-by-case basis.

FACTS: The debtor, Maxwell Communication (P), was headquartered and managed in England and incurred most of its debt there, but 80 percent of its assets were in the United States. Less than ninety days before filing for Chapter 11 bankruptcy, several transfers were made to European banks with whom it had credit arrangements. Maxwell (P) later sought to avoid these pre-petition transactions. Parallel and cooperative proceedings were commenced in England, and administrators were appointed to manage the affairs and property of the corporation. An examiner (P) was appointed to mediate among the various parties and a plan for orderly liquidation was produced. The reorganization plan was approved in both the United States and England. The plan did not, however, resolve all the problems that might arise from concurrent proceedings, such as which substantive law would govern the resolution of disputed claims by creditors, and whether the debtor could set aside pre-petition transfers to certain creditors. When Maxwell (P) commenced adversary proceedings to recover the funds under the theory that they were avoidable transfers under Bankruptcy Code § 550(a)(1), the banks (D) filed motions for dismissal, alleging that applying the Bankruptcy Code to these transactions would violate the presumption of extraterritoriality and that dismissal was also warranted on grounds of comity. The bankruptcy court granted the motions. The district court affirmed. Maxwell (P) and the examiner (P) appealed.

ISSUE: May bankruptcy courts best be able to effectuate the purposes of the bankruptcy law by cooperating with foreign courts on a case-by-case basis?

HOLDING AND DECISION: (Cardamone, J.) Yes. Bankruptcy courts may best be able to effectuate the purposes of the bankruptcy law by cooperating with foreign courts on a case-by-case basis. Where a dispute involving conflicting avoidance laws arises in the context of parallel bankruptcy proceedings that have already achieved substantial reconciliation between the two sets of laws, comity argues decidedly against the risk of derailing that cooperation by the selfish application of our law to circumstances touching more directly upon the interests of another forum. The doctrine of international comity precludes application of American avoidance law to transfers in which England's interest has primacy. There is an alternative mechanism for avoiding preferences under English law. Maxwell's (P) insolvency did not jeopardize the United States' interests because its holdings were sold as going concerns, because most of the creditors were not residents of the United States, and because the two countries' preference laws in any event serve similar ends and England had a greater interest in applying its own laws. Affirmed.

ANALYSIS

This is a unique case. International cooperation in insolvency matters dates back to the Bankruptcy Reform Act of 1978. The United Nations Commission on International Trade Law Model Law on Cross-Border Insolvency provides for recognition and standing of foreign representatives of insolvency estates.

Quicknotes

COMITY A rule pursuant to which courts in one state give deference to the statutes and judicial decisions of another.

Glossary

Common Latin Words and Phrases Encountered in the Law

A FORTIORI: Because one fact exists or has been proven, therefore a second fact that is related to the first fact must also exist.

A PRIORI: From the cause to the effect. A term of logic used to denote that when one generally accepted truth is shown to be a cause, another particular effect must necessarily follow.

AB INITIO: From the beginning; a condition which has existed throughout, as in a marriage which was void ab initio.

ACTUS REUS: The wrongful act; in criminal law, such action sufficient to trigger criminal liability.

AD VALOREM: According to value; an ad valorem tax is imposed upon an item located within the taxing jurisdiction calculated by the value of such item.

AMICUS CURIAE: Friend of the court. Its most common usage takes the form of an amicus curiae brief, filed by a person who is not a party to an action but is nonetheless allowed to offer an argument supporting his legal interests.

ARGUENDO: In arguing. A statement, possibly hypothetical, made for the purpose of argument, is one made arguendo.

BILL QUIA TIMET: A bill to quiet title (establish ownership) to real property.

BONA FIDE: True, honest, or genuine. May refer to a person's legal position based on good faith or lacking notice of fraud (such as a bona fide purchaser for value) or to the authenticity of a particular document (such as a bona fide last will and testament).

CAUSA MORTIS: With approaching death in mind. A gift causa mortis is a gift given by a party who feels certain that death is imminent.

CAVEAT EMPTOR: Let the buyer beware. This maxim is reflected in the rule of law that a buyer purchases at his own risk because it is his responsibility to examine, judge, test, and otherwise inspect what he is buying.

CERTIORARI: A writ of review. Petitions for review of a case by the United States Supreme Court are most often done by means of a writ of certiorari.

CONTRA: On the other hand. Opposite. Contrary to.

CORAM NOBIS: Before us; writs of error directed to the court that originally rendered the judgment.

CORAM VOBIS: Before you; writs of error directed by an appellate court to a lower court to correct a factual error.

CORPUS DELICTI: The body of the crime; the requisite elements of a crime amounting to objective proof that a crime has been committed.

CUM TESTAMENTO ANNEXO, ADMINISTRATOR (ADMINISTRATOR C.T.A.): With will annexed; an administrator c.t.a. settles an estate pursuant to a will in which he is not appointed.

DE BONIS NON, ADMINISTRATOR (ADMINISTRATOR D.B.N.): Of goods not administered; an administrator d.b.n. settles a partially settled estate.

DE FACTO: In fact; in reality; actually. Existing in fact but not officially approved or engendered.

DE JURE: By right; lawful. Describes a condition that is legitimate "as a matter of law," in contrast to the term "de facto," which connotes something existing in fact but not legally sanctioned or authorized. For example, de facto segregation refers to segregation brought about by housing patterns, etc., whereas de jure segregation refers to segregation created by law.

DE MINIMIS: Of minimal importance; insignificant; a trifle; not worth bothering about.

DE NOVO: Anew; a second time; afresh. A trial de novo is a new trial held at the appellate level as if the case originated there and the trial at a lower level had not taken place.

DICTA: Generally used as an abbreviated form of obiter dicta, a term describing those portions of a judicial opinion incidental or not necessary to resolution of the specific question before the court. Such nonessential statements and remarks are not considered to be binding precedent.

DUCES TECUM: Refers to a particular type of writ or subpoena requesting a party or organization to produce certain documents in their possession.

EN BANC: Full bench. Where a court sits with all justices present rather than the usual quorum.

EX PARTE: For one side or one party only. An ex parte proceeding is one undertaken for the benefit of only one party, without notice to, or an appearance by, an adverse party.

EX POST FACTO: After the fact. An ex post facto law is a law that retroactively changes the consequences of a prior act.

EX REL.: Abbreviated form of the term ex relatione, meaning upon relation or information. When the state brings an action in which it has no interest against an individual at the instigation of one who has a private interest in the matter.

FORUM NON CONVENIENS: Inconvenient forum. Although a court may have jurisdiction over the case, the action should be tried in a more conveniently located court, one to which parties and witnesses may more easily travel, for example.

GUARDIAN AD LITEM: A guardian of an infant as to litigation, appointed to represent the infant and pursue his/her rights.

HABEAS CORPUS: You have the body. The modern writ of habeas corpus is a writ directing that a person (body) being detained (such as a prisoner) be brought before the court so that the legality of his detention can be judicially ascertained.

IN CAMERA: In private, in chambers. When a hearing is held before a judge in his chambers or when all spectators are excluded from the courtroom.

IN FORMA PAUPERIS: In the manner of a pauper. A party who proceeds in forma pauperis because of his poverty is one who is allowed to bring suit without liability for costs.

INFRA: Below, under. A word referring the reader to a later part of a book. (The opposite of supra.)

IN LOCO PARENTIS: In the place of a parent.

IN PARI DELICTO: Equally wrong; a court of equity will not grant requested relief to an applicant who is in pari delicto, or as much at fault in the transactions giving rise to the controversy as is the opponent of the applicant.

IN PARI MATERIA: On like subject matter or upon the same matter. Statutes relating to the same person or things are said to be in pari materia. It is a general rule of statutory construction that such statutes should be construed together, i.e., looked at as if they together constituted one law.

IN PERSONAM: Against the person. Jurisdiction over the person of an individual.

IN RE: In the matter of. Used to designate a proceeding involving an estate or other property.

IN REM: A term that signifies an action against the res, or thing. An action in rem is basically one that is taken directly against property, as distinguished from an action in personam, i.e., against the person.

INTER ALIA: Among other things. Used to show that the whole of a statement, pleading, list, statute, etc., has not been set forth in its entirety.

INTER PARTES: Between the parties. May refer to contracts, conveyances or other transactions having legal significance.

INTER VIVOS: Between the living. An inter vivos gift is a gift made by a living grantor, as distinguished from bequests contained in a will, which pass upon the death of the testator.

IPSO FACTO: By the mere fact itself.

JUS: Law or the entire body of law.

LEX LOCI: The law of the place; the notion that the rights of parties to a legal proceeding are governed by the law of the place where those rights arose.

MALUM IN SE: Evil or wrong in and of itself; inherently wrong. This term describes an act that is wrong by its very nature, as opposed to one which would not be wrong but for the fact that there is a specific legal prohibition against it (malum prohibitum).

MALUM PROHIBITUM: Wrong because prohibited, but not inherently evil. Used to describe something that is wrong because it is expressly forbidden by law but that is not in and of itself evil, e.g., speeding.

MANDAMUS: We command. A writ directing an official to take a certain action.

MENS REA: A guilty mind; a criminal intent. A term used to signify the mental state that accompanies a crime or other prohibited act. Some crimes require only a general mens rea (general intent to do the prohibited act), but others, like assault with intent to murder, require the existence of a specific mens rea.

MODUS OPERANDI: Method of operating; generally refers to the manner or style of a criminal in committing crimes, admissible in appropriate cases as evidence of the identity of a defendant.

NEXUS: A connection to.

NISI PRIUS: A court of first impression. A nisi prius court is one where issues of fact are tried before a judge or jury.

N.O.V. (NON OBSTANTE VEREDICTO): Notwithstanding the verdict. A judgment n.o.v. is a judgment given in favor of one party despite the fact that a verdict was returned in favor of the other party, the justification being that the verdict either had no reasonable support in fact or was contrary to law.

NUNC PRO TUNC: Now for then. This phrase refers to actions that may be taken and will then have full retroactive effect.

PENDENTE LITE: Pending the suit; pending litigation underway.

PER CAPITA: By head; beneficiaries of an estate, if they take in equal shares, take per capita.

PER CURIAM: By the court; signifies an opinion ostensibly written "by the whole court" and with no identified author.

PER SE: By itself, in itself; inherently.

PER STIRPES: By representation. Used primarily in the law of wills to describe the method of distribution where a person, generally because of death, is unable to take that which is left to him by the will of another, and therefore his heirs divide such property between them rather than take under the will individually.

PRIMA FACIE: On its face, at first sight. A prima facie case is one that is sufficient on its face, meaning that the evidence supporting it is adequate to establish the case until contradicted or overcome by other evidence.

PRO TANTO: For so much; as far as it goes. Often used in eminent domain cases when a property owner receives partial payment for his land without prejudice to his right to bring suit for the full amount he claims his land to be worth.

QUANTUM MERUIT: As much as he deserves. Refers to recovery based on the doctrine of unjust enrichment in those cases in which a party has rendered valuable services or furnished materials that were accepted and enjoyed by another under circumstances that would reasonably notify the recipient that the rendering party expected to be paid. In essence, the law implies a contract to pay the reasonable value of the services or materials furnished.

QUASI: Almost like; as if; nearly. This term is essentially used to signify that one subject or thing is almost analogous to another but that material differences between them do exist. For example, a quasi-criminal proceeding is one that is not strictly criminal but shares enough of the same characteristics to require some of the same safeguards (e.g., procedural due process must be followed in a parole hearing).

QUID PRO QUO: Something for something. In contract law, the consideration, something of value, passed between the parties to render the contract binding.

RES GESTAE: Things done; in evidence law, this principle justifies the admission of a statement that would otherwise be hearsay when it is made so closely to the event in question as to be said to be a part of it, or with such spontaneity as not to have the possibility of falsehood.

RES IPSA LOQUITUR: The thing speaks for itself. This doctrine gives rise to a rebuttable presumption of negligence when the instrumentality causing the injury was within the exclusive control of the defendant, and the injury was one that does not normally occur unless a person has been negligent.

RES JUDICATA: A matter adjudged. Doctrine which provides that once a court of competent jurisdiction has rendered a final judgment or decree on the merits, that judgment or decree is conclusive upon the parties to the case and prevents them from engaging in any other litigation on the points and issues determined therein.

RESPONDEAT SUPERIOR: Let the master reply. This doctrine holds the master liable for the wrongful acts of his servant (or the principal for his agent) in those cases in which the servant (or agent) was acting within the scope of his authority at the time of the injury.

STARE DECISIS: To stand by or adhere to that which has been decided. The common law doctrine of stare decisis attempts to give security and certainty to the law by following the policy that once a principle of law as applicable to a certain set of facts has been set forth in a decision, it forms a precedent which will subsequently be followed, even though a different decision might be made were it the first time the question had arisen. Of course, stare decisis is not an inviolable principle and is departed from in instances where there is good cause (e.g., considerations of public policy led the Supreme Court to disregard prior decisions sanctioning segregation).

SUPRA: Above. A word referring a reader to an earlier part of a book.

ULTRA VIRES: Beyond the power. This phrase is most commonly used to refer to actions taken by a corporation that are beyond the power or legal authority of the corporation.

Addendum of French Derivatives

IN PAIS: Not pursuant to legal proceedings.

CHATTEL: Tangible personal property.

CY PRES: Doctrine permitting courts to apply trust funds to purposes not expressed in the trust but necessary to carry out the settlor's intent.

PER AUTRE VIE: For another's life; during another's life. In property law, an estate may be granted that will terminate upon the death of someone other than the grantee.

PROFIT A PRENDRE: A license to remove minerals or other produce from land.

VOIR DIRE: Process of questioning jurors as to their predispositions about the case or parties to a proceeding in order to identify those jurors displaying bias or prejudice.

Casenote Legal Briefs

Administrative Law	Breyer, Stewart, Sunstein & Vermeule
Administrative Law	Cass, Diver & Beermann
Administrative Law	Funk, Shapiro & Weaver
Administrative Law	Mashaw, Merrill & Shane
Administrative Law	Strauss, Rakoff, & Farina (Gellhorn & Byse)
Agency & Partnership	Hynes & Loewenstein
Antitrust	Pitofsky, Goldschmid & Wood
Antitrust	Sullivan & Hovenkamp
Bankruptcy	Warren & Bussel
Business Organizations	Allen, Kraakman & Subramanian
Business Organizations	Bauman, Weiss & Palmiter
Business Organizations	Hamilton & Macey
Business Organizations	Klein, Ramseyer & Bainbridge
Business Organizations	O'Kelley & Thompson
Business Organizations	Soderquist, Smiddy & Cunningham
Civil Procedure	Field, Kaplan & Clermont
Civil Procedure	Freer & Perdue
Civil Procedure	Friedenthal, Miller, Sexton & Hershkoff
Civil Procedure	Hazard, Tait, Fletcher & Bundy
Civil Procedure	Marcus, Redish & Sherman
Civil Procedure	Subrin, Minow, Brodin & Main
Civil Procedure	Yeazell
Commercial Law	LoPucki, Warren, Keating & Mann
Commercial Law	Warren & Walt
Commercial Law	Whaley
Community Property	Bird
Community Property	Blumberg
Conflicts	Brilmayer & Goldsmith
Conflicts	Currie, Kay, Kramer & Roosevelt
Constitutional Law	Brest, Levinson, Balkin & Amar
Constitutional Law	Chemerinsky
Constitutional Law	Choper, Fallon, Kamisar & Shiffrin (Lockhart)
Constitutional Law	Cohen, Varat & Amar
Constitutional Law	Farber, Eskridge & Frickey
Constitutional Law	Rotunda
Constitutional Law	Sullivan & Gunther
Constitutional Law	Stone, Seidman, Sunstein, Tushnet & Karlan
Contracts	Ayres & Speidel
Contracts	Barnett
Contracts	Burton
Contracts	Calamari, Perillo & Bender
Contracts	Crandall & Whaley
Contracts	Dawson, Harvey, Henderson & Baird
Contracts	Farnsworth, Young & Sanger, Cohen & Brooks
Contracts	Fuller & Eisenberg
Contracts	Knapp, Crystal & Prince
Copyright	Cohen, Loren, Okediji & O'Rourke
Copyright	Goldstein & Reese
Criminal Law	Bonnie, Coughlin, Jeffries & Low
Criminal Law	Boyce, Dripps & Perkins
Criminal Law	Dressler
Criminal Law	Johnson & Cloud
Criminal Law	Kadish, Schulhofer & Steiker
Criminal Law	Kaplan, Weisberg & Binder
Criminal Procedure	Allen, Hoffmann, Livingston & Stuntz
Criminal Procedure	Dressler & Thomas
Criminal Procedure	Haddad, Marsh, Zagel, Meyer, Starkman & Bauer
Criminal Procedure	Kamisar, LaFave, Israel, King & Kerr
Criminal Procedure	Saltzburg & Capra
Debtors & Creditors	Warren & Westbrook
Employment Discrimination	Friedman
Employment Discrimination	Zimmer, Sullivan & White
Employment Law	Rothstein & Liebman
Environmental Law	Menell & Stewart
Environmental Law	Percival, Schroder, Miller & Leape
Environmental Law	Plater, Abrams, Goldfarb, Graham, Heinzerling & Wirth
Evidence	Broun, Mosteller & Giannelli
Evidence	Fisher
Evidence	Mueller & Kirkpatrick
Evidence	Sklansky
Evidence	Waltz & Park
Family Law	Areen & Regan
Family Law	Ellman, Kurtz & Scott
Family Law	Harris, Teitelbaum & Carbone
Family Law	Wadlington & O'Brien
Family Law	Weisberg & Appleton
Federal Courts	Fallon, Meltzer & Shapiro (Hart & Wechsler)
Federal Courts	Low & Jeffries
Health Law	Furrow, Greaney, Johnson, Jost & Schwartz
Immigration Law	Aleinikoff, Martin & Motomura
Immigration Law	Legomsky
Insurance Law	Abraham
Intellectual Property	Merges, Menell & Lemley
International Business Transactions	Folsom, Gordon, Spanogle & Fitzgerald
International Law	Blakesley, Firmage, Scott & Williams
International Law	Carter, Trimble & Weiner
International Law	Damrosch, Henkin, Pugh, Schachter & Smit
International Law	Dunoff, Ratner & Wippman
Labor Law	Cox, Bok, Gorman & Finkin
Land Use	Callies, Freilich & Roberts
Legislation	Eskridge, Frickey & Garrett
Oil & Gas	Lowe, Anderson, Smith & Pierce
Patent Law	Adelman, Radner, Thomas & Wegner
Products Liability	Owen, Montgomery & Davis
Professional Responsibility	Gillers
Professional Responsibility	Hazard, Koniak, Cramton & Cohen
Property	Casner, Leach, French, Korngold & VanderVelde
Property	Cribbet, Johnson, Findley & Smith
Property	Donahue, Kauper & Martin
Property	Dukeminier, Krier, Alexander & Schill
Property	Haar & Liebman
Property	Kurtz & Hovenkamp
Property	Nelson, Stoebuck & Whitman
Property	Rabin, Kwall & Kwall
Property	Singer
Real Estate	Korngold & Goldstein
Real Estate Transactions	Nelson & Whitman
Remedies	Laycock
Remedies	Shoben, Tabb & Janutis
Securities Regulation	Coffee, Seligman & Sale
Securities Regulation	Cox, Hillman & Langevoort
Sports Law	Weiler & Roberts
Taxation (Corporate)	Lind, Schwartz, Lathrope & Rosenberg
Taxation (Individual)	Burke & Friel
Taxation (Individual)	Freeland, Lathrope, Lind & Stephens
Taxation (Individual)	Klein, Bankman & Shaviro
Torts	Dobbs & Hayden
Torts	Epstein
Torts	Franklin & Rabin
Torts	Henderson, Pearson, Kysar & Siliciano
Torts	Schwartz, Kelly & Partlett (Prosser)
Wills, Trusts & Estates	Dukeminier, Johanson, Lindgren & Sitkoff
Wills, Trusts & Estates	Dobris, Sterk & Leslie
Wills, Trusts & Estates	Scoles, Halbach, Roberts & Begleiter